NETHERLANDS

Ruhr

Essen
·Düsseldorf

WEST GERMANY

Rhine River

· Frankfurt

Moselle River

LUXEM-
BURG

SAAR

Saarlouis
Saarbrücken

Saar River

Rhine River

FRANCE

SWITZERLAND

STANFORD BOOKS IN WORLD POLITICS

———————— GRAHAM H. STUART, *Editor* ————————

THE
Saar
Battleground and Pawn

THE
Saar
Battleground and Pawn

*

F<small>RANK</small> M. R<small>USSELL</small>

STANFORD UNIVERSITY PRESS
Stanford, California

GEOFFREY CUMBERLEGE : : OXFORD UNIVERSITY PRESS
LONDON

STANFORD UNIVERSITY PRESS, STANFORD, CALIFORNIA
London: Geoffrey Cumberlege, Oxford University Press

THE BAKER AND TAYLOR COMPANY, HILLSIDE, NEW JERSEY
HENRY M. SNYDER & COMPANY, 440 FOURTH AVENUE, NEW YORK 16
W. S. HALL & COMPANY, 457 MADISON AVENUE, NEW YORK 22

PREFACE

This study had its more remote origin in 1919. The author became intrigued by the ingenious provisions of the Treaty of Versailles embodying the solution of the Saar controversy. These provisions were unique. They sought to provide an impartial international government for the Saar Territory which might be perpetuated at the end of fifteen years if the inhabitants voted for its continuation. The experiment was to be initiated by the League of Nations, itself a new and ambitious experiment in international co-operation, and was to be conducted under its control. The actual government of the Saar was to be entrusted to an international commission whose members were to be drawn from several different nations. And, however able they might prove to be, they certainly could not be expected to be familiar with the problems of international administration with which they would be confronted. Moreover, they would have to function during a period of inflamed postwar passions, exacerbated nationalism, economic disturbances, and, inevitably, under the impact of power politics. What obstacles! But also what possibilities for a world growing in political and economic interdependence!

The chief interest of the author was then and still is in the interplay of political and economic forces across national frontiers and in the possibilities of fruitful and sustained international collaboration where problems of the nature of those encountered in the Saar demand solution. Merely technical problems of international administration or of economic adjustment have, therefore, been left to others more concerned and more competent to deal with such matters.

The present study could not possibly have been written had it not been for an earlier one by the present author on the International Government of the Saar, published by the University of California Press in 1926. However, this work did not cover developments beyond 1923. The present study deals with the period during which the Saar Basin Governing Commission functioned, the organization and supervision of the plebiscite, the World War II period, and the present experiment under French auspices. Obviously, much more space has been given to an account of the fifteen-year period during which the Saar was ruled under international auspices. In addition to this having been a most interesting experiment, nearly all of the chief forces and influences that must be taken into account today in any

vii

10770

attempt to diagnose the Saar problem were clearly revealed during the period of the Governing Commission's rule.

At one time or another I have become indebted to a number of persons who have given aid in obtaining information on one or another aspect of the Saar problem. Many whom I consulted in the early 'twenties, and who were kind enough to enlighten me about significant matters not to be found recorded in public documents, are no longer living. Among them should be mentioned the three members of the Committee of Experts appointed to draft the Saar section of the Treaty of Versailles. Dean Charles Haskins talked with me frankly in an interview at Harvard in 1923, and in the same year I was privileged to discuss the question in London with Sir Cuthbert Headlam-Morley of the Historical Section of the British Foreign Office. André Tardieu granted me an interview in Paris and made it possible for me to meet and talk with all the original appointees to the Governing Commission at Saarbrücken and the French mining officials in the Saar, and to enjoy the hospitality of General Brissaud-Desmaillet and his officers at the headquarters of the French garrison on the outskirts of Saarbrücken. Finally, in my omnivorous pursuit of information and ideas, a helping hand was extended at all times by individual members of the Secretariat of the League of Nations. Nor do I forget the helpfulness of Miss Florence Wilson, at that time the courteous and efficient head of the League of Nations Library.

Likewise, in the United States in the early 'twenties many persons gave me needed assistance of one kind or another. Among them were Chancellor David Starr Jordan, President Ray Lyman Wilbur, and others of Stanford University, including E. D. Adams, director of the Hoover War Library, Ralph Lutz, later director of the Hoover Institute and Library on War, Revolution, and Peace, and Professors Frank Golder, Graham H. Stuart, and V. J. West. To former President David Prescott Barrows of the University of California I owe a debt of gratitude for his general helpfulness, and to Dean Frank Probert of the College of Mining at California for useful assistance in comprehending the nature and significance of the mineral resources of the Saar. Others whose co-operation and assistance are gratefully acknowledged are Miss Sarah Wambaugh, Professor Manley Hudson, David Hunter Miller, and Ray Stannard Baker. Needless to say, all of them should be exempted from responsibility for any sins of commission or omission in the pages that follow.

As this task reaches completion I should like to record that Mrs. Hildegarde Millar, Librarian of the Bureau of International Relations at the University of California, has organized prompt searching parties for elusive materials whenever she has received an SOS from me. Likewise, my wife has always cheerfully recognized the priority of this international enterprise over matters of merely domestic concern. But the editor of the series of Stanford Books on World Affairs, Graham H. Stuart, deserves a special citation. It was he who coerced me by degrees to try to bring the Saar story up to date and who, because of his interest and understanding of the significance of the problem it poses, has been of the greatest assistance at all times.

FRANK M. RUSSELL

BERKELEY, CALIFORNIA
June 1, 1951

TABLE OF CONTENTS

THE
Saar
Battleground and Pawn

I

BATTLEGROUND AND PAWN

The people of the Saar whose political fate and economic life are once more caught in the shifting tides of power politics seem resigned for the moment to the demand of Germany's historic rival that they should once more live within the French orbit. Although they voted to rejoin the Reich in the plebiscite of 1935, the present state of Germany is such that they seem to welcome rather than shrink from the renewal of the French connection. For it will guarantee them bread, afford them security, and relieve them of the heavy burdens their kinsmen in occupied Germany will have to carry.

The Saar region is part of that "debated ground," lying west of the Rhine between Switzerland and the North Sea, for the possession of which Germans and Frenchmen have at one time or another battled since the partition of Mersen in 870 when it was united to the German Empire. However, the real challenge to Germany did not come until the latter half of the sixteenth century and the seventeenth century, when a strong, unified French state came into existence and was able to confront a crumbling German Empire.

In 1552, Henry II of France invaded Germany and seized the bishoprics of Metz, Toul, and Verdun for the Emperor Charles V. Although none of these acquisitions comprised any part of the Saar, the town of Saarbrücken, at present the chief city of the region, was at the time a fief of the bishopric of Metz. In 1648, the peace of Westphalia confirmed the title of the three bishoprics to France "in full sovereignty." However, Louis XIV determined to follow the glory road, and in 1679 he set up *Chambres de Réunion* at Metz and other places to investigate and pass favorably upon his title to additional territories that were at the time or "ever had been" dependencies of his new possessions. As the *Chambres* were subservient French courts, this early type of peaceful penetration or, as Lord James Bryce described it, this "pleasant euphemism for robbery in time of peace," was highly successful. In fact the Metz *Chambre* was so expeditious in finding that Saarbrücken and other "dependencies" legally belonged to France that the grand monarch found it necessary to admonish his judges to the effect that there was no hurry, and that it would make a better impression on Europe if they were to reach their decisions after more deliberation.

In the year in which the *Chambres* were meeting (1680) Louis XIV began to build the town of Saarlouis, one of several fortified cities which were to serve as military outposts along the eastern frontier of France. Saarlouis was to remain continuously in French hands until 1815, and become the center of French influence in the Saar. It was the seat of Louis' high court of justice as well as the headquarters of the chief provincial administrative officers, and the French like to recall that it was the birthplace of Marshal Michel Ney.

The annexations of Louis in this region formed the heart of a new French province, the Province de la Sarre, which during the sixteen years of its existence seems to have been governed chiefly with military needs rather than civilian considerations in mind. However, the other powers, alarmed and angered at the expansionist policies of Louis, formed a Grand Alliance against him in 1688, and after nearly ten years of warfare forced him in 1697 to withdraw to the west bank of the Rhine and disgorge most of the territories he had seized. In the Saar he was allowed to retain only the Saarlouis district. The remainder went back to the German Empire, although feudal ties, royal subsidies, ethnic affinities with the inhabitants of Lorraine, and the attractions of the court of Louis tended to make the princes gravitate within the French orbit in spite of their connection with the German Empire.

The French Revolution was variously received in the Saar as well as elsewhere in Germany. Proclaiming the rights of man and the abolition of special privilege, it evoked fear and hostility among the governing classes of Europe. On the other hand, the lowly and oppressed, the intellectuals, and in general the middle class greeted it with enthusiasm as the harbinger of a better day. Thus, as the armies of revolutionary France marched across the frontiers to bring *liberté*, *égalité*, and *fraternité* to all peoples in their path, they were met in the Saar as elsewhere with communal petitions asking for union with France. Plebiscites confirming these petitions were taken in various districts but in most instances, since they were held under French military occupation, it is questionable whether they accurately reflected in all instances the wishes of the people.

During the period of the Reign of Terror, which started in 1793, people in the Saar as well as Frenchmen in France were to endure the brutal excesses and arbitrary processes which came in the wake of a bloody social revolution. Nevertheless, the revolution left the middle class and peasants of the Saar, as in other occupied territories, in a much improved position materially and socially. In this connection Hermann Oncken, in *The Historical Rhine Policy of France*, declares that "in the sections of Germany which they occupied, the French broke up a backward world of feudal territories with a superannuated class system, a crippled form of public life, and stagnant economic conditions. What they put in place of this decaying order meant, in more than one respect, political progress, for they abolished feudal burdens and promoted equality before the law, material prosperity, individual freedom, and territorial consolidation."

The Napoleonic phase of the revolution had important consequences for the Saar. As a result of the young Napoleon's military genius, which enabled him to win brilliant victories over the Italians and Austrians, the French were able—in secret articles of the Treaty of Campo Formio of 1797—to induce the German emperor provisionally to cede territory on the left bank of the Rhine south of Coblenz and including the Saar, which was now organized as one of four departments of the Rhine. The French then carried on intensive propaganda among the inhabitants of these departments to induce them to declare for union with France. Whether or not the petitions which were forthcoming from various communes would have been regarded as decisive by an impartial tribunal, the French secured the left bank of the Rhine by the Treaty of Lunéville in 1801, and in 1802 accorded full French citizenship rights to the inhabitants.

During the period of French sovereignty, following the Treaty of Lunéville, the mining and iron and steel industries of the Saar received their first great impetus. The demands of war were chiefly responsible for this development. Napoleon founded the École des Mines in order to exploit the coal resources, which in turn were necessary in the manufacture of steel. Besides peaceful implements, swords and guns and cannon balls were the end products.

Louis XIV's Province de la Sarre lasted sixteen years; the Département de la Sarre of revolutionary France existed for thirteen years, coming to an end with the Peace of Paris after Napoleon's abdication in the spring of 1814. Although the French frontiers were in general to be pushed back to the line of 1792, France was left in the possession of the district of Saarbrücken with most of the coal mines then under exploitation. Napoleon's return from Elba and his bid for the recovery of his power in Europe alarmed the powers allied against him and resulted, after Waterloo, in their determination to get rid of Napoleon and, likewise, to take various measures to keep the French henceforth in check. Among the territorial decisions made with this end in view was that which gave practically all of the Saar region, including not only Saarbrücken but also Saarlouis and the area of the chief coal deposits to Prussia.

Between the installation of Prussia in the Saar and the Franco-Prussian war of 1870, French influences in the region declined sharply. Many Frenchmen left their homes to take up residence in France or elsewhere, particularly from the Saarlouis district, although Saarlouis remained the center of French culture in the Saar, and French aspirations to repossess the region did not die. The energetic —and, to the French, offensive—Prussians, however, sent in their efficient administrative officials, exploited the coal mines under state ownership, brought the younger generation up under Prussian teachers, and in the course of time put a Prussian stamp upon the social and economic life of the region.

The war of 1870 further confirmed Prussian influence and strengthened Prussian economic control. The swift and crushing victory of the Germans resulted not only in the levy of a large war indemnity against France but in the annexation of Alsace and Lorraine. Bismarck seemed to foresee future trouble in the insistence of the German military authorities that Lorraine should be included in the annexationist demands made upon France, when he deplored "the idea of having so many Frenchmen in our house against their will." Actually the French were never entirely to be reconciled to the loss of Lorraine and were determined to repossess it when the opportunity came during World War I. More than that, as we shall see, when victory came they were vigorously to press their claim to the control of the adjacent Saar territory. Once more the people of the Saar were to find that they were but pawns in the game of power. And so do they appear to be today, after World War II.

2

STRUGGLE AND COMPROMISE

On the seventh day of May 1919, the representatives of the triumphant Allied and Associated Powers invited the German plenipotentiaries to the Trianon palace to receive the decisions of the victors of World War I, as embodied in a document referred to by the President of the Peace Conference, Georges Clemenceau, as the "Second Treaty of Versailles." The Germans well understood that the phrase was to remind them of the humiliating treaty forced on France at the conclusion of the war of 1870—in this same Hall of Mirrors—and to foreshadow a hard peace. But though humiliated in turn, they had no recourse, and bowing unwillingly to *force majeure* they affixed their signatures to the treaty.

The struggle over the Saar at the Peace Conference and the compromise—an inharmonious mingling of French realism and what the French called "Wilsonian idealism"—resulted largely from French fears of a resurgent and unregenerate Germany which, when restored to strength, would again spring at the throat of France. Germany, therefore, must be weakened territorially, buffer states must be erected on her frontiers, and she was to be saddled with a huge bill for reparations, the payment of which could for a long time absorb the energies of the Germans and prevent their building another military machine for conquest. On the other hand, France and her allies were to be strengthened at the expense of Germany, territorially and otherwise, so that the "Huns" would not dare to unleash another war. The insistence of the French that they should control the Saar was chiefly motivated by this preoccupation with the German menace, although, as will appear, other considerations did enter into French calculations with respect to the settlement as a whole and the Saar in particular.

It has been intimated that in the period between the war of 1870 and that of 1914 the French were never entirely reconciled to the loss of Alsace and Lorraine. For a long time French school children grew up with textbooks propounding the idea that these "two sisters," taken from France by force, would one day return; but in the course of time the loss came to be rather generally accepted and, without doubt, only a few chauvinists were willing to go to war to repossess them. If this seemed to be true with respect to Alsace and Lorraine, it was even more certainly so as regards the Saar. François Aulard,

7

writing at the end of the war of 1914, after France had occupied the Saar, states that he was troubled and "scandalized a little, as a historian and as a Frenchman," that French newspapers in describing the entry of the French into Landau and Saarlouis should refer to these as German cities. It is safe to say, however, that few, if any, Frenchmen on the eve of World War I considered any part of the Saar as French territory to be redeemed from a despoiler.

The German attack on France in 1914 had the effect of reopening the old account. Slumbering memories were reawakened; old ambitions, vitalized perhaps more by fear than by cupidity or a desire for revenge, were revived. In 1916, Ferdinand Engerand, a member of the French Chamber of Deputies, anticipating the end of the war, published *L'Allemagne et le fer*, which was incidentally intended to help the French case at the peace table. In this book the author traced the sources of German power to the Reich's abundance of coal and iron. On the other hand, he pointed out that France suffered from the loss of the Saar coal in 1815 and from the further loss of part of the Lorraine iron in 1871. He then argued for the "natural frontier" of the Rhine (which would include the Saar) as a boundary, at once "defensive and profitable" for France.

In 1917 another Frenchman, Georges Launay, in *France-Allemagne*, recalled that the Saar was old French territory taken from France in 1815, asserted that it was a natural annex of Alsace-Lorraine, and pointed out that as most of the mines of the Saar were state-owned, their return to France would present no difficulty. The requisition of the Saar coal basin, said another French writer in the same year, would be a proper act of restitution on the ground that it was a territory wrested from France by force and against the wishes of the local inhabitants. In the following year Louis Madelin wrote a detailed historical account of the Rhine, intended to prove that France should have the Rhine river for her eastern boundary. As a legal basis for this position he asserted that when in 1914 Prussia indulged in tearing up treaties she tore up those of 1814 and 1815 as well as that of 1871. Thus there were no treaty obstacles to the extension of the French frontier to the Rhine.

That the foregoing views were not held exclusively by a few individuals with no direct official responsibility but were shared by the French government as early as February 1917, is evident from certain secret conversations and correspondence leading to an understanding between the French and Russian governments in March 1917. Each of the two governments pursued particular objectives of no concern to the other, and it was not difficult to strike a bargain.

Russia had long nourished an ambition to control Constantinople and the Straits. Moreover, she desired "complete liberty in establishing her western frontiers." France agreed to support her in these matters after Russia had assured the French Republic that she would support the demand that Alsace-Lorraine be restored to France and, further, that the republic's frontiers were "to be drawn up at the discretion of the French Government so as to provide for the strategical needs and for the inclusion in French territory of the entire iron district of Lorraine and of the entire coal district of the Saar valley."

These arrangements were to prove not only valueless but even embarrassing to France at the time of the Peace Conference. Neither in the public declarations of war aims by the Allied Powers on December 21, 1916, and January 10, 1917, nor in the French parliamentary resolution of June 1917 was the acquisition of the Saar mentioned as a war aim of France. Shortly after the Soviets had published the secret correspondence between Russia and France, the Socialists launched an attack in the Chamber of Deputies and demanded that the government state its war aims. Etienne Pichon, minister of foreign affairs, replied under pressure that France cherished no ambitions for foreign territories, but that lands which had been taken from France by force should be returned and, consequently, the "reintegration" of Alsace-Lorraine must be demanded. Was the Saar "foreign" territory? André Tardieu was to argue later that it should not be so regarded. What did Minister of Foreign Affairs Pichon mean by "reintegration"? The statement seemed ambiguous, but at the Peace Conference the meaning became clear when French regional geographers were cited to show that from a geographic and economic point of view the Saar should be regarded as a part of Lorraine.

On January 9, 1918, President Woodrow Wilson formulated a peace program in his "Fourteen Points" address. This program was later accepted, with two reservations—neither of which involved the Saar—by the Allied Powers, including France, as embodying their aims in the struggle with the Central Powers. The only reference to the eastern frontier of France was contained in the eighth point which called for the righting of "the wrong done to France by Prussia in 1871 in the matter of Alsace-Lorraine." The secret arrangements of 1917 between France and Russia were still troubling some Englishmen, however, and in May 1918 the question was raised in the House of Commons whether the frontier line of 1814 was among the war aims of the Allies. Foreign Secretary Arthur James Balfour arose and made a categorical denial, saying at the same time that the secret Franco-Russian conversations were not made known to the British

Government until long after they had taken place, and that they had no international standing. He then gave it as his opinion that the 1814 line never had been "a very fixed or solid part of the foreign policy for any length of time of any French government." The Quai d'Orsay did not see fit at this time to question the accuracy or validity of the British foreign secretary's statements.

In November 1918, when the Allies formally accepted President Wilson's Fourteen Points, with the two reservations noted, as the basis for a peace settlement with the Central Powers, Point Eight still remained without any official interpretation and no reservations were being offered by France with respect to it. However, the French attitude at the forthcoming Peace Conference was foreshadowed on December 29, 1918, in the Chamber of Deputies, in the remarks of Franklin Bouillon, president of the Committee on Foreign Affairs of the Chamber. He said in substance that Alsace-Lorraine in 1870 and the Saar constituted one question; that the taking of the Saar in 1815 by Prussia was a theft, just as the annexation of Alsace-Lorraine in 1870 was a theft; that the date was not important. If it were suggested that 1815 was far in the past and that France had lost her rights by prescription, yet it was agreed on all sides that the wrong done to Poland by the treaties of 1772 should be repaired. Then why should the wrong done to France in 1815 not be righted?

However, France entered the Peace Conference prepared to encounter opposition to her stand on the Saar issue both from Great Britain and from the United States, and her case was weakened rather than strengthened by the secret arrangements she had made with tsarist Russia. The Bolshevists who had exposed these arrangements were now entrenched in power, and they would not have been disposed to support the French claims even had they been represented at the Peace Conference. As regards Britain, certain to have great influence in the peace settlement, the Balfour declaration had made it clear that the British Government did not consider itself under any obligation to support France on the issue. Finally, President Wilson refused to recognize the validity of any secret agreements as far as the United States was concerned. Tactical considerations, therefore, dictated that France should make her fight for the Saar from a more tenable position; and André Tardieu, who argued the French case on this as well as other issues in *The Truth About the Treaty,* though publishing other secret documents pertaining to the Saar, did not mention the secret arrangement of 1917 with Russia.

When the Peace Conference met, the French engaged the various delegations in individual interviews in order to sound them out on the question. After this preliminary reconnaissance they mapped out their plan of campaign and began their attack in March 1919. Tardieu prepared a memorandum based upon the studies of the question made by his colleagues of the Comité d'Études, and distributed it to the heads of the delegations at the conference. This was followed shortly by a verbal presentation of the French case to the Council of Four composed of David Lloyd George, Woodrow Wilson, Georges Clemenceau, and Vittorio Emanuele Orlando. Since Orlando was preoccupied with pressing the claims of Italy, and was not interested in the Saar question, the struggle was narrowed and became a campaign to win over two men, Wilson and Lloyd George, to the French point of view. However, in the final analysis, the task before the French was to convince President Wilson. For where British interests were not involved, Lloyd George was usually not disposed to resist French claims. On the other hand, in matters in which the interests of the British Empire would not be adversely affected, the British Prime Minister tended to support Wilson's stand especially on issues which the President was not disposed to yield.

On March 25, Lloyd George circulated a memorandum entitled "Some Considerations for the Peace Conference Before They Finally Draft Their Terms." Referring to the Saar, the British Prime Minister suggested that the French should be given the 1814 frontier or "the present Alsace-Lorraine frontier with the use of the coal mines in the Saar Valley for a period of ten years." Moreover, Germany must guarantee that after the expiration of the ten-year period she would not interfere with the sale of Saar coal to France.

The French case was clearly presented and logically argued in the memorandum prepared by André Tardieu and his associates. They felt they were entitled to the entire industrial region of the Saar. They argued for the frontier of 1814 on the ground that the region between the line of 1815 and that of 1814 had been taken from France by force; that the inhabitants by petitions and by other manifestations at the time and since had expressed an affection for France and a desire to be reunited with her; and that in spite of the systematic colonization of the country by Prussians and the efforts of Prussia to stifle French sentiment, a passionate attachment to France had survived among the middle class and peasant element. As a matter of restitution, therefore, the French demanded the frontier of 1814 as a minimum.

Under the head of "Reparation" an additional claim was presented. Attention was called to the fact that part of the mining and industrial region of the Saar lay beyond the frontier of 1814. The political and economic severance of one part of the region from the other would not be sensible and it would be injurious to the region itself, since the different parts were economically dependent upon one another. That France should have the entire mining region seemed logical and just to Tardieu and his associates. During the war, when the Germans were retreating, they had deliberately flooded and ruined the French coal mines, which had had an output of about twenty million tons a year. It would be a number of years before they could again begin to produce. France had had to import about twenty-three million tons of coal before the war. With the return of Alsace-Lorraine her needs would be greater. If the Saar mines were not given to her she would be compelled to import fifty million tons a year.

The French argued further that Germany was rich in coal and her economic equilibrium would not be disturbed by the cession of the Saar fields. On the other hand France, poor in coal and made even poorer by the wanton acts of the Germans, was entitled to special reparation in kind. Moreover, the invaders had devastated much of France over which their armies had marched, and the Saar mines offered an opportunity to collect something in satisfaction of the "general reparation" account.

The official position taken by France received the support of Marshal Ferdinand Foch and other military men. Actually, from their point of view, the Saar, though not unimportant in itself, was but a part of the large area west of the Rhine, over which the French must have control. In Parliament the extreme Right adopted a stand similar to that of the military, and the Radical Republican and Radical Socialist parties, though not in complete accord as regards the status of the Rhineland, were in favor of effective French control of the Saar Basin. Only the Socialists remained opposed to any form of annexation, although they, too, agreed that France was entitled to the coal of the Saar as reparation in kind.

In President Wilson the French were to meet the most determined and sustained opposition. As John Maynard Keynes, the British economist expressed it, the President was "capable of digging his toes in and refusing to budge" on basic matters upon which he had made up his mind. He did it now. A great principle was involved, a democratic principle, an old American principle which had been accepted by the Allies, and which should be honestly applied to the territorial settlement. In a speech before Congress, more than two years before, he had declared, "national aspirations must be respected; people may now be dominated and governed only by their own consent. 'Self-determination' is not a mere phrase. It is an imperative principle of action . . . . peoples and provinces are not to be bartered about from sovereignty to sovereignty as if they were mere chattels and pawns in a game . . . ." Thus the French were put on notice at this time, as well as on numerous other occasions when President Wilson spoke of the forthcoming territorial settlement, that the President would expect the Saar settlement to conform to this principle.

The President rejected most of the French contentions. Consistently with the principle that only "open covenants openly arrived at" should receive international recognition and form the basis of legal rights in international affairs, the President pointed out that since France had never claimed the frontier of 1814 "in any public document," and had accepted the eighth of the Fourteen Points which referred to the wrong she had suffered in 1871, she was debarred from raising the question of the 1814 frontier. He further expressed the opinion that the historical argument was a dangerous one for the French to use—the Germans had used it in 1871 in justification of their annexation of Alsace-Lorraine. Moreover, from an economic point of view the 1814 frontier was unsatisfactory, for it would cut the coal basin in two and ruin it. Under these circumstances a cession of territory without an immediate plebiscite to test the sentiments of the inhabitants was inadmissible. On the other hand, the President would admit that France was entitled to have the right to exploit the mines for a specified period in order to obtain reparation in kind for the damage to her own mines.

Clemenceau, president of the Peace Conference, headed the French delegation and, as one of the Council of Four, made decisions along with his other three colleagues at the top level. He seldom spoke in the debates, ordinarily leaving the statement of the French case to his lieutenants, but ultimately the decision with respect to the French position lay with him. The "Tiger" had had a long and tempestuous career in French politics and by temperament was inclined to fight through to a decision rather than to compromise. Perhaps he more nearly resembled Wilson in this than in anything else. But his fundamental outlook was quite different from that of the optimistic American President. Wilson was determined that Versailles should produce peace rather than a truce between never-ending wars, and he scrutinized each item on the agenda of the Peace Conference from the point of view of its contribution toward that end. But Clemenceau was a European. Moreover he was old and completely disillusioned. Over a long career he had seen national conflicts break out time and again. War would never be eliminated. It could only be postponed by erecting and holding as long as possible balances of power. As for Wilson's fourteen-point peace program, "*Le bon dieu* was content with ten commandments, but Wilson must have fourteen!"

After he had allowed the French experts to take issue with President Wilson on various points concerning the Saar question, Clemenceau intervened and put the discussion on a philosophical-psychological plane. He began by saying that he had a serious reservation to make with respect to the President's position, and then remarked, "You eliminate sentiment and memory. The world is not guided by principles alone . . . . economic interests are not everything. The history of the United States is glorious but brief. One hundred twenty years is a very long period for you; for us it is a short one. Our conception of history cannot be quite the same as yours. . . . . The point at issue is not material reparation only; the need for moral reparation is no less great." And pointing up his remarks with an assertion that was designed to impress the apostle of self-determination, he declared that there were one hundred and fifty thousand Frenchmen in the Saar who desired to live under the French flag and whose right to justice should also be considered. But Wilson, the philosopher-king, the man of principle, the peace-seeker, was not much impressed; nor was Lloyd George. The French, therefore, decided to abandon their fight for the 1814 frontier and take up new positions on firmer ground. They now demanded ownership of the coal mines, a special political administration for the entire territory, in order that they would not be hindered in the exploitation of their property by the Germans, and finally, "safeguards for the rights of the inhabitants."

The new French stand was apparently designed to appease President Wilson and to reach him where he was most vulnerable. The French realized that he regarded the creation of a League of Nations, which, among other things, should be given supervisory powers in relation to the execution of the terms of the peace treaties, as the paramount task and crowning work of the Peace Conference. He was also committed to the mandates system as one of the most constructive tasks of the League in the cause of peace. They did not propose, therefore, that the "special political administration" for the Saar should be French, in the sense of outright annexation, even for a period of years. They did propose that France should have a mandate from the League of Nations for fifteen years, under which she would have the right to occupy the Territory with her military forces and veto acts of the local administration.

During this period inhabitants desiring French nationality could have it conferred upon them individually, and "when in each of the principal administrative sections the majority of the electors shall have French nationality, or rather when the district council shall ask for annexation to France, this annexation will occur *de jure* upon its acceptance by the League of Nations." No demand for reunion with Germany would be considered, according to this plan, until after fifteen years. Then those inhabitants who had not already expressed a choice were to be given an opportunity to do so. The fifteen-year period was "fixed precisely with a view to allowing events to shape themselves and the population to decide justly and freely as to its sovereignty." Prussia had had "one hundred years to consolidate her work of violence." France would undo that work by exposing the people of the Saar to the institutions of freedom.

These proposals were to prove unacceptable to President Wilson, but, eventually, he had difficulties sustaining his uncompromising position. Lloyd George had warned the French against insisting on the frontier of 1814 lest this "create another Alsace-Lorraine," but he was disposed to approve the compromise arrangement put forward. Wilson's historical expert, Charles Haskins, even thought that the French should have the frontier of 1814 as a matter of justice, and that there should be a "minimum of French political authority" in the Saar district beyond, in order that France should be assured the necessary coal from the mines, which should be transferred to her. On the other hand, the American economic expert, Bernard Baruch, argued against the transfer of the coal mines to France, pointing out the dependency of the metallurgical industries of the Saar as well as the gas works of southern Germany on the coal of the Saar Basin. If France were to be given ownership of the mines she would have the power to injure these industries and disturb generally the economic life of both the Saar and Germany. On the other hand he recommended that "Germany should be required to supply to France an amount of coal sufficient to make up the deficit in the normal production of the Lens and Pas de Calais fields during the period of their restoration." The mines should be restored within about five years. More than this, "Germany should be required to deliver to France seven million tons a year, the amount which France imported annually before the war."

In the face of French opposition and the conflicting advice of his experts, Wilson finally agreed to the transfer of the coal mines of the Saar and likewise to the guaranty of adequate economic facilities for their exploitation by France. But as regards the political proposals he remained obdurate, insisting: "I have no right to hand over to her [France] people who do not want to go to her, or to give them a special government, even if it is better for them, if they do not want it."

The President's concessions were substantial, but they did not include the delicate and difficult matter of political control. A special Committee of Three, consisting of André Tardieu of France, Charles Haskins of the United States, and Sir Cuthbert Headlam-Morley of Great Britain, was given the matter for study and report. Tardieu seems to have won his colleagues over to the French viewpoint, although Haskins probably needed little if any persuading. In any event, upon Tardieu's request the committee made a declaration at the end of the report to the effect that unless a special political and administrative regime were established, the social and economic clauses the committee had drawn up for the Saar could not be applied without "serious difficulties and conflicts." As for the French, they were willing to agree either to the erection of an independent state of the Saar attached to France by a customs union, or to a French mandate under the League of Nations. In the event the former proposal should be accepted, France would be assured of a buffer state which might be drawn further and further into the French orbit. If the latter alternative, as outlined by the French, were agreed to, the gradual legal absorption of the entire territory would be a possibility which France would labor to make a reality.

Both proposals were distasteful to President Wilson. Evidently he could not reconcile them with the principle of national self-determination which he considered of fundamental importance in making a just and lasting peace. The President thought that French fears of German sabotage and unwillingness to live up to the terms of the economic provisions could be allayed in other ways. Differences arising between Germany and the French Mines Administration should be submitted to an arbitration commission established for the purpose. This was quite unsatisfactory to the French, who argued that such a commission could not prevent disputes from constantly arising between Germany and France, and that it would actually usher in a "regime of perpetual lawsuits." Therefore they insisted that German sovereignty must at least be suspended for a period of fifteen years and a special political and administrative regime established.

The Saar issue was but one of many in which the American President found himself at odds with one or more of the nations at Paris. To "realists" on both sides of the Atlantic, he was a naïve knight-errant, unfamiliar with the facts of life in international politics. Henry Cabot Lodge wanted the United States to help dictate a quick, hard peace with Germany, but otherwise leave matters to the Europeans and bring the boys home. This must have given heart to Clemenceau and Wilson's other opponents who thought they knew better than he what the situation required. Thus the President found himself in conflict with France over the Rhineland and the Saar, with the Italians over Fiume, with the Japanese over Shantung, and on certain matters even with the British. However, the deadlock with the French over the Saar very nearly brought the Peace Conference to the breaking point. Actually it was at the most critical period in the Saar discussions that Wilson apparently decided that further efforts to get the kind of treaty he felt essential to guarantee a durable peace would be futile. He therefore ordered the *George Washington* to Brest, with the evident intention of returning to the United States should the French be unwilling to retreat from their position.

It now appeared that the victors in the war would be unable to write a peace. However, Wilson made one more effort to break the stalemate by proposing that the Saar be governed for fifteen years by an international administrative commission. During this period the French were assured that German sovereignty in the territory was to be suspended, the inhabitants would no longer be represented in the Reichstag, and the international commission was to be vested with full governing power. This compromise proposal was apparently intended to remove French fears that the Germans would be left in a position to sabotage the exploitation of the coal mines. On the other hand it would prevent possible use of the temporary economic rights of France in the Saar to acquire permanent political control. It was not what the French would have preferred, but it did represent concessions to the French point of view that might well prove of substantial value. Therefore they accepted it in principle and agreed to leave the drafting of the proposal to the Committee of Three which had previously been called upon for advice on the Saar. When they had completed their labors, Tardieu, the French member, declared that this section of the Treaty of Versailles "sets forth . . . . the principles which . . . . France had defended before the Conference." The criticisms that were directed against it not only by the Germans, but by the Socialists of France, General Jan Christiaan Smuts, Bernard Baruch, and others, give evidence that Tardieu accurately summed up the situation and that the French apparently had won the substance of their contentions. On the other hand, it was generally supported as, on the whole, the best possible solution of a difficult problem, having the merit—since a plebiscite was to be held after fifteen years—of not foreclosing the political future of the *sarrois*.

3

FRANCE, THE SAAR, AND THE LEAGUE

The Saar Territory, as defined in the Treaty of Versailles, was an artificial creation corresponding to no political or administrative unit or division that had ever existed in the past. It was formed out of portions of the territories of two German states, Prussia and Bavaria, and its boundaries were so drawn as to give it as far as possible economic unity. Thus not only the Saar Valley in large part but also an area extending north beyond St. Wendel and east to the town of Homburg were included. On the west and south it was bounded by Lorraine, on the north it faced Rhenish Prussia—from which it was for the most part carved—and to the east lay the Bavarian Palatinate, a small portion of which was included in it. Altogether it was smaller than Rhode Island, with an area of 723 square miles, but the controversy over its political disposition, as we have seen, almost wrecked the Peace Conference. The chief reasons for this have been suggested, but a fuller picture will make the treaty provisions concerning the Territory more understandable and at the same time more significant.

Although the French did not emphasize the strategic importance of the Saar to France when they presented their case at the Peace Conference, their diplomats and the military in particular did not lose sight of the area's significance for future defensive purposes. Perhaps their concentration on other aspects of their case grew out of a realization that President Wilson, at any rate, was less likely to be moved by considerations of "strategic frontiers" than by arguments giving the greatest weight to the welfare and the wishes of populations and to arrangements designed as far as possible to emphasize co-operation rather than conflict between nations. However, the French remembered that the German attack in 1870 was launched through the military route of the Saar, the first battle occurring in Lorraine about three miles from Saarbrücken, the chief city of the Saar. Their strategists therefore did not want to take the risk that in "the next war" it would serve as a springboard for an attack on Lorraine and the heart of France. They had always viewed the decision of 1815 at the Congress of Vienna as highly detrimental to the safety of France, since it had forced on her a weak frontier. That the Germans felt much the same way, regarding Lorraine as a base from which French troops could readily march into Germany, might also be true, but it could not be expected that Frenchmen in 1919 would have thought this relevant. The French had no designs on Germany, but after 1870 and 1914 they made their plans so that it would not "happen again." The Saar entered into their military calculations for another reason already mentioned—its "black gold." For coal and other minerals are essential to the prosecution of modern war, and the nation without ready accessibility to them is at a disadvantage in a contest of arms.

Prior to World War I the Saar was the third most important coal-producing district in Germany. If the Lorraine portion of the Saar field were to be included, the total output of 1913 was between seventeen and eighteen million tons. The area placed under the League of Nations in 1920 accounted in 1913 for approximately thirteen million tons, nearly one-third of the total production of the mines of France in that year. It has been estimated that the coal reserves of the Saar total sixteen and a half billion tons, probably greater than the entire coal reserve of France but small in comparison with the other rich coal resources of Germany. However, the Saar coal, although entirely adequate for factories, illuminating gas, and other domestic purposes, is not suitable for making coke. In steel manufacture, therefore, it has had to be mixed with coal from the Westphalian mines, until recently at any rate. The French now assert that they have developed a process for making high-grade coke from unmixed Saar coal, although the Germans dispute this claim. The importance of the mines in the life of the inhabitants of the Saar is revealed by the fact that the livelihood of about one-third of the population depended upon them. Looking at the economy of the Saar as a whole, it is evident that the mines were of the most vital importance to the entire population. In 1913, about one-third of their output was consumed in the Saar, Germany taking a total of 82 percent. Alsace-Lorraine, at that time a part of the Reich, absorbed about 12 percent of the total production of the mines.

The Saar has been fortunate in that the iron mines of Lorraine are only about thirty miles away, and thus only a short haul is required to bring the ore to the cokeries in the Saar. Hence, it has been possible to establish great iron and steel works, employing thousands of workers. One of the oldest industries in the Saar was glassmaking. In 1913 it ranked next in importance to metallurgy, also employing several thousand workers. The ceramic industry, producing tiles, pottery, porcelain, terra cotta, etc., occupied third place. Other minor but not insignificant industries were the chemical industry, explosives plants, and paper mills.

The coal and manufacturing industries have enabled the Saar to support a dense population. According to the census of 1922 it had 713,105 inhabitants, about 987 to the square mile for the Territory as a whole. The industrial area was and is the most concentrated in Europe. In the central and eastern parts food is grown on numerous small farms, and many of the miners and industrial workers have plots upon which food is grown by the family. However, the food-growing area has been sufficient to feed the crowded industrial population for only about forty days a year. The Saar has thus had to seek most of the food for its population ouside its own borders.

As regards the origins, ethnic character, and sentiments of the inhabitants of the Saar, French and German historians are in almost complete disagreement. Georges Clemenceau's assertion in the heat of the controversy at the Peace Conference that there were one hundred fifty thousand Frenchmen in the Territory was undoubtedly an exaggeration. On the other hand, in the Saarlouis district, French as well as German was spoken, and many of the inhabitants were either French or of mixed French and German ancestry. However, taking the Saar as a whole, the inhabitants at the time of the Peace Conference were overwhelmingly German in language and outlook. Politically, the Center (Clerical) party claimed the allegiance of the greatest number of the population. As one would infer, a large majority of the inhabitants were of the Roman Catholic faith. According to the census of 1922 there were over five hundred thousand Catholics and slightly less than two hundred thousand Protestants.

The foregoing historical data and a great deal more detailed information were available to the experts at the time they worked out the arrangements for the Saar, which were with slight modifications written into the Treaty of Versailles. Undoubtedly, these data were of service, especially in the determination of the administrative provisions of the Saar statute. Where political considerations were involved, they probably counted for less. At any rate, it was evident that, unless a clearly formulated vital principle were involved, political issues were likely to be resolved in favor of the French. André Tardieu was an able man and a skilled negotiator. Charles Haskins, the American member of the drafting committee, had previously in the negotiations indicated general concurrence with the French point of view rather than with that of President Wilson. The position of Sir Cuthbert Headlam-Morley, the British member of the committee, is not as well known, but it may perhaps be inferred that it reflected the apparently disinterested position of his chief, Lloyd George.

The first article dealing with the Saar in the treaty was at once a judgment on Germany and an iron-clad economic guaranty to France.

"As compensation for the destruction of the coal mines in the north of France and as part payment towards the total reparation due from Germany for the damage resulting from the war, Germany cedes to France in full and absolute possession, with exclusive rights of exploitation, unencumbered and free from all debts and charges of any kind, the coal mines situated in the Saar Basin . . . ." The stipulations interpreting and supplementing this article were such as might be regarded as reasonable on the assumption that the Germans would be disposed to sabotage the efforts of the French administration of the mines, which was to displace that of the Germans. But they also armed France with means of coercion against the local population, which could be used for political as well as economic ends. The mines became the "complete and absolute property" of the French state and it was assumed that the latter would exploit them as such. However, under the treaty France had complete liberty not to work the mines as well as to work them. If it desired to transfer the right to exploit them to a third party, the treaty sanctioned it. If it wished to import labor from outside the Territory to work in the mines or in their accessories, it was free to do so. Moreover, France was allowed complete liberty to determine the distribution and price of the products of the mines and their accessories and subsidiaries.

The Governing Commission of the Saar, as will appear, was purposely endowed with extensive executive and legislative powers in order that it might discharge its responsibilities without being handicapped by obstruction from the Germans or by undue interference from the Council of the League of Nations. However, in relation to France, the owner of the principal resource of the Territory, the Commission's powers were greatly circumscribed. For example, it could not exercise the power of eminent domain, nor might it take any measures which would affect the property rights of France in the mines and other immovables that might become the property of the French state. On the other hand, the Governing Commission had certain positive obligations. It was required to provide the equipment and personnel necessary for the transportation of the products of the mines and their accessories and of the employees and workmen of the French state. If in the opinion of France the improvement of any of the railways or waterways in the Saar should become necessary in connection with the transportation of the products of the mines, no obstacle was to be placed in the way of such improvement by the Governing Commission. Additional roads, electric lines, and telephone connections might be established by the French state itself, if it considered them necessary for the exploitation of the mines; and its freedom to exploit the new means of transportation and communication was not subject to restrictions.

The foregoing rights and privileges of the French state could perhaps be regarded partly as reasonable safeguards and partly as logical corollaries of the ownership of the coal mines by a power which considered that it had to assume German hostility as an established fact. However, other concessions to France, which seemed to have political overtones of considerable significance, were written into this section of the treaty. The French state was to be permitted to establish, as incidental to the mines, primary and technical schools for employees and their children and provide that instruction in these schools be given in the French language and in accordance with French educational ideas. Was this intended to be or might it become a means of de-Prussifying the Saar? The Germans, whose record with regard to the Poles and other nationalities in the late nineteenth century presumably qualified them to be judges in such matters—and who were aware that Tardieu and other Frenchmen in high places had expressed confidence that, given time, France could win the loyalty of the *Saarländer*—thought that here was an opening wedge designed for the purpose.

Two other stipulations in the treaty seemed to be intended to bring the Saar into the French economic orbit and to link the material welfare of the inhabitants so intimately with that of France that the closest political as well as economic association would be forged. The French state was to have the right to substitute French for German money in making payments, purchases, and contracts in connection with the mines or their accessories and subsidiaries. Given the economic rights of France and the intimate connection of various industries with the mines, this provision might well presage an eventual battle for survival between the German mark and the French franc over the entire territory. Of even more far-reaching importance was the provision that the Saar was to be subjected to the French customs regime. However, a five-year transitional period was provided during which, with some qualifications, products would be allowed to pass to and from Germany duty free. Although the treaty forbade export taxes on metallurgical products or coal exported from the Territory to Germany, or on German exports for the use of the industries of the Saar, the customs provisions were apparently intended to insure French control over the economic life of the inhabitants.

The government of the Saar Territory was placed under the League of Nations, as trustee, for a period of fifteen years. At the termination of this period a plebiscite was to be held, to give the inhabitants an opportunity to indicate their choice of either returning to Germany, or being united to France, or remaining under the government of the League of Nations. It may be observed that it was not specified in whose interest the League was to act as trustee. Remembering the constant insistence of France that a Saar regime must be established fully capable of guaranteeing her complete freedom in relation to the mines, the French, no doubt, thought of the trusteeship as properly intended to safeguard their interests. There were other interests, however, that were likewise considered by the non-French members of the committee that drafted this section of the treaty—namely, the interests of the inhabitants of the Saar and those of Germany. And, in the broadest sense, it would seem that there was the intent that the League should consider in its government of the Saar the stake of all nations in the peace and stability of the European community.

It was obvious to the framers that the League would have to entrust the actual government of the Territory to a body other than itself—a body in a position to develop an intimate knowledge of the problems which would inevitably arise with the enforcement of the terms of the treaty. It was therefore decided that there should be a Governing Commission, appointed by the Council of the League of Nations, which should "sit in the territory of the Saar Basin." The Commission was to consist of five members, and was to include "one citizen of France, one native inhabitant of the Saar Basin, not a citizen of France, and three members belonging to three countries other than France or Germany." Thus the country that had been granted extensive property rights and economic privileges was always assured of representation on the Commission, as was the Saar population which was subject to the new regime. But three places remained. The members appointed to these places were presumably intended to represent general rather than special interests, and since the Commission could take decisions by majority vote, they were theoretically in a position—whenever necessary—to hold the Commission to a disinterested course as against the special pleadings and preoccupations of the French or Saar members. The control over the Governing Commission by the League was insured by the provision that the members of the Commission were subject to annual appointment as well as removal by the Council of the League. However, it seems that the committee which drew up this section of the treaty had assumed that, as a rule, the members of the Governing Commission would be reappointed for a number of years. Considering the nature of the Commission's tasks and the necessity for a steady administration of the

Territory this was a sound policy, which the League Council was to follow as far as circumstances would permit.

Except for the limitations on its freedom of action in relation to the special position of France in the Saar, the Commission was granted extensive powers. The inhabitants of the Saar were completely severed from political connection with Germany, losing their right to be represented in the Reichstag and the Prussian and Bavarian legislatures. Henceforth they were to look to the Governing Commission as the legal authority for the protection of their rights and interests in the Territory and to it likewise for insuring the protection of their interests abroad. The powers of the Governing Commission of an executive and administrative nature included the appointment and dismissal of officials, the administration and operation of railways, canals, and the different public services, and the "full right of user of all property other than the mines." The Commission's legislative powers included the creation of administrative and representative bodies at discretion, the power to modify legislation pertaining to the mines in force in the Territory, after consultation with the French state, and to effect modifications in other laws and regulations in force on November 11, 1918, after consulting the elected representatives of the inhabitants. It likewise could fix the hours and conditions of labor of men, women, and children, and had the sole power of levying taxes and dues. Although judicial functions were left to the existing courts, the Commission was required to establish a civil and criminal court of appeal which was also to have original jurisdiction in matters for which the existing courts were not competent. Finally, the new government under which the people of the Saar were to live would be responsible not to them but to the League of Nations. However, the people were given certain political, civil, economic, and religious guaranties designed to afford them protection against arbitrary actions on the part of the Governing Commission and France. In particular instances, too, their rights were established as against Germany.

The bill of rights and guaranties deserves further attention, since it afforded the inhabitants of the Saar specific guaranties which could serve as a basis for appeal to the League of Nations. This saved them from having to endure without recourse the rule of an international commission imposed from the outside and, with one exception, composed of foreigners. It was perhaps the chief contribution of the Anglo-American members of the Committee of Three, and was actually to be invoked frequently, especially in the earlier years of the new regime.

As has already been noted, it was the intention of the framers of the Treaty of Versailles to sever completely the political connection between the Saar and Germany. However, there was no intent to force new local political institutions on the people. Thus, the local assemblies of the Saar inhabitants were expressly recognized, although they were to be retained "under the control of the Governing Commission." It was also specifically provided that every inhabitant over twenty years of age was to have the right to vote for representatives to these assemblies. The existing nationality of the inhabitants was preserved, but France was undoubtedly responsible for the qualification that no hindrance should be "placed in the way of those who wish to acquire a different nationality." Probably Tardieu and his French colleagues hoped that in the course of the fifteen-year period many of the inhabitants could be won to seek French nationality, and this, should it happen, would contribute toward France's success in the eventual plebiscite.

A number of economic guaranties were also included in the bill of rights. The Governing Commission, though having the power to fix the hours and conditions of labor in the Territory, was required "to take into consideration the wishes expressed by the local labor organizations, as well as the principles adopted by the League of Nations." The rights which the inhabitants had acquired to social insurance or pensions were to be preserved and continued by "Germany and the Government of the Territory of the Saar Basin." As has been observed, the Governing Commission alone had the power to tax, but all taxes and dues had to be applied to the needs of the Territory. Moreover, with the exception of customs duties, it was forbidden to impose new taxes without previously consulting the elected representatives of the inhabitants. And net receipts from customs on goods for local consumption must be included in the budget of the Territory. In view of the inexpediency of immediately severing the Saar economy from that of Germany, which would have undoubtedly worked a cruel hardship on the Territory, the following provisions were of greatest importance: No export tax might be imposed on coal and metallurgical products exported from the Saar to Germany or from Germany to the Saar, provided that such exports were for the use of Saar industries. Natural or manufactured products originating in the Saar were not to be subject to customs duties in transit over German territory, and products coming from Germany were not to be subject to transit charges over the Saar. For five years there were to be no import duties on products originating in the Basin and exported to Germany, and for the same period German products imported into the Saar for local consumption were to admitted duty free. It is interesting, however, to observe that this provision did not specifically forbid Germany from prohibiting the import of products from the Saar and, conversely, there was apparently no legal obstacle to the barring of German goods from importation to the Saar.

In addition to receiving guaranties of religious liberties, freedom of schools, and use of language, the inhabitants were completely freed from military burdens and expenditures. Neither compulsory nor voluntary military service was to be allowed, the construction of fortifications was prohibited, and it was expressly laid down that "only a local gendarmerie for the maintenance of order may be established." The protection of persons and property was an obligation of the Governing Commission, presumably to be discharged by means specifically allowed in the treaty. Finally, at the end of fifteen years the inhabitants were to be accorded the right to vote, "by communes or districts," on the question of their political destiny, the League of Nations rendering the final verdict after taking into consideration their wishes, as expressed at the polls. Thus not only were the basic rights of the population to be protected during the specified fifteen-year period, but at its conclusion they were to be allowed to express themselves on the fundamental question of their future political allegiance.

German critics of the treaty have often referred to it as the *Diktat* of Versailles. Certainly it was not a negotiated treaty except as among the victorious Allied and Associated Powers. Germany was not represented at Paris, nor were German officials consulted during the Peace Conference. However, when the draft treaty had been completed, the German government was given an opportunity to offer criticisms, and, even prior to the submission of the entire text, the Saar provisions of the treaty were handed to the Germans. The Germans, regarding this as a test case which would reveal whether the Allies were willing to soften the treaty at any point, were quick to press the attack: The Saar was inhabited by an "unalloyed German population." It should not be torn from Germany, especially since the German government recognized that France was entitled to reparation in kind and was prepared to guarantee deliveries of coal to France until such time as the French mines should be restored. Under the circumstances, to submit such a territory to foreign rule was "odious," no matter how humane such a rule might be.

Georges Clemenceau, replying for the Allies, pointed out that the "odious" administration to which the Germans referred was that of the League of Nations. The arrangement constituted a "prompt, secure, and businesslike method of compensation for the destruction of the French coal mines." At the same time it exacted "a definite and exemplary retribution" for this act of destruction. However, the arrangements were for a term of years, at the end of which the inhabitants were to be entitled to determine their final form of government. To the fear expressed by the Germans—that in the event of a favorable plebiscite they might not be able to buy back the mines within the period designated in the treaty and that the Territory would then not be returned to them—Clemenceau answered that the Allies might be willing to change the provisions of the treaty at this point so that it would be possible for Germany to meet her obligations and not lose the Territory.

The final and amplified position of the German government concerning the Saar was set forth in its "Comments on the Conditions of Peace" of May 29, 1919. After a reiteration of the usual German ethnic and historical claims and the desire of the inhabitants to remain in the German Reich, specific provisions of the Saar statute were singled out for criticism, such as the character and composition of the Governing Commission: "This Commission, whose seat need not even be in the Saar district, is not responsible to the population for its actions. Only *one* of its members must be a native and a resident of the Saar district, an arrangement which offers no security whatever that he may not be one of the few foreigners living in the country. This member is not to be elected by the people but appointed, subject to recall, by the Council of the League of Nations. Along with four representatives of other States, this member shall decide on the fate of the population with a power practically unlimited. A representative of the people with any legislative competence does not exist."

The fear of the Germans that France looked forward to future annexation of the Territory, and that the treaty provisions not only provided no safeguards against such a development but actually paved the way for it at certain points, was also expressed: "The importation of foreign laborers, which endangers the interests of German workmen, is not subject to any restrictions. Facilities are offered for the acquisition of an alien nationality. All this, together with undefined prescriptions about customs conditions, coinage, administration, railway traffic, and many other arrangements, offers every possibility to sever completely the connection between the Saar district and the remainder of the Empire."

Not only did the German government make the foregoing rejoinder, but the representatives from the Saar in the Reichstag also addressed an appeal directly to the Peace Conference. However, the

Allied and Associated Powers took the position that the German observations revealed "a complete misapprehension of the spirit and purpose of this section of the treaty," reiterated the reasons for including the criticized articles, and called attention once more to "the fact that the whole arrangement is temporary, and that at the end of fifteen years the inhabitants will have a full and free right to choose the sovereignty under which they are to live."

It might well have been conjectured from the German attitude at the Peace Conference, as well as from the character of German nationalism developed in the course of the nineteenth century, that the German government would not be convinced by Allied arguments as to the necessity and justice of this or any other unfavorable section of the treaty. For the moment, however, Germany was militarily impotent, and there was nothing to do but submit and await a favorable opportunity to reopen the argument. It could not now be resumed, for, as Frederick the Great had remarked, "negotiations without arms are like notes without instruments."

4

INTERNATIONAL CONTROL AND GERMAN
NATIONALISM

The framers of constitutions, no matter how wise they may be, cannot altogether anticipate in the fundamental law the needs of government in relation to the governed. Nor can they produce an instrument of government free from all ambiguities. Moreover, where others take over and begin to apply the instrument to actual situations, the process of interpretation and elaboration starts, and at this point in some degree a government of laws ends and a government of men begins. It would have been surprising, too, if the non-German framers of the Saar statute, drawn as they were from different nations and differently motivated, could have produced a document representing throughout a single point of view and quite clear in its meaning to all. On the whole, the framers did a workmanlike job as to clarity and precision. Such trouble as was to be encountered in carrying out the Saar provisions of the Versailles Treaty arose rather from a refusal of the Germans to accept the Peace of Versailles as a just settlement and, in particular, from their opposition to the application of certain of the Saar provisions.

The government of the Saar could not be put into operation until the Treaty of Versailles had come into force and the League of Nations had been organized. Specifically, the Council of the League, which was vested with the power of initiating and implementing the new regime, had to take action first. Thus it was not until February 1920, more than a year after the Armistice, that the first formal steps toward the establishment of the new government were taken. On that date Demetrius Caclamanos, the Greek representative on the Council of the League, who was asked to make proposals for initiating the Saar government, made a number of recommendations. His report was accepted, and the first step in the application of this section of the treaty was taken.

The first recommendation of Caclamanos, though it was accepted at the time seemingly as a matter of course by the Council, was later to be attacked by the Germans as unsound in principle and as having worked badly in practice. This recommendation was that the chairmanship of the Governing Commission should go to the French member. The reasons given for it, though plausible to the members of the

29

Council, did not impress the hostile and suspicious Germans: "The welfare of the population of the Saar and the necessity of maintaining order in this region require a close collaboration between the French Government, which by the Treaty controls a very important part of the economic life of the Basin, and the Governing Commission, to which the Council entrusts its administration. This collaboration cannot be better ensured than by the relations which a French Chairman of the Commission would maintain with the French Government, by his knowledge of the details of French administration . . . . and by the guarantee of a good understanding with France which, as a Frenchman, he would naturally possess."

Although, as has been observed, the rights and duties of the Commission were specified in the treaty, the Council adopted on the recommendation of its *rapporteur* "certain instructions and suggestions of a general nature for the use of the members of the Commission." These supplemented the treaty provisions at certain points and, though relating to procedural matters, were of the greatest importance in so far as they insured regular rather than sporadic accounting by the Commission to the Council of the League and publicity with respect to the administration of its responsibilities. This, it may be added, could never have been realized before 1920 in connection with the activities of any international commission, since no international organization, such as the League of Nations, capable of receiving and scrutinizing the reports and criticizing the policies of international agencies responsible to it, was at hand for the purpose.

The Council of the League provided that the Governing Commission of the Saar should meet in permanent session. Its administrative and other responsibilities obviously required that it exercise continuous supervision. The instructions, however, anticipated problems of sufficient importance, which the Council apparently did not desire to leave to the discretion of the Commission. Thus the Commission was instructed that decisions involving, for example, the interpretation of the provisions of the treaty relating to the Saar "must not be taken except in the presence of all the members of the Commission." And should the enforced absence of a member of the Commission necessitate the appointment of a substitute, "the appointment shall be made by the Council of the League of Nations." The French and Saar members, however, might in case of urgency appoint their own temporary substitutes, provided that the other members of the Commission were agreed in each case that the absence was justified. The secretary general of the League was to be informed by telegraph of such an appointment, and he in turn was to inform the Council of the

League. The latter was then to decide whether the appointment should be confirmed.

At another important point the treaty provisions were supplemented by the Council's instructions to the Commission. The treaty did not expressly require reports from the latter to the former. The Council, therefore, directed the Commission to report to it, through the secretary general, "in order to keep the League informed on all questions of interest." This the Commission was to do in quarterly reports throughout the fifteen years of its existence. Finally, it was enjoined to "have no occupation and no interest except the welfare of the people of the territory of the Saar Basin."

At the time these instructions were given to the Commission the Council of the League took the position that others might be issued as experience should indicate their necessity, but that the authors of the treaty provisions on the Saar intended that the Commission, at all times in close touch with the Saar people and their affairs, should have "the maximum power of appeal and judgment." The power of the Council to scrutinize its work at frequent intervals and, in its discretion, to change the personnel of the Governing Commission each year, fully protected the League from any possible danger that the Commission would become lax or prone to dispense favors to one side, contrary to the intent of the treaty provisions. It may be added that the League had been given many different responsibilities under the Covenant and the peace treaties and, "instead of burdening itself with too many details, should concern itself only with the most important matters and act chiefly as a supreme court of appeal."

There now remained the question of the personnel of the Governing Commission. In a sense, the decision of the Council at this point was more important than at any other; for at the time it appeared that the Commission, once appointed, would be given a free hand in governing the Saar and in interpreting the extent of its powers under the terms of the treaty. That any commission appointed by the Council would favor the German viewpoint in the course of its administration was as unlikely as that the Germans in and outside the Saar would co-operate and loyally support the fifteen-year League regime. The League Council for the first few years of the League's existence was for most purposes under the direction and control of Great Britain and France. Germany was not a member of the League and had no influence in the Council. The United States, the only other power capable of exerting a strong influence, had disassociated itself altogether from the peace settlement and never occupied the "vacant place" at the Council table. Japan, though a member of the League and of the Council, was for the most part a disinterested observer of European affairs. The small states, represented at one time or another on the Council, were seldom able to exercise any influence on its decisions. Thus Great Britain and France, owing to their power and prestige and their legal position as permanent members of the Council, enjoyed an unusual position. As long as they maintained their wartime solidarity and were in substantial agreement with respect to the policy to be followed toward Germany, they were likely to be in accord on the Saar; and this meant that Britain would go along with the French point of view.

The first appointments to the Governing Commission, as well as the decision that the French member should be its chairman, strongly suggest that the French influence in the Council of the League was powerful and perhaps decisive. Victor Rault, a French administrative official, was made chairman of the Commission, and given charge of the key posts of interior, foreign affairs, commerce, industry, and labor. Whatever may have been Rault's administrative competence, he was a single-minded French nationalist, who was charged with having openly pronounced in favor of annexation of the Saar at the time of the Peace Conference. As chairman of the Commission, he was to prove inflexible and unimaginative. He was not equipped with a knowledge of the German language, and seemingly had little understanding of the mentality of the people over whom he and his colleagues were to rule. Two other members of the Commission selected at this time were pro-French in their sympathies and could be expected to support Rault and thus insure a majority of votes in the Commission for measures desired by him. They were Major Lambert, a Belgian, who was to have as his assignment the other key posts of public works, railways, and the postal service; and Count Adam de Moltke Hvitfeldt, a Dane, whose country had been neutral in the war but who was a resident of Paris, and thoroughly sympathetic with the French point of view. He was apparently inclined to support at all times a pro-French policy in the Commission and, as far as possible, also the French propaganda efforts designed to counter those of the Germans. The latter regarded him as "an entirely Frenchified Dane." He was given charge of public education, ecclesiastical affairs, charities, health, and social insurance. Landrat Alfred von Boch, of Saarlouis, was selected to represent the Saar. He was not a very forceful man; and, in any case, the position of the Saar representative was delicate and difficult, especially in the earlier years of the Commission's existence. If he seemed to co-operate with his three colleagues in matters on which the majority of the Commission was at odds with the leaders of the Saar population, he was certain to earn the enmity of the latter. On the other hand, if he supported the position of the Saar leaders and organizations on the many issues which divided the Commission and the population, he would constantly find himself battling alone or almost alone in the Commission. Under the circumstances it is not surprising that the turnover in the post of Saar representative on the Commission was to be quite frequent during the early, more troublesome years. The fifth member of the Commission was to be Richard Deans Waugh, a Canadian, who did not arrive in the Saar until April 1920. The Departments of Justice, Agriculture, and Supply were reserved for him. He was a staunch League of Nations man and wanted to see the terms of the treaty with respect to the Saar carried out by the Governing Commission without fear or favor. He was to find himself frequently at odds with the chairman and the majority of the Commission, whom he charged with following a pro-French course. In consequence, he resigned in 1923.

The members of the Commission were to face a skeptical if not completely hostile population from the first. The day before assuming power—probably in anticipation of an unfriendly reception and of possible attempts by the Saar leaders to test its resolution—the Commission proclaimed in the newspapers of the Territory its concept of its duties and its determination to fulfill them. The clauses of the treaty relating to the Saar were to be enforced "in letter and in spirit," and the Commission was "firmly resolved to impose respect for its authority." The proclamation continued that "it will fearlessly suppress all attempts, from whatever source, to disturb or mislead the population. It will tolerate neither open violence, intrigue, nor passive resistance. The Treaty of Peace does not leave it without the necessary authority, and the powers conferred will permit the Commission to devote itself to its task without being troubled with useless and criminal opposition."

If the proclamation had concluded on this militant and challenging note, the Commission might well have been criticized. The inhabitants had chafed under French military rule, which had aggravated their hatred and distrust of France. A successful civil administration of the Territory would now have to depend upon the dissipation of this hatred by a conciliatory and constructive policy with emphasis upon the well-being of the people. No doubt, Rault and his colleagues were apprehensive of appearing before the German population with an olive branch rather than a sword. Germans obviously respected the sword. Therefore, only after first showing the sharp edge of the Commission's authority did the proclamation give the inhabitants a glimpse of the olive branch. The people were assured that in its administration the Commission would be "inspired by the principles that directed the establishment of the League of Nations." However, it could not be expected that, with Germany excluded from the League, the people of the Saar would be favorably impressed by this statement. Undoubtedly, it was of more interest to them that the Commission pledged itself to enforce respect for their rights and well-being and to pay particular attention to the development of industry and the improvement of working conditions.

On the occasion of the official entry of the Governing Commission into Saarbrücken, which it selected as the seat of government, delegations of officials and representatives of organizations of the Territory came to pay their respects and to promise loyal collaboration. Chairman Rault, on behalf of the Commission, replied to these courtesies by elaborating the principles contained in the proclamation of the day before. However, from the point of view of establishing cordial and confident relations with the population it was unfortunate that he also felt it necessary to make a point of paying a public tribute to the highly unpopular French military in the person of General Henri Wirbel, who had been the supreme administrator of the Saar during the military occupation.

Rault's tribute seemed to be a not-too-subtle reminder that the French military was at hand and at the disposal of the Commission, should the latter be forced to resort to it. Nevertheless, the first acts of the Commission indicated that it intended to set up a civil regime and, if possible, dispense with military procedures. It retained a reduced staff of army officials, as a temporary measure, but asserted that these would gradually be replaced by Saar civilians "under the direction of a few heads of services from other countries, chosen for their professional ability." Moreover, it immediately restored freedom of movement within the Saar, abolished postal censorship, took steps to re-establish the freedom of the press and right of assembly, dissolved the military police courts, and gave assurance that henceforth no inhabitant of the Saar would be summoned before a court-martial. Finally it promulgated an amnesty ordinance, covering sentences pronounced by the military police courts, and announced that other similar "measures of grace" would follow.

The installation of the new civilian regime raised the problem of establishing a central administration to replace the military administration which had been in operation since the Armistice. And since the Saar Territory defined by the treaty corresponded to no previous political entity, it was necessary to organize certain services and reorganize others to correspond with the newly made Territory over which the Commission was to govern. Unquestionably, in this connection, Rault's previous administrative experience was highly useful to the Commission. His study of the entire problem of necessary administrative reorganization led to recommendations which were adopted by the Commission and effected the "administrative and judicial autonomy of the Territory."

One of the matters demanding immediate attention was the reconstitution of local assemblies, for political as well as civil rights had been in abeyance during the military regime, and the treaty required that the Governing Commission consult the elected representatives of the inhabitants before modifying the laws and enactments in force on November 11, 1918. Rault, after an investigation of the local customs and a study of the electoral laws enacted in Germany since the Revolution of 1918, had a draft law prepared for discussion by the Commission and for the comments of the party leaders of the Territory. Consequently, prompt arrangements were made, so that elections under this law could be held before July 20, 1920.

The Commission, from the first, encountered economic problems which were difficult to solve and for which it was not responsible. Nevertheless it had to bear the brunt of criticism for their not being eliminated promptly. The transfer of the mines to France and the setting up of the new French customs necessarily disturbed the normal course of business and brought embarrassment to many interests. The German mark depreciated, working hardship especially on persons living on fixed incomes and resulting in prohibitive prices for French goods. To make matters worse, the German government decided in April 1920 to close the frontiers to both exports and imports. As the Saar was dependent upon Germany for the major part of its food and merchandise, this was serious; and the Governing Commission, with some misgivings, provisionally admitted a representative of the German commissioner for exports and imports into the Chamber of Commerce of Saarbrücken. This official was empowered by the German government to make adjustments and thereby facilitate the transactions of the trading interests of the Territory.

Additional economic difficulties were encountered. Under the provisions of the treaty, the French Mines Administration was obligated to supply a certain amount of coal to the Saar factories. This proved to be quite inadequate, but the Commission was powerless to remedy the situation. The steelworks suffered too from the failure of Germany to furnish them with more than a fraction of the amount of coke formerly supplied. In consequence they were compelled to reduce their output, and this in turn meant throwing workers out of employment. At the same time, labor demanded higher wages, which employers declared they were unable to grant. Still other economic problems cropped up, which will be described later.

In the meantime, in certain directions where it was not hampered by treaty restrictions or inhibited by political considerations, the Commission took resolute steps, calculated to improve conditions in the Territory and to give evidence of its good will toward the inhabitants. It reorganized the food supply services for the benefit of the population, took measures to relieve the housing shortage, and, in one instance, it successfully intervened with the French government to permit the entry into the Saar of certain much-needed articles of daily use, which could be obtained only from Germany. The French government had in this instance issued a decree forbidding such imports into the Saar, but withdrew the prohibition at the request of the chairman of the Governing Commission.

Nevertheless, when the Commission reported to the League of Nations in June 1920, it was apparent that it had made no progress toward reconciling the principal elements in the Saar to the new regime. According to the Commission, actual hostility was encountered chiefly among "the officials, the teaching profession, the clergy, and the higher industrial and commercial classes." It was also asserted that certain German organizations "whose purpose it is to oppose by all possible means the putting into force of the Treaty of Peace in the plebiscite areas" were at work in the Saar, and that they were carrying on their propaganda through the most widely read local newspapers. Actually, the Commission had not been in the Saar a month before plans were made by the Saar leaders to organize all classes in the Territory against the Governing Commission and the alleged annexationist designs of the French. Several mass meetings were held in Saarbrücken at this time to protest the Commission's policies, and measures were soon taken to unite all *Saarländer,* whether living in the Territory or residing in the Reich, to work for the return of the Saar to Germany. The resulting Saarverein, which was later to become the Bund der Saarvereine, had its headquarters in Berlin and local chapters throughout Germany. It published a biweekly periodical, the *Saar-Freund,* and gave the widest publicity to criticisms of the Governing Commission and the French Mines Administration.

The inference to be drawn from the report of the Governing Commission was that had these disturbing elements not continuously carried on agitation against the Commission, the Treaty, and the League of Nations, the people of the Saar would have understood and appreciated the efforts of the Commission to minister to their welfare. This, to say the least, was doubtful. Granting a certain docility of Germans in general toward their German governors, the automatic transfer of this habit of obedience to an alien government imposed upon them by a victorious enemy was not to be expected. And even with the very best intentions and the most intelligent effort, the Governing Commission, working within the limitations of the treaty and confronted with economic and social problems arising from the war, could not hope to find more than an unwilling submissiveness on the part of Saar Germans, who had known better days under a German government. Furthermore, German leaders, within and outside the Territory, were determined that the population of the Saar should retain its German nationalist feeling and remain sensitive to patriotic appeals. These appeals against the French military and the policies of the Governing Commission began almost immediately after the Commission reached the Saar, and caused it soon to recede from the liberal stand it had taken at the outset.

The first trouble started in April when the *Volksstimme,* a Socialist paper, published a bitter attack on the French army, in which it accused French troops of atrocities at the time of the occupation of Frankfurt. The general in command of the French troops in the Saar could not let the matter pass without retaliatory action. Did the Commission see any "political objections" to the institution of court-martial proceedings against the offending editor? The Commission replied that it saw no such objections, and since the paper refused to withdraw the charge, the Commission "allowed military justice to take its course." Reporting to the League on the affair, it pointed out that it was still dependent on French troops for keeping order in the Territory, since it had as yet been unable to organize a local police force, and that it could not allow aspersions to be cast on the French military forces. Moreover, the civil and criminal court, which the Commission was required by the treaty to establish, had not yet come into being, and if the case had been tried before the ordinary tribunal at Saarbrücken, the Commission foresaw that the offending editor would have been "ostentatiously acquitted."

On another matter the Commission itself threatened to take drastic action. Anticipating a railway strike, it issued a decree warning the railway men that should a strike occur, a state of siege would be proclaimed, civilian personnel would be requisitioned to assure continuance of service, and all workmen and employees would be required to obey the instructions of the authorities responsible for the maintenance of order. Recognizing that such extreme measures by a civil administration in time of peace called for explanation and justification, the Commission pointed out that the stoppage of transportation would imperil the population's food supply as well as endanger the public peace. Moreover, it would hamper the French in the exploitation of the mines and interfere with vital communication of the Allied Armies of Occupation.

This action of the Governing Commission is explicable as a necessary preventive measure, designed to protect the public interest and welfare of the Saar population and to safeguard French and Allied interests. It may be emphasized again that the Commission seems to have been convinced that most of the trouble in the Saar was due to the presence and activity of nationalist organizations and to agitators (acting in sympathy with or as agents of the German government) sent into the Territory for the purpose of stirring up opposition to the authority of the Governing Commission and discrediting it in the eyes of the population. It therefore took steps to control the admission of foreigners and to curtail the movement of those in the Territory. Naturally, these measures were unpopular and were branded as autocratic. However, the Commission acted within its rights in taking them, and its members seemed to be agreed on their expediency under the circumstances.

The first serious and open challenge to the Commission came in August 1920, six months after it began to exercise authority, in the form of a strike of the public officials of the Territory protesting the promulgation of an unpopular statute issued in July 1920. There were about thirty thousand officials of all grades in the Saar. Many of them had been sent into the Territory originally as appointees of the imperial, Prussian, or Bavarian governments. They still looked to these governments for aid in obstructing the Governing Commission, and, no doubt, for advancement when the Saar should return to the Reich. But under the treaty, all of them became officials of the Governing Commission, which had the power of appointment and dismissal. Undoubtedly, the Commission would have preferred to dismiss officials who were not native inhabitants of the Saar, in furtherance of its announced policy of making the Saar completely independent of Germany. But these Prussian and Bavarian officials had been carefully trained for public service, and there were not many natives of the Saar with the requisite qualifications. Consequently, the Commission requested the German, Prussian, and Bavarian governments to place their officials in the Saar at the Commission's disposal. It then reappointed them, requiring at the same time that they take an oath of fidelity to the Governing Commission.

As the services became permanently organized, the Commission planned gradually to introduce "inhabitants of the Saar" into them, although choosing the directing heads from skilled administrators drawn from other countries. In practice, these heads were selected principally from France. For the Central Administration the Commission adopted a rule that three-fourths of the positions available should be reserved for candidates from the Saar Territory. These measures were consistent with the over-all objectives of the Commission. As will be indicated later on in some detail, the Commission was determined to cut the political ties and as far as practicable loosen the various other bonds that held the people of the Saar in close and intimate association with their German kinsmen across the border. Possibly it was hoped that the *sarrois* would appreciate and take pride in having their "public servants" largely recruited from among inhabitants of the Saar. In 1920, however, it may well have seemed to the people of the Saar that the situation had only changed for the worse— in place of German administrative heads there now were French and a scattering of other foreigners. Moreover, their leaders never allowed the people of the Saar to forget that the French were plotting their eventual absorption into France, and that this—as well as all other policies of the Commission—was in reality directed to that end.

The grievances of the striking public officials, as publicly announced, centered about the method of selection, discipline, and dismissal adopted by the Governing Commission. The importation of foreigners was denounced, the disciplinary councils which the Commission had set up were opposed as being nonrepresentative, and the Commission's right to dismiss officials whom it considered disloyal was challenged. The Commission had taken the position that its officials might not belong to associations outside the Territory without permission. The officials on the other hand insisted that they should have the right to belong to any organization they desired.

It was evident that the Commission saw in the strike, which was apparently deliberately timed to synchronize with a Soviet offensive against Poland and with railway labor trouble in the Ruhr, something more sinister than a mere protest against certain of its administrative decisions. Chairman Rault, in his report to the League, explained it as "in the nature of an offensive prepared long beforehand, with the object of destroying the authority of the Governing Commission and of proving that the regime provided by the Treaty of Peace for the administration of the Saar Territory could not be established. The strike was intended to deprive the Governing Commission of the co-operation of all its officials, to reduce it to impotence, and to prove that a government established by the League of Nations in pursuance of the Treaty of Versailles would not be able to survive." The Commission, therefore, acted. A state of siege was proclaimed, the police were placed under the control of the military, the services of the railway employees were requisitioned, and a field railway company from the French Army of the Rhine was procured in order to insure uninterrupted train service. The military garrisoned in the Saar were likewise utilized. General Georges-Henri Brissaud-Des-maillet, commander of the French troops in the Saar, expelled about one hundred allegedly notorious Pan-Germans, for the most part German agitators whose regular residence, according to Chairman Rault, was not in the Saar. Further measures included prohibition of public meetings, censorship of the press, and the suspension of two newspapers which had published articles without the general's permission. In the meantime, Chairman Rault sought to prevent the spread of the strike to the miners and metalworkers by explaining to the unions the Commission's conviction as to the origin of the strike.

The strikers soon yielded before the resolute stand of the Governing Commission. However, they issued a manifesto that their action was not to be interpreted as an acceptance of the Governing Commission's position. Moreover, a general twenty-four-hour strike took place, to express the sympathy of the workers of the Territory for the officials and to protest against the action of the civil and military regime. Yet, the Commission considered that its tactics had preserved its prestige and averted disorders in the Territory. Chairman Rault, in reporting the outcome to the League Council, was apparently overjoyed at what seemed to him the realization of a new tranquillity in the Territory.

It was to become clear, however, that beneath the surface, at any rate among the Saar leaders, there persisted the resolve to oppose the Governing Commission and to discredit its policies. Actually, the Commission always drew a distinction between the common people of the Saar and the leaders who tended to follow instructions emanating from the Reich. And a few months later it came into the possession of a confidential circular alleged to have been issued by the German minister of the interior and intended for the officials of the Saar. The circular, after advising them that they remained "German officials," declared that they would be promoted by the German government independently of the Governing Commission, that their oath of allegiance to the Commission was not to affect their status in relation to Germany, that disciplinary action by the Commission was void, and that special advantages would be secured to the officials by the German government. The Commission learned that similar circulars were distributed to the German Saar officials allegedly by the Prussian and Bavarian governments. The German governments, of course, were not in a position to do very much for the Saar officials who received the circulars, but the latter were reminded that Germany, the Fatherland, had not forgotten and would not forget them.

Germany was not at this time a member of the League, and consequently could not take issue directly with the Governing Commission, but it did not fail on this and other occasions when Saar issues were before the Council or when Saar grievances were being aired to enter the lists against the Governing Commission. The expulsions by the military authorities were condemned as contrary to the laws in force in the Saar concerning liberty of movement and residence. It was argued that even a state of siege could not justify expulsions from the Saar Territory. Moreover, it was claimed that the Governing Commission had exceeded its authority by extending its decrees to cover the occupied Rhine provinces, which were outside its jurisdiction. The transfer of executive powers to a French general was likewise held incompatible with the provisions of the Treaty of Versailles, which called for the maintenance of order by means of a local gendarmerie.

The measures of the Governing Commission broke the strike of the public officials. The latter took the oath of loyalty to the Commission and accepted the statute of July 1920, the promulgation of which was the occasion for the walkout. Having won a clear-cut victory, the Governing Commission was disposed to be generous. Chairman Rault revised the list of expulsions ordered by the military authorities and removed many names. General Brissaud-Desmaillet pardoned others who had been sentenced to court-martial. The Governing Commission even decided to pay the officials and workers in the public services for the days during which they were on strike, although, as the Chairman explained to the League Council, it "was obliged to send back to their former governments several officials . . . . who continued their dangerous agitation."

5

IMPLEMENTATION AND RESISTANCE

No doubt, the leaders of the Saar would have grudgingly accepted a civilian international government, provided it were willing and able to follow a policy of laissez faire for the specified fifteen-year period and provided it were transitory. Certainly it would have been less onerous than the extended military occupation other parts of Germany had to endure under the treaty. However, as we have already seen, the Saar Commission was given such extensive governing powers under the treaty that, subject to review by the League of Nations, it could, if it wished to do so, cajole and coerce the inhabitants to turn their eyes eventually toward France. At any rate, the provision for a plebiscite at the end of fifteen years, to be administered by an alien government which they assumed would be intent on serving French interests, aroused foreboding among Germans and caused resistance all along the line to the policies of the Governing Commission.

One of the most bitter issues arose from the decision of the Commission to keep French garrison troops in the Territory for an indefinite period. On this question the Germans could base their appeal on the explicit terms of the treaty itself, which forbade both compulsory and voluntary military service in the Saar and specified that "only a local gendarmerie for the maintenance of order" was permissible. In rebuttal, the Commission could point to the fact that under the treaty it was required "to provide in all cases for the protection of persons and property in the Saar Basin." Conceivably it might find itself powerless to fulfill this primary obligation if it were to comply immediately and strictly with the terms of the treaty with respect to military forces.

The Council of the League of Nations recognized the dilemma that would confront the Commission should it have to rely upon the German communal and municipal police to start the enforcement of the treaty. It therefore decided that until the Governing Commission should be able to form the local gendarmerie stipulated in the treaty, it might have recourse in its discretion to the French troops stationed in the Territory. Accordingly, the Commission decided to retain the French troops until it could organize a gendarmerie of its own, but pointed out that henceforth these would have the status of garrison troops and not that of troops of occupation. As such, they would presumably be under the control of the Commission and could not employ arbitrary military procedures, such as might be used by foreign troops in occupied Germany.

The vigilant German government immediately protested this arrangement as a violation of the treaty and, in particular, objected to the exercise of French military jurisdiction over the inhabitants. It argued that justice in the Territory must be rendered in accordance with German law (French courts-martial operated under French law) and in the name of the Governing Commission. Thus, the only tribunals having jurisdiction in the Saar were the civil and criminal courts operating in the Saar when the Governing Commission began to function and the courts which it should set up under the treaty.

Chairman Rault justified the Governing Commission's position on legal as well as practical grounds. The treaty had not restricted the Commission as to the means it should employ in discharging its duty to assure protection to persons and property in the Territory. Rault also pointed out that the troops were entirely distinct from those making up the Army of the Rhine, and that their commander must comply with all requests made by the chairman of the Governing Commission. Moreover, the Commission could not dispense with these troops, because it was unable to recruit a local police force of four thousand men—which was estimated as the minimum needed. There were two reasons for this. In the first place, there was more attractive and remunerative employment in the mines and workshops; and secondly, the upkeep of such a large force would be "a crushing charge upon the resources of the Territory." This burden was being borne by France, which, according to Chairman Rault, was maintaining nearly seven thousand troops in the Saar to insure the safety of the mines. It was evident, also, that Rault was reluctant to recruit a local gendarmerie, pointing out "the defects inherent in police obtained by local recruiting," and reminding the League Council that the municipal police and local gendarmerie had gone on strike along with the other public officials.

The political parties of the Saar immediately took issue with the Governing Commission in a memorial to the League of Nations. A police force of fifteen hundred men would be adequate in a peaceful and law-abiding community, such as the Saar, and there should be no difficulty in recruiting and paying such a force of dependable men. They also asserted that although the French government was paying its troops in the Saar out of the French treasury, many communes suffered hardship through being required to furnish dwellings for the French military.

There followed a rejoinder by the Governing Commission and a memorandum in rebuttal by the political parties. Moreover, the German government sent a note to the League in support of the position of the political parties, pointing out that the Commission, although it had established a local gendarmerie by its decree of July 7, 1920, was proceeding so slowly that it would take about sixty years to bring the gendarmerie to full strength. Thus French troops would be called on to provide "an atmosphere free from undue influence" in the plebiscite of 1935. The point was then made that the maintenance of order in the Saar by the troops of a power greatly concerned in the outcome of the plebiscite was absolutely incompatible with the status of the Territory. The political parties also contended, contrary to the assertions of the Governing Commission, that it was possible to recruit a sufficiently large local gendarmerie, and offered as proof that there had been a large number of applications for appointment to such a force. It was also declared that the Commission's estimate of the expense of a normal police force was too high. The cost of an adequate force could be and would willingly be borne by the people of the Saar. However, as a result of the Commission's oppressive policies, it had been obliged to pay salaries to its employees higher than would otherwise be necessary, in the hope of securing a pliant body of civil servants. The memorandum concluded that the true cause of the presence of French troops in the Saar was to support intense French propaganda in the Territory and to try to intimidate the population so that they would vote for France at the time of the plebiscite.

German suspicions were further evidenced by protests of the German government against the employment of French military police by the Governing Commission. This body was composed of from 75 to 100 men and was intended primarily for the policing of French troops. However, it was given additional duties, such as supervision of frontier traffic and was called on to perform other tasks assigned to it by the chairman of the Governing Commission in the interest of general security. The German government asserted that this additional military force was not provided for in the treaty, that it formed an integral part of the French army through its discipline and organization, and that it was employed by the Commission as a special political police. Thus, it was alleged, the Commission delegated to this body such tasks as the gathering of confidential information about applicants for positions in the communal administration and the investigation, at one time or another, of the attitude of the population. These assertions were denied by the Commission, and the League Council apparently saw no reason to interfere.

On the other hand, the Council regarded the retention of French troops in the Territory more seriously. Actually, it developed that the Commission itself was not unanimous on the issue. Waugh, the Canadian member, was in favor of dispensing with French troops, pointing out that they could be stationed just outside the Saar and therefore made available to the Commission in the event of an emergency. Normally they would not be utilized in the Territory and, thus, one source of irritation would be removed from the field of controversy. The majority of the Commission evidently felt differently. Chairman Rault reported that the local gendarmerie would be enlarged as the financial situation permitted, but that the Commission was convinced of the necessity of retaining under any circumstances the garrison force of forty-five hundred men in the Territory. Nevertheless, the League Council began to exert pressure through the adoption of repeated resolutions advising the Commission to increase the strength of the local gendarmerie to the point where French troops might be withdrawn. However, as will be shown later, it was several years before full compliance with the Council's request was achieved.

The tenacity with which the majority of the Governing Commission held to their resolution to keep French troops in the Saar had an obvious and less sinister explanation than that suggested by the German government and the German political leaders of the Territory. The Commission, anticipating trouble at the time of the plebiscite, may well have desired a strong and reliable military force at hand to prevent intimidation of the voters. But it had another, more immediate and compelling reason. It was determined from the first to follow a policy of making the Saar "an autonomous country independent of Germany," and to take all the necessary steps to implement that policy; steps which, as it knew, were almost certain to meet with opposition and obstruction. Under these circumstances it wanted to have an adequate force on which it could depend at any time for the support of unpopular measures that it was resolved to take.

At the first opportunity, the Commission decided to adopt "certain measures designed to emphasize the political autonomy of the Saar Territory." Perhaps some of the members desired to foster a distinct Saar patriotism or at least emphasize the Territory as a political unit quite separate from the Reich. The Saar was furnished with a new flag and coat of arms as well as new "Saar" postage stamps. The treaty required the Commission to undertake "the protection abroad of the interests of the inhabitants . . . . by such means and under such conditions" as it should think best. In complying, the Commission took another highly unpopular step: It entrusted these interests to France. However, the Commission can hardly be blamed for failing to set up its own diplomatic and consular establishment. Such a move would have been expensive and, all things considered, unjustified. And to have entrusted these tasks to Germany, whose influence in the Saar the Commission desired to reduce rather than enhance, was unthinkable, and would in any event not have been consistent with the apparent intent of the framers of the Saar section of the treaty. The designation of a neutral power might well have offered the solution, and it was said unofficially that the Commission approached Switzerland, which declined the bid. As stated by Rault in his report to the Council, the Commission found it "natural, therefore, to confide the protection of the foreign interests of the Saar Territory to one of the Great Powers represented on the Governing Commission and possessing agents accredited to all the Powers." It appears that the French chairman, who also had the portfolio of foreign affairs, was deferred to by the other members of the Commission in the decision to ask the French government to accept the responsibility.

Another early decision of the Commission brought criticism from the Saar leaders on the ground that it was prejudicial to German nationals, and in particular would affect them adversely at the time of the plebiscite. The term "inhabitant of the Territory of the Saar Basin" was employed several times in the treaty, but "inhabitant" had never been defined. What was the status of an "inhabitant"? How might it be acquired, and how lost? The Commission decreed that persons born in the Territory and those resident in the Territory on November 11, 1918, were inhabitants by right. Other persons residing in the Territory for a period of three years might become inhabitants. And in the case of public officials and others able to prove that they held "a position which requires that their main residence be in the Territory" the period of residence was reduced to one year. Thus German nationals unable to meet these requirements were henceforth considered as foreigners.

The Commission brought the draft decree before the local assemblies, as it was obligated to do under the treaty, in order that they might express an opinion. The Commission stated frankly that inhabitants of German nationality had enjoyed "considerable privileges in comparison with the nationals of other states," and therefore that it thought it necessary "to lay down that nationality should no longer be a hindrance to the inhabitants of the Saar Territory." As was to be expected, the local assemblies opposed the decree. The political leaders denounced it as discriminating against German nationals and favoring "immigrating foreigners." Under its terms German nationals who did not possess the status of inhabitants, as defined by the Commission, were classified as aliens. Altogether, the decree was obnoxious to the Saar representatives, but it was nevertheless adopted by the Commission.

It has been noted that the Commission was obligated under the treaty to consult the elected representatives of the inhabitants whenever it found it necessary to modify the laws and regulations in force in the Territory at the time of the Armistice. The manner in which the Commission interpreted and carried out this obligation brought constant protest from the Saar leaders that it was arbitrary, autocratic, and evasive. They complained that too frequently the Commission did not consult them at all, and when it did, it did so in a devious way, and, in any case, it freely disregarded their advice. However, the treaty had only required the Commission to consult the elected representatives of the inhabitants in such a manner as it might deem expedient, thus leaving the Commission full discretion in the matter. It might consult the various local assemblies or set up a general assembly for the Saar Territory. The Commission decided on the former, pointing out that the moment was not opportune for summoning a general assembly and that it "seemed more practicable, as well as more in accordance with the spirit of the treaty," to invite the local assemblies to give their opinions on proposals submitted to them by the Commission.

The Saar leaders, who often found themselves defending what they argued was the intent of the treaty as against the interpretation put upon it in any particular instance by the Governing Commission, at once declared that the Commission was evading its obligations. The piecemeal consultation, they strongly hinted, was intended to obscure rather than elicit the true views of the population, for the Commission consulted the people of the Saar by requiring eight different governing bodies to confer separately on issues put before them. The Saar leaders contended that to get a clear comprehension of public opinion, the Commission should provide for a parliament of the Saar. The local assemblies finally even threatened to refuse to examine any proposal of the Commission if it should not accede to their request.

The Governing Commission was not disposed to yield to the request, arguing first of all that it was not the intent of the framers of the treaty to have such an organ of government created. Moreover, since the Governing Commission possessed with respect to the Saar the legislative powers formerly belonging to the German Empire, Prussia, and Bavaria and might decide as well as put into effect all modifications of the laws, it doubted the wisdom of setting up an elected parliament in competition with the League government. And finally, the Commission reminded the German leaders that the Saar was a plebiscite area deliberately placed under a strong international government "above all parties and all currents of opinion," in order that the inhabitants might give free expression to their wishes in 1935; and if the proposals of the leaders of the Saar were adopted, the whole object of the regime would be defeated.

The Saar political leaders were nevertheless persistent. In March 1922 they called a conference representative of the principal political parties of the Saar, including delegates of the local assemblies. At this meeting a resolution was adopted, calling for the creation of a popular assembly which should have "full rights of participation in the government." Moreover, voters and candidates for this assembly must be of German nationality. In the event of disagreement between this new organ and the Governing Commission, it was proposed that the matter should be referred to the League of Nations for final settlement.

In the meantime, the Governing Commission itself came to the conclusion that it was not practicable to submit its draft decrees to the numerous local assemblies, and decided to establish a single assembly for the whole Territory. However, this took the form of an advisory council quite different in selection and composition from what the Saar leaders had demanded. It was to be composed of thirty representatives elected by the Territory as a whole for a three-year term, and only persons more than twenty years of age who could claim the status of "inhabitants of the Saar" could take part in the election. Moreover, to qualify for a seat on the Advisory Council one was required to be a native inhabitant of the Territory and to have no elective or public post outside the Saar. Finally, the Commission itself was to appoint the chairman from among the inhabitants of the Territory.

As for its competence, the Advisory Council was to be limited to the consideration of such proposals as the Commission should submit to it under the stipulations of the treaty. It was provided that it should meet every three months, but it could only be convened by the chairman of the Commission and had to confine its discussions to the agenda with which the chairman presented it. Any discussion on other subjects, such as decrees of the Governing Commission, was to be considered null and void. The Advisory Council was, thus, far from being a parliament; it was not even a debating society.

The solicitude of the Commission, however, caused it to decide to create a second body, the Technical Committee. The latter was "to provide the inhabitants with the possibility of taking an interest in administrative, political, and financial matters, in which, according to the terms of the Treaty of Peace, the representatives elected by the people are not called upon to take a part." The Technical Committee was to be small, it was to be composed of native inhabitants of the Saar, and its members were to be further selected on the basis of their experience and acquaintance with local conditions in the Territory. The members were to hold yearly appointments from the Commission and were to assist the latter on all matters of a technical nature submitted to it.

The decree establishing these two bodies, far from appeasing the Germans, aroused the greatest resentment, and was bitterly attacked by the newspapers and political parties of the Territory. For a time it seemed likely that the parties would abstain from taking part in the elections, though eventually they decided to participate. But the representatives they selected for membership on the Advisory Council utilized the occasion of the first meeting to review their grievances against the Governing Commission and state the price of their co-operation with it. As for the Advisory Council, a spokesman of the Center party declared that "it limits our political rights much more strictly than does the Treaty of Versailles." There was a general demand that the Advisory Council be given the right to ask questions, to present grievances, and to participate in the drawing up of the agenda for its meetings. Other demands were for the right of initiative and for parliamentary immunity. Strong protests were voiced against the appointment of its chairman by the Governing Commission and against Germans not born in the Saar being ineligible to sit on it. The Social Democratic party also protested against the establishment of a Technical Committee, which it regarded as an antidemocratic institution, designed to discount the views of the representatives of the elected body, the Advisory Council.

The occasion of the first meeting of the Advisory Council was employed to censure the Governing Commission for its "Frenchifying policy," as a representative of the Center party expressed it, and for its aim to separate the Saar from its mother country and have it annexed by France. The Social Democratic party's representative delivered an ultimatum—which in substance seemed to express the sentiments of the representatives of the other parties—in the following language: "The indispensable condition for the co-operation of the Social Democratic Party is that the Governing Commission should cease to follow the French annexationist policy, which leads it openly to propose to transform the Saar Territory, in fifteen years, into a country politically and intellectually ripe for annexation to France." Thus the "new era" in the relations between the Governing Commission and the Saar inhabitants was not ushered in with the creation of the Advisory Council. On the contrary, the use to which the occasion of the first meeting of that body was put indicated rather that the old struggle was likely to go on, the Germans simply utilizing a new piece of machinery, in so far as it might be serviceable, to aid them in the fight.

It is difficult to see how the Governing Commission could possibly have fulfilled its obligations under the treaty short of the steps it took in setting up the Advisory Council; although it might well be argued that the concession it made in this instance was formal rather than substantive in character. Nevertheless, its action was censured not merely by the Germans but for quite different reasons by right-wing French elements as well. A French commission sent into the Rhineland in 1922 pointed out the various safeguards the Governing Commission had provided to protect its position in relation to the Advisory Council, but concluded nevertheless that it was a grievous mistake to set up such a council at all. For how could the Commission prevent an elected assembly from passing resolutions and from publishing them far and wide? And might not elections to the Advisory Council be utilized to interrogate the people and give to these elections the character of a plebiscite? Moreover, the inhabitants were not to be consulted piecemeal by districts, which would make it possible "to avoid a great current of opinion, to split it up in some way," but on the basis of a single list for the whole Territory. Thus, there existed the danger of a premature plebiscite with unfortunate results. Implicit in this argument was a censure of the Governing Commission, which on this as on other occasions was to find that it could please neither the ardent French nationalists nor the equally ardent German patriots.

The Governing Commission also took certain steps in the early period which, in the view of the Saar leaders, were designed to further the alienation of the Territory from Germany and orient it toward France. Under the terms of the treaty it was in a position to take certain decisions with respect to the Saar educational system, and it lost no time in the adoption of measures designed to separate this system from that of the Reich and make it autonomous. Within a few months after taking office, the Commission decided that a general reform of the public educational system was necessary, and appointed a committee of resident professors and teachers to draw up a reorganization scheme. It also decided to place in charge of the Department of Education a priest of the Saar Territory rather than a German from the Reich. Among reforms it projected was the founding of a higher technical school for the Territory. The Commission pointed out that Prussia had deliberately avoided setting up such a local school in order that students seeking such training would be compelled to attend establishments in the interior of Germany. However, the Commission contended that such an institution was indispensable in a mining and industrial region like the Saar, and that its establishment would give satisfaction to "people of the Saar Territory who are desirous of completing their professional education in their own country." The phraseology seemed to suggest that Germany was not the country of the *sarrois*, at least not any longer, and undoubtedly had the effect of deepening the suspicions of the Saar leaders.

However, the most serious cleavage between the Commission and the Saar leaders, as regards education, grew out of the Commission's interpretation of the scope of its power under the provision of the treaty empowering the French state to establish and maintain, as incidental to the mines, primary or technical schools giving instruction in the French language for the mining employees and their children. The French Mines Administration made use of the opportunity and opened free primary and technical schools of its own, where instruction was given in the French and German languages. According to the Governing Commission, many requests were received from parents of German nationality that their children be permitted to attend these schools. As a result, it decided to issue certain decrees making this possible. One decree permitted children of employees of the Mines Administration, regardless of nationality, to satisfy the compulsory education requirement by attending the schools of the Mines Administration. A second decree allowed children of persons not employed in the mines to fulfill the educational obligations prescribed by law by enrolling in these schools.

The Governing Commission reported that the Department of Education received a great many applications from parents who desired to have their children attend the schools of the state mines, and that Count de Moltke Hvitfeldt, who was in charge of public education, was "convinced . . . . that a large part of the population wishes to see the study of French introduced into the primary schools." Count Moltke's pro-French bias was well known, and his enthusiasm for the French cause may have been responsible for his optimistic estimate. However, the Commission took what would seem to be a sound position when it pointed out that in a frontier community, such as the Saar, "a knowledge of two languages confers an obvious superiority and represents a real advantage." Accordingly, it decided to institute optional courses in French for children from ten to thirteen years of age attending the regular primary schools. In addition to this provision, special classes were organized in the primary schools to meet the needs of pupils "who desire, before leaving the primary schools, to prepare themselves for going on at the age of thirteen or fourteen to secondary schools in which French is a compulsory subject."

It should occasion no surprise that these measures aroused alarm and led to resistance by the German leaders. For most of the children attending the schools and affected by these decrees would in the natural course of things be voters in 1935, at the time of the plebiscite. From the German standpoint, therefore, they must be vigilantly shielded from French influences and the German cultural inheritance must be passed on to them. Thus, the German language was to be maintained, and educational innovations and experiments foreign to the German pattern were to be opposed. As far as one may be able to judge by the protests of important organized groups in the Saar, the population regarded the actions of the Commission and of the French Mines Administration as most reprehensible. There were strong protests, not only from the political parties but also from the trade unions, the press, the teachers, and the clergy. In the ensuing struggle the German government, as was its custom, supported the Saar leaders by drawing the attention of the League of Nations to the matter and arguing the illegality of the Commission's action.

It was pointed out that by the provisions of the treaty the inhabitants of the Saar were to retain their schools and language, and that the Commission was therefore under an obligation to maintain "the fundamental principles governing the school organization at the time of the coming into force of the Versailles Treaty." Contrary to this, it was asserted, the Governing Commission was pursuing a policy aiming at a fundamental modification of the entire school system, and it had introduced innovations and "made experiments of all kinds" that were of questionable value from an educational standpoint. Moreover, the Commission's decrees, enabling not only the children of German miners but also the offspring of persons not connected with the mines to attend the schools of the French state mines, had never been submitted to the elected representatives of the Territory, who should have been consulted in accordance with treaty requirements. Actually, it was argued, these French schools were, according to the treaty, to be "incidental to the mines," and therefore open only to the French children of the Mines Administration's employees, but not to children of the miners themselves, who were, of course, German.

Likewise, it was contended that French schools in the Saar that were neither primary nor technical should be abolished.

The German government not only accused the Commission of violating the treaty, but also charged the officials of the French state mines with a policy of favoritism and bribery designed to lure German children into French schools. It was asserted, for example, that the regular schools of the Saar were placed at a disadvantage, for the French state mines' schools offered "pocket money, free school outfits and clothes, Christmas presents, favorable treatment of parents who send their children to the French schools, and detrimental treatment of those who refuse to do so." Moreover, it was charged that in the French schools there was less severe discipline, that nonattendance was treated with great leniency, and that promises or rewards were made to individual children if they would induce other children to attend.

Chairman Rault made a spirited and, on the whole, rather effective defense of the Governing Commission's position to the League. He stated that the Commission was governed in the first place by the conviction that parents "should be free to choose a school for their children and that anxiety for their children's future might often lead the parents to send them to a school maintained by the Mines, having regard to the proximity of the French frontier, and the important part played by France in the economic life of the Territory through the Mines, the customs, and certain industries which she possesses . . . ." However, the Commission had advised parents on the application form for admission to the French schools that it was highly unlikely that graduates of these schools would be allowed to continue their studies in Germany or secure administrative posts in the Reich. Chairman Rault produced figures to show that while the number of parents desiring to send their children to the French schools was not so negligible as to be ignored, they were small in proportion to the total public-school attendance. Thus, in January 1923 there were 4,408 children on the registers of the mines' schools, of whom 3,798 were of German nationality. But as against this number, there were 123,000 attending the national schools. Assuming the substantial accuracy of these figures, the charge of the German government that "the national schools of the Territory have become positively deserted" seemed rather grotesque.

The Council of the League of Nations considered the question during 1923 and 1924, finally adopting the report and conclusions of its *rapporteur*, in which he said, "I rely on the wisdom of the Governing Commission, and I am fully confident that it will find a means of allaying the anxiety which this matter seems to have aroused in certain sections of the Saar population." This seemed to say that the Council would not interfere but would rely upon the Commission to correct anything that needed correcting. Whether or not this was a delicate suggestion that the Commission should re-examine its policy in relation to education, it undoubtedly was responsible for a decision which the Commission took shortly thereafter. Reasserting its legal right to grant permission to parents not employed in the mines to send their children to the primary schools of the French Mines Administration instead of to the public schools, the Commission now declared that henceforth it would not grant such permission except in extraordinary circumstances. This concession, or capitulation, as the German leaders preferred to regard it, removed this question from the area of serious controversy for several years.

Another source of friction between the Commission and the political leaders, and the clergy as well, was the policy of the Commission in relation to the religious groups in the Territory. The Commission announced its intention to relieve the population from dependence "to any extent or in any way . . . . upon authorities situated outside the Basin . . . ." The extension of the idea of autonomy for the Saar to the religious sphere met with immediate resistance from religious as well as political quarters. Over 70 percent of the people were Roman Catholics, owing direct obedience to the bishops of Trier and Speyer. The Protestants also were under the Evangelical church organization of the Rhine Province. It is understandable that the Commission, which had so energetically set about severing the political conections of the Saar with Germany, should look with a certain amount of apprehension on the religious ties linking the great majority of the population to their old country. The disciplined and docile Catholics of the Saar could be expected to look for and follow the instructions of their German bishops rather than the Governing Commission in any and all matters of controversy. The Commission therefore decided to approach Rome with the request that a separate diocese, quite independent of the German hierarchy, be established for the Saar Territory. However, the Commission failed in this attempt and had to face political opposition and hostility from the Reich bishops as well as from the Catholic clergy in the Territory, although the latter were paid from the treasury of the Territory. An early and spectacular instance of this opposition occurred in 1923. On *Katholikentag* seventy thousand Catholics gathered at Saarbrücken and staged a great demonstration against the Governing Commission. The Bishops of Trier and Speyer were present and lent encouragement to the host of marchers who protested against the ecclesiastical policy of the Commission and swore to maintain the connection with Bavaria and Prussia. That the German bishops were aligning themselves with the political leaders in the struggle against the Governing Commission was indicated in other ways too. For example, the Bishop of Speyer intervened in the school controversy by sending a pastoral letter to be read in the churches of his diocese in the Saar, calling upon Catholic parents to withdraw their children from the schools of the Mines Administration and send them to the national schools. The bishop may have been influenced by doctrinal considerations at this time, since children allowed to attend the French mines' schools might be lost to the Church. In any event, his action reinforced and gave a religious sanction to the deliberate and sustained policy of the political leaders of attacking the Commission whenever possible.

On certain economic issues the Commission also came into collision with Saar leaders, in spite of the fact that in the economic domain it had fewer opportunities to take decisive initiative. The economic provisions of the section of the treaty pertaining to the Saar were at once so minute and so sweeping—André Tardieu and his advisers no doubt saw to that—that on most vital matters there was little left for the Governing Commission to do. It could, on the one hand, stand by and see that the rights and privileges granted to France were not denied her, and, on the other hand, it could take such action as it might to reduce the hardships and uncertainties involved in the severance of old economic relationships and the establishment of new ones. But if the Commission seemed to be shorn of power in the economic sphere, this power was not vested in the people of the Saar but was conferred on France. However, as will appear, the decisions of the French officials and the Mines Administration could and often did leave the Commission no choice but to take political decisions obnoxious to the Germans. The significance of these decisions, in view of the future plebiscite, was of course not lost on the Germans, who, at the same time, saw in the Commission's actions fresh proof of an evil design.

It will be recalled that a most important and unusual provision in the treaty forbade the prohibition or restriction of the circulation of French money in the Saar. This provision becomes understandable if one bears in mind that the French state owned and operated the mines, that their exploitation and prosperity were vital to the entire economic life of the Territory, and that there was the desire to protect France at every turn in her use of her property. The French state mines were not tardy in availing themselves of the privilege granted by this provision. In July 1920 they began to pay the miners in francs and from then on conducted all their financial transactions in French currency. Of course, it could be pointed out that the mark was depreciating while the franc was stable. Actually, the miners recognized that they would be better off with the French currency and favored the change. The decision, however, resulted in about seventy thousand workers of the Saar receiving wages in a currency of higher value than the mark and caused a rise in the cost of living. And as the mark continued to depreciate, the miners came to occupy a privileged position, and workers in other industries began to complain that their wages were inadequate.

The first demand that wages be paid in francs came from the metalworkers' Socialist trade unions. They, too, wanted to get more goods, still selling in mark currency, for their money. The Governing Commission regarded the matter as outside its jurisdiction and was not disposed to intervene. At first, the employers would only agree to an increase in wages paid in marks. However, within a few months the ironworks and some of the foundries yielded and consented to pay their workers in francs. Finally, although the employers in some types of finishing works still refused to pay wages in francs, the great majority of the working population were being paid in French currency. The procedure was not unfeasible after all, for some important industries, notably the steelworks, were under French control and thus were disposed, other things being equal, toward the introduction of the franc. On the other hand, the iron- and steelworks depended upon Germany for their chief market, which meant that they were paid for their products in depreciated marks while they had to purchase their ore and coal, and now pay their workmen, in francs. This forced them to seek new markets, and as a by-product of this situation French capital found an easier entry to the Saar.

In the meantime the Governing Commission could not remain indifferent to developments. In December 1920, Chairman Rault submitted a report to the Commission in which he predicted that the franc was certain to oust the mark, and that as an employer of labor the Commission itself must face the question of paying its employees in francs. According to Rault, a number of officials of the Central Administration had already requested that they be paid in francs. Therefore he suggested that the whole question be studied, and the Commission followed by appointing a committee to investigate the situation and make recommendations. In the meantime, events more or less indicated the path which the Commission was to take in the following months. In March 1921, the minister of public works submitted a report pointing out serious budgetary difficulties confronting the Commission as a result of the retention of the depreciating mark, and recommending that the salaries of railway, postal, telegraph, and telephone employees be paid in francs, and that charges for service also be reckoned in French currency. The Commission agreed. A short time later it took a similar step with respect to the salaries of officials of the Central Administration, the constabulary, the Saar police, and the employees of the water system. Later still, in August 1921, it accorded legal recognition to the *de facto* dual currency system by substituting in the Civil and Commercial Codes "the two currencies of the country" for "the currency of the Empire." The franc was now well on the way to complete victory.

The decision to adopt the French franc as the sole legal tender of the Saar was foreshadowed in subsequent reports of the Commission to the League. In December 1921 it pointed out the difficulties arising from the circulation of two currencies, one of them constantly depreciating, and recalled that on January 10, 1925, importations from Germany would be subject to French customs duties and that prices undoubtedly would rise. For that reason "there should be as many persons as possible in the Territory in the possession of francs." A year later the Commission reported that the situation resulting from the depreciation of the mark was greatly aggravated; that it had become "impossible to balance a regular budget," either for government or for commercial and industrial enterprises, as long as the fluctuating mark was used as currency. Moreover, the necessity for constant revision of salaries paid in marks had given rise to labor disturbances and demonstrations, and a committee of the Free Syndicates and the Socialist and Communist parties had demanded either that the double currency system be abolished or that the French currency be established as the sole legal tender. A short time later, in June 1923, the German currency was eliminated by action of the Commission, and the franc became the only legal currency of the Saar Territory. This action was taken without consulting the elected representatives of the people, who undoubtedly would have strongly opposed it.

The Commission's early attitude of benevolent neutrality toward the franc, which finally developed into decisive support for that imported currency in its winning battle against the mark, met the same distrust and hostility from the German government and from German leaders in the Saar as had all other acts of the Commission that could be regarded as in any way adverse to the maintenance of an unimpaired connection between the Saar and the German Fatherland. They severely criticized the Commission in the first place for having failed to consult the people's elected representatives before introducing the franc into the public services. They questioned that the officials and workers had asked for the introduction of the franc, but in any event, they declared, the situation had been created by the Commission itself, because it had refused to grant necessary increases of wages and salaries in marks. The critics asserted that even under the existing circumstances 71 percent of the railway employees had voted against the franc, and that the allegedly representative Saar Economic Council had taken a decided stand against it. And, first and last, they contended that under the treaty the German mark must be retained as the only official currency of the Territory, use of the French franc being allowed only in exceptional cases in transactions of the French state mines.

It had thus become clear over a three-year period that the Commission's policies and, in fact, the Commission itself were unwelcome and suspect, at any rate as far as the German government and the political leaders of the Saar were concerned. These forces were against the regime itself, the treaty provisions under which it operated, and the whole *Diktat* of Versailles, which by various devices and in different ways "enslaved" the German people.

6

APPEAL AND MEDIATION

It is obvious from what has already been recounted that no commission for the Saar would have been able to function effectively and perhaps even survive for its full life of fifteen years had there been no over-all international institution, such as the League, to give it advice, supervision, and assistance. While it cannot be contended that the Saar Basin Governing Commission was entirely removed from international politics by being attached to the League, it did have a measure of freedom and a security of tenure as a corporate body, such as previous international commissions had not possessed. The members of these earlier commissions were the appointees of national governments, and could be recalled and replaced at will by their governments. To be sure, if they dealt exclusively with technical matters, removed from the field of political controversy, they might work with comparative freedom, and expect renewals of their limited tenure. But the individual members of these commissions owed allegiance to the governments of the states which appointed them, and if national interests were assumed to be involved, they could hardly function freely as representatives of international interests or as international agents.

The members of the Saar Basin Governing Commission were theoretically at liberty to discharge their responsibilities without instructions from any national government. On the other hand, they were required to render a regular accounting for their actions to the international body which appointed them, the Council of the League of Nations. In practice, the French member of the Commission, and, it is to be inferred, the Saar member, sought or received advice from the parties whose interests they were expected to safeguard—France and the Saar Territory. But, as in the case of the others, they were bound by the relevant provisions of the Treaty of Versailles and owed allegiance to the League of Nations. Moreover, such control as France or any other government might legally exert over members of the Commission could only be exercised collectively. Any member of the League of Nations represented on the Council was, as has been stated, in a position to participate in the selection of the personnel of the Commission as well as in the determination of their salaries, and could collaborate with the other members of the Council in their supervision. Likewise, the representative of a Council member participated with his colleagues in the consideration of the quarterly reports of the Commission, in the examination of petitions, memorials, complaints, and other matters relevant to the work of the Governing Commission and to conditions in the Saar Territory.

Up to this point the League and the Council have practically been referred to interchangeably in their relation to the Saar. However, the Council, though sharing with the Assembly the leading position, was but one of several bodies making up the League of Nations. And although it was designated in the treaty as the agency responsible for establishing the government of the Saar Territory and maintaining a certain supervision of that government, it was itself subject to the scrutiny of the League membership represented in the Assembly. Actually the treaty vested the government of the Saar in the League of Nations, which was to act "in the capacity of trustee." Likewise, it was the League of Nations, rather than the Council specifically, that was entrusted with deciding after the plebiscite the sovereignty of the Saar. However, the apparent intent of the framers of the treaty was that the Council should have sole jurisdiction as regards the Saar, and the League acted upon this assumption from the beginning to the end of the Saar regime. At the same time it must be pointed out that the Council annually reported on the government of the Saar, as on other matters for which it was responsible, to the Assembly. It was recognized almost from the first that the Assembly had the right "to discuss and examine any matter which is within the competence of the League," and that it was within its province to concern itself with any matter "affecting the peace of the world." Actually it rarely gave attention to the Saar, an indication perhaps that it had confidence in the regime of the Governing Commission and in the adequacy of the Council's supervision. However, Lord Robert Cecil, at the time representing the Union of South Africa, and always a vigorous champion of faithful adherence to the covenant of the League, arose in the Third Assembly in 1922 and made the suggestion that the Saar member of the Governing Commission be appointed in collaboration with the Saar Advisory Council. On this occasion other aspects of the Saar situation were also discussed, and Lord Arthur Balfour, the British member of the Council, defended the Governing Commission. It was one of the few times the General Assembly touched even briefly upon the Saar question.

On the other hand the Secretariat of the League, through its Administrative Commissions Section, played from the beginning an indispensable if inconspicuous part in the consideration and adjustment of Saar problems by the Council. Its functions and methods were essentially those of a civil service. It had no independent executive powers but, like any other body of administrative experts, it collected, appraised, and made available to the Council data upon which the latter chiefly relied in reaching decisions. For the members of the Council were busy national officials, delegated by their governments to attend meetings several times a year for but a few days. In most instances they had no opportunity or time to study in advance of their arrival the items on the agenda. And when they reached Geneva, where most of the Council meetings were held, usually a variety of problems confronted them, which they had to grapple with during the brief sessions. Under the circumstances, the Council came of necessity to lean heavily on the Secretariat in the preparation of resolutions and reports, for technical assistance, for information, and on occasion even for advice. For the Secretariat, contrasted with the Council and Assembly, was a body of experts acting in an international capacity rather than as representatives of particular national states, and it was the only organ of the League which, so to speak, was always on the job. During twelve months of the year its different sections were keeping in close touch with situations in regions, such as the Saar, in which the League had responsibilities. By means of correspondence, meetings with officials, and occasional field trips, the Secretariat sought to temper animosities, mitigate differences, and ease tense situations. Thus, the Administrative Commissions Section received the reports of the Saar Governing Commission, the minutes of meetings, and the *Amtsblatt* (official journal of the Commission) containing texts of its decrees, ordinances, and proclamations; and as need arose, the Secretariat's officials conferred with the chairman or individual members of the Commission. They received and brought to the attention of the Council of the League written protests and memoranda from the German government and petitions and memorials from organizations in the Saar; and they met with delegations from the Saar.

The processes and procedures developed by the League in general and applied to the Saar in particular were such that captious and irresponsible criticism was not encouraged, but on the other hand opportunity to expose alleged injustices or violations of rights was guaranteed. Representatives of the Saar inhabitants were not privileged to address petitions and protests directly to the League—these were to be sent to the governing authority, which was the Commission—but the latter was then obligated to forward the material to the secretary general of the League with such comments as it deemed appropriate. Thus there was no opportunity to suppress them; they were put into the record. The German government could send protests not only to the Governing Commission but directly to the League Secretariat. In the latter event, it was customary for the secretary general to forward a copy to the Commission and ask for any comments or observations it cared to make. It seems likely that these requirements of publicity and opportunities for public scrutiny operated at one time or another as a brake on the Governing Commission, causing it to act with more care and circumspection than it might otherwise have done. And on occasion, as the record shows, the Commission was forced to recede from a position which it had taken or had to modify its stand after questions had been raised by the Council.

In certain instances it seems clear that pressure from League quarters during the first formative years stimulated the Commission to alter certain of its policies to conform to the specifications or apparent intent of the treaty. For example, there is reason to believe that the Commission's rather tardy and reluctant decision to create a general assembly (Advisory Council) for the Territory, while due in part to the refusal of the local assemblies to be "consulted," was in part inspired by the Secretariat and by the attitude of the Council. Chairman Rault, to be sure, gave specific reasons for revamping the policy, intended to leave the impression that the Commission made its decision in the light of experience and changed conditions. But this was at most only partly true, for, as has been observed, Rault argued against such change for two years. Face-saving, however, is regarded as important not merely in the Orient but in political circles of the West as well. And the Council, in this as in other instances in which it dealt with Saar matters, took occasion through its *rapporteur* to congratulate the Commission on its "initiative" in creating the Advisory Council.

The important decision of the Commission to retain French troops in the Territory and the tenacity with which Chairman Rault stuck to his guns on this issue have been discussed, but the part played by the League in the gradual abandonment of this position should be made clear. The original attitude of the Council, it will be recalled, was that the troops might be retained until a local gendarmerie, specified in the treaty, could be established. Rault estimated that a force of over four thousand men would be needed to maintain order and to protect lives and property. Evidently, the French troops would be needed indefinitely, for only 155 men had been recruited for the local gendarmerie after about a year and a half, and thereafter its growth remained practically stationary. Of course vigorous protests came from the German government. The Council answered these protests in June 1921 by holding that the maintenance of order in the Territory was "paramount," and that the Commission must be the judge of what means it employed for this purpose. However, the Council reiterated that it did "not contemplate the maintenance of a foreign garrison as a permanent feature of the organization of the Saar," and that its policy was to dispense with such a garrison as soon as a local gendarmerie could be formed. It then pointedly requested the Governing Commission "to insert in the periodical reports of the Commission to the Council detailed information as to the development of the local gendarmerie and as to the prospects of reducing the French troops." But when at the instance of the German government the Council again placed the question on the agenda for its meeting of February 1, 1923, it found that although the number of French troops had been considerably reduced, the local gendarmerie was making no progress at all. After considering the situation, the Council continued its pressure on the Commission by reaffirming its previous resolutions, requesting the latter to increase the strength of the local gendarmerie, and giving notice that "at its next session it will consider the program drawn up by the Commission." This put Rault under the necessity of a concrete response, and shortly thereafter he submitted a program for increasing the local gendarmerie from 155 to 355 men during the year 1923. Obviously this increase would not enable the Governing Commission to dispense with French troops, and it was natural to ask whether the Commission planned to rest at this point, and if not, what its program would be for succeeding years. The Council, therefore, adopted a resolution to the effect that the proposed increase was to be regarded as only a beginning, and that before adopting its budget for 1924–1925 the Commission should submit for the consideration of the Council its proposed increase for that period. At the Inquiry of 1923, which will shortly be considered, Rault was to show a far less compliant attitude.

Such situations, in which the Council of the League employed pressure to secure a modification or change of policy on the part of the Commission, were, of course, exceptional. For the most part the Council did not intervene but left the Commission full discretion. Moreover, the Council sought in every appropriate way to give the Commission moral support. An outstanding example of this may be found in a step taken by the Council in 1922 and designed to afford greater security of tenure for the members of the Commission. Although the treaty provided for annual appointments, the policy of the Council had been to reappoint as a matter of course the members of the Commission on the expiration of their terms. This was not only in accord with the intention of the framers of the Saar section, but was obviously a sound practice. However, in 1922 the Council concluded to give the members of the Governing Commission a more definite assurance by stating that it would, barring exceptional circumstances and reserving its rights under the treaty, renew their mandates up to the beginning of 1925. This decision was apparently based on the belief that a five-year tenure was necessary to enable the Governing Commission to complete the program it had started, insure continuity of policy, calm the situation in the Saar, "and diminish the political difficulties which necessarily arise from annually renewing the Commission." If the problems and difficulties facing the Commission had been of an administrative rather than of a political nature, the move would have been undoubtedly very helpful; but unfortunately such was not the case.

The famous Inquiry of 1923, for which the Council summoned the members of the Governing Commission to Geneva to account for the manner in which they were administering the Saar trust, was full of significance. It was admittedly an extraordinary procedure, indicative of a belief in British and other quarters that more light on the situation in the Saar was needed than had been emanating from Saarbrücken and Berlin, and that either a League commission of investigation should be sent to the Saar or the members of the Governing Commission should be called to Geneva. It was also symptomatic of a break in the entente between France and Great Britain, and of a disposition on the part of the latter to take issue with her former wartime ally on Raymond Poincaré's and the French nationalists' policy of building up French power and extending French influence on the Continent. The occupation of the Ruhr was the occasion and perhaps the chief cause of the estrangement as well as of the development of British criticism of the Saar Governing Commission, for only the year before, Lord Balfour had risen in the League Assembly to give an unqualified endorsement of the Saar regime. And it may be added that it was due to British support or acquiescence in the Council that France enjoyed from 1920 to 1923 almost as much power in matters pertaining to the Saar as she would have possessed had the protectorate demanded by her in 1919 been granted. But now all was changed.

Although other matters contributed toward the British demand for the inquiry, a repressive decree issued by the Commission relative to a coal strike in the Territory brought matters to a head. The occupation of the Ruhr in January 1923 had been followed one month later by a strike of one hundred thousand workers in the Saar. Rault and the French were convinced that the strike was a political maneuver of the Germans designed to embarrass France in the Ruhr and the Rhineland as well as in the Saar. Convinced likewise that restrictive measures were necessary to forestall serious disorder in the Territory, Rault and his Danish and Belgian colleagues voted a provisional decree for the maintenance of public order and security. Interestingly enough, the acting Saar representative, Julius Land, did not vote on the decree, but the Canadian representative, Waugh, voted against it. The decree was so drastic that it gave free ammunition to the Germans, who from the first had denounced the "autocracy" of the Commission and who could now point to its inhumanity. For by the terms of the decree it became a serious offense, punishable by imprisonment for five years and a possible fine in addition, for a person publicly to offer adverse criticism of the Treaty of Versailles! Moreover, it was provided that to insult or traduce the League of Nations, or any of its members, or the states which signed the Treaty of Versailles (evidently Germany herself needed protection against the *Saarländer*) was likewise an offense for which the same punishment would be meted out. Other provisions were scarcely less Draconian. Finally, it was provided that cases under the decree were to be tried before a special court appointed by Chairman Rault himself.

On the initiative of Hjalmar Branting of Sweden the question was placed on the Council's agenda for its April meeting. As was to be expected, Gabriel Hanotaux of France defended the action of the Commission and Branting expressed disapproval. Edward Wood, the representative of Great Britain, though cautious in his remarks in the Council, later reported to the House of Commons that he disapproved of the decree quite as much as Mr. Branting did, but that he also wanted to avoid encouraging German propaganda in the Saar, which Chairman Rault, his only source of information, had charged was responsible for the criticism against the Commission. However, Wood asked a question at the Council's session which may have been inspired by information received from Saarbrücken sources. He wanted to know whether the entire Commission had agreed on the necessity of the decree! And he "wondered" whether it was likely to inflame or soothe public feeling in the Saar. He was sure that in his own country such a decree would have rendered the position of the government more difficult.

The matter was also debated in the British House of Commons, in May 1923, on which occasion the entire Saar regime—from the personnel of the Governing Commission to its policies—was subjected to the most vigorous and outspoken criticism. Edward Wood, who was a member of Parliament at that time, revealed that he had been opposed to the appointment of Julius Land, sponsored in the Council by Hanotaux of France. (Branting had also voted against Land's appointment to the Governing Commission of the Saar.) He objected to the fact that the only name submitted was Land's, thus leaving the Council no choice, and proposed that the matter be tabled until inquiries designed to discover other eligible persons for the post could be made. Wood then explained to the House that he had never been satisfied "that he [Julius Land] discharged or discharges what I conceive to be the principal functions for which a member of the Governing Commission should exist, namely, the function of being able to act, and being accepted as acting for the population of the Saar." The discussion in the House of Commons was far from perfunctory, Herbert Asquith, Sir John Simon, Lord Robert Cecil, and others taking part in it. Asquith denounced the decree as "in entire defiance of all the principles which all democratic countries and all free countries have been endeavoring to practice." Lord Robert Cecil more pointedly stated that it was "one of the examples of the spirit that has been produced by the recent action in the Ruhr in regard to the whole of European affairs . . . . and worthy of Prussian militarism at its worst." Both the government and the opposition participated in denunciations of the decree, and there were suggestions that the League should consider the two questions of the Saar and the Ruhr at the same time, since they were "very closely linked together." Finally Wood announced that it was the government's intention to propose to the other governments represented on the Council that there should be "an impartial inquiry conducted by the machinery of the League into the question of the general administration of the Saar Territory."

The French reaction to this announcement was immediate and unfavorable. Philippe Millet asserted in *L'Europe Nouvelle* that the treaty provisions concerning the Saar were complicated and paradoxical, and that had it not been for *"l'esprit politique"* of the French and the majority of the members of the Commission, there would have been more trouble than had now occurred. He charged that the movement for an inquiry had as its indirect object the removal of the chairmanship from France, and asserted that a new arrangement was desirable, giving the mines to France in perpetuity and the territory to Germany, subject to certain controls. Léon Bourgeois was quoted in *Le Temps* as arguing that the treaty endowed the Governing Commission with sovereign power, and that while the Council had the right to appoint and dismiss members of the Commission, it had no right of direct intervention in the administration of the Territory. Furthermore, an inquiry such as had been proposed would ruin the authority of the Governing Commission and destroy the possibilities of utilizing any international administration in the future. Other writers helped to swell the chorus of French disapproval.

However, the British government had openly committed itself to such an inquiry, and the state of English public opinion at the time was such that the government could hardly have withdrawn its proposals even if it had been so inclined. Accordingly, in June Britain presented a memorandum to the League, pointing out the necessity of examining certain provisions of the treaty so that there might be a "clear agreement" as to their meaning. The point was made that since the League of Nations had been made trustee for the Saar, and since the Governing Commission represented the League, the Council had a duty to make sure that the treaty provisions were being carried out. As for the form of the inquiry, the Council should determine the matter. At the next Council meeting, which was a closed one, Lord Robert Cecil, the British representative, asked for permission to present the proposals of his government at a "public session." This precipitated a debate with Gabriel Hanotaux, who argued that such a "delicate question" should first be discussed confidentially and only later at a public session. Lord Cecil was a strong believer in the Wilsonian concept of "open diplomacy," and he and Hanotaux, who was of a different persuasion, argued the matter at more than one League session, with reference to various "delicate questions" with which League agencies had to deal. In this instance, after a protracted debate in which other members of the Council sought to mediate between the conflicting viewpoints of the British and French representatives, an agreement was finally reached to hold a public session on July 3, 1923, for the hearing of the British proposals.

As was to be expected, the principal spokesmen in the discussion at this public session were Lord Robert Cecil and Gabriel Hanotaux, although the alert and active Swedish representative, Hjalmar Branting, rose before the close of the meeting in support of Lord Cecil's position. The latter, in a restrained and altogether temperate speech, in which he praised the Governing Commission for its administrative achievements in the Saar, nevertheless criticized by implication the Commission and its chairman. He pointed out that according to the Saar provisions of the treaty and the explanations given by Clemenceau in answer to German criticisms at the time of the Peace Conference, the Governing Commission, including its chairman, was responsible solely to the League of Nations and not to France. Cecil also drew the conclusion from Clemenceau's remarks that it was the duty of the Council of the League of Nations to supervise the government of the Saar. As for the provisional decree, he expressed the view that there should be further investigation of the circumstances surrounding its promulgation, and the Council itself should conduct the inquiry rather than entrust it to a special commission. If such a special commission were sent to the Saar, the Governing Commission could hardly carry on its administration with any degree of effectiveness. The British representative also cautioned that the appointment of an investigating commission would be an expensive step and would needlessly complicate the machinery of the League. Inquiry by the Council should be thorough; and all members of the Governing Commission rather than the chairman alone should be invited to Geneva and questioned as to the manner in which they had been discharging their responsibilities. Also, minutes of the Commission's meetings should be submitted to the Council at the inquiry.

Gabriel Hanotaux, the representative of France, rose to a general defense of the Governing Commission. After quoting extensively from previous remarks of Council members—particularly the different British representatives who had sat on the Council—to show that they had uniformly approved and even praised the Commission for the way in which it was handling a difficult task, he asserted that there had been "complete agreement between the Council and the Governing Commission" prior to the time of the strike and the issuance of the provisional decree. This was certainly an exaggeration; for, as has already been observed, at one time or another the Council and the Commission majority were not in agreement, and the inquiry was shortly to make this evident—at least as far as individual members of the Council and the Governing Commission were concerned. By this time the strike which provoked the decree had ended, after a wage increase which had at first been refused was granted. Hanotaux took occasion to praise the Governing Commission, whose wise policy, he asserted, had been responsible for the prevention of serious disorders and for the eventual settlement of the strike itself.

Turning to the question of the legal justification of the Commission's action, Hanotaux reminded the Council that the Commission was not merely an administrative organ but a "real government." And he stated frankly that "there is one point which governs the whole situation, namely, that France has particular rights in the Saar." She was the proprietor of the mines and the treaty made it clear that she had the right to exploit them without hindrance. Moreover, there was the guaranty of a plebiscite at the end of fifteen years. In the meantime, the League of Nations exercised a trusteeship on behalf of the Allied Powers and had the responsibility of maintaining these rights. On the other hand, Hanotaux felt it necessary to warn his colleagues that the Germans were perpetually raising questions and carrying on propaganda with the purpose of "nibbling away at the Treaty of Versailles." Members must be on guard against these insidious efforts to weaken the treaty by attacking it first at one point and then at another, so as to "ruin the very foundation of the existing European system."

As for the proposed examination into the affairs of the Saar, Hanotaux declared, he welcomed it. But it must not take the form of an *enquête,* which in France implied a suspicion of guilt. It must be merely an *examen,* or extension of the work of the Council, for in the case at issue there was no question of guilt. Moreover, the French representative cautioned his colleagues against any attempt to govern the Saar from Geneva "with texts." For the "art of government is, beyond everything else, the art of understanding the psychology of the peoples . . . . You can only govern on the spot and with men."

After this lecture on government and applied psychology, Hanotaux's Swedish colleague, Hjalmar Branting, spoke briefly in support of the position taken by the British Government. He surmised that, as Lord Robert Cecil had said and as Hanotaux had emphasized, an inquiry would undoubtedly reveal that from a "technical point of view" the administration of the Saar had been praiseworthy. But he personally believed that the Commission had not succeeded in "collaborating with the population and in gaining its confidence," and that if it should develop more democratic processes these would lead to improved relations with the people of the Saar. He thought Hanotaux's warning about German propaganda was an injustice to the Saar population, in that it suggested that the elected representatives of the Territory were merely agents of outside interests.

At the conclusion of the discussion it was unanimously agreed in principle "that an inquiry should be held in order to put an end to misunderstanding and to arrive at a final settlement of the controversies which have arisen." The Secretariat of the League was directed to send for the members of the Governing Commission and instruct them to bring the necessary documents to the next Council meeting. On Hanotaux's request it was decided to hold the inquiry behind closed doors. Lord Robert Cecil, whose bias in favor of open sessions was well known and who was expected to insist on an open hearing, offered no objection in this instance, since "personal questions might be raised." The decision deprived newspaper correspondents of the opportunity to get any very sensational copy, assuming of course that the participants would have spoken their pieces as freely in an open as in a closed hearing. On the other hand, a closed session would have no international audience, and thus any temptation to make campaign appeals would be removed. The Germans, no doubt, would have preferred an open session. They sent a delegation from the Saar to Geneva, headed by the steel magnate Hermann Röchling, and had prepared to seek a hearing and present their case before the Council. However, the Council decided to confine itself to a lengthy interrogation of the members of the Governing Commission behind closed doors.

This session of the Council was so revealing of the actual functioning of the Saar government—and of the points of view of both Commission and Council members—that it deserves close attention. The inquiry began on July 6, 1923, with all members of the Governing Commission present. Lord Robert Cecil examined the chairman of the Commission, Victor Rault, at some length, inquiring particularly into his conception of the role of chairman and his understanding of the proper relationship of the chairman to the Governing Commission, on the one hand, and to the French government, on the other. It was apparent that the questioner was intent on getting to the heart of the matter, and Rault's frank replies to these and other questions furnished an insight into the spirit and inner workings of the Saar government, such as had not hitherto been so candidly or so completely revealed. Lord Cecil first wanted to know how the work of the Commission had been organized, and whether all members considered all questions or whether certain matters were handled individually. Rault explained that as chairman of the Commission he had been in a position to extend his powers and might have concentrated all important administrative matters in his own hands, but that he had considered it better and more in accord with the spirit of the treaty to distribute the duties of government among the members of the Commission. In the assignment of portfolios, however, as has already been noted, Rault fared rather well; and he now explained that, as he was both French member of the Commission and chairman, he was obliged to take the portfolio of foreign affairs. In addition to this department, the Ministries of the Interior and of Public Safety had been assigned to him at his express request. And he had also been in charge of commerce, industry, and labor.

As regards the internal arrangements with his colleagues, Rault reported that each member of the Commission had been considered master of his own particular ministries, except that some of the higher public officials had been chosen by the member concerned with the agreement of the chairman or by the Commission as a whole. On ordinary matters of administration, each member was free to act; but if a change of law or regulation was involved, or if a matter required the expenditure of money, or if some question was of interest to the whole Commission—a determination apparently in the discretion of the chairman—it was brought before the weekly meeting of the Commission. As for the Commission's periodical reports to the Council, during the first year they had been drawn up by the chairman alone, by his authority as executive of the Commission. Rault explained that, in view of his numerous duties, his work necessarily formed the greater part of these reports. However, during the subsequent two years, a different procedure had been adopted. Each member of the Commission submitted what he wanted put into the report concerning his department, and the chairman inserted these notes into the final draft without change. Still more recently, Rault had inaugurated a procedure applicable when the Commission was not in agreement on a question of exceptional gravity. For example, the Commission had not been unanimously in favor of the promulgation of the recent controversial decree, and Rault had read it to the Commission after he had drafted it. He was quite willing to adopt the same procedure for future reports, should his colleagues desire it.

Lord Cecil continued his interrogation, seeking to learn what relations the chairman of the Governing Commission had with the French government. Rault stated that it was evident that the French member of the Commission had special duties to fulfil. He had to see that the advantages secured to France under the treaty were maintained. Consequently, it was clear that he would have to maintain relations with his country and pay attention to indications given him by France relative to the defense of her special interests in the Saar. But, stated Rault, he acted in two different capacities. From the standpoint of general administration, he acted not as the French member but as the chairman of the Commission. And he pointed out that the chairman, whatever his nationality, must have relations with certain French ministries. When it came to a question of taxing the mines, for instance, he must enter into negotiations with the French Minister of Public Works. As the Saar was within the French customs zone, it was inevitable that he deal with the French Ministry of Finance. Furthermore, in January 1925, when the French tariff between the Saar and Germany would go into effect, it would become necessary for the chairman to make arrangements with the French Ministry of Commerce and Industry and even with the ministry presided over by the premier of France. Moreover, he must be continuously in touch with the French government for other reasons as well, such as problems arising from the Ruhr occupation. Decisions of the Interallied High Commission in the Rhine territories affecting the commerce of the Saar made it necessary to enter into negotiations with the French government in order to protect Saar interests. It was likewise necessary to have relations with other governments. For example, the chairman was in correspondence once or twice a week with the German government.

It was evident that Lord Cecil was well informed on the whole question, whatever may have been the source of his information. He remarked that he had heard that the Governing Commission had established an office in Paris, and he thought Rault could give further information about this action. The chairman obliged. It had been set up at the Paris office of the League to serve him and his colleagues when they went to Paris. It also promoted the economic interests of the Saar. Businessmen seeking information about the Saar could have their questions answered here.

Lord Cecil then wanted to know whether it had been Monsieur Rault's practice to communicate the content of letters and correspondence between him and other governments to the members of the Governing Commission. Rault answered that such correspondence was forwarded to individual members as their duties required it, and was brought frequently before the entire Commission. Whenever a decision had to be made on a question, the correspondence was placed before the Commission as a whole. Lord Cecil then inquired whether Monsieur Rault would see any objection to communicating all his correspondence with the French government to the entire Governing Commission. At this point Rault fell back upon the distinction between the functions of the chairman of the Commission and the French member of the Commission. The French member might have to make certain observations to the French government on a given question, possibly even enter into discussions with it. It would not be possible even in the general interest to communicate these letters. Everything addressed to the chairman of the Governing Commission, as such, could be communicated to the Commission; but this would not apply to letters addressed by France to the French member of the Governing Commission.

The question of the issuance of the provisional decree was also raised by Lord Robert Cecil. Rault denied first the charge that it had been inspired by the French government; he had merely informed the French authorities of the decree after it had been issued. It had been discussed by himself and Count de Moltke Hvitfeldt, the member in charge of the Department of Justice, and they had issued the decree on their personal responsibility. There had been violent attacks on the Commission in the Saar press, hatred against the French inhabitants of the Saar had been fomented, and the situation had become intolerable. From the point of view of the general interest of the Saar and of the special interests which Rault, in his capacity as French member of the Commission, represented, he thought such violence on the part of the press impermissible. Had he submitted the decree to the Advisory Council—which he had been censured for not doing—that body would not have acted promptly, and a wave of protest in the Territory would have ensued. He had wanted to avoid renewed agitation; and the High Administrative Court had ruled that it was proper to issue the decree at once. Therefore it was promulgated on March 7, 1923. Why had it not been submitted to the Advisory Council when the latter body met on March 12? The agenda of this body had been prepared ten days in advance of its meeting, and it could discuss only matters included in the prepared agenda. The decree had been submitted to the Technical Committee in April, and after the Advisory Council had finished the agenda already referred to, the decree had been submitted to it. Moreover, the decree had been applied with moderation. In his capacity as Minister of the Interior, Rault explained, he had suspended four newspapers for twenty-four hours as a warning. These papers had published violent denunciations of the French and Belgian troops in the Ruhr. On renewal of the offense, one paper had been suspended for a week and another one for a fortnight. An appeal was taken against these decisions to the High Administrative Court. This tribunal, judging each case on its merit, had sustained Rault's decisions. He was convinced that the decree had had a good effect: the strike had ended without a single incident.

The question which from the first had engaged the attention of the Council and caused it much concern, namely, the retention of French troops in the Saar, was raised once more. Lord Cecil remarked that the presence of French garrison forces in the Saar was anomalous, and that they ought not to be retained longer than was necessary. But Gabriel Hanotaux, coming to the defense of Rault and the Governing Commission, reminded the members present that the Council had taken a decision by which it approved the presence of the troops. Lord Cecil differed. According to his interpretation, the Council had always held that these troops were an additional force not to remain permanently in the Territory, and that as soon as possible the maintenance of order should be entrusted to a local gendarmerie. Rault voiced a doubt as to whether the Council had always expressed itself in such a precise manner. He made it plain that, in any event, he was not disposed to grant that the Council had any right to decide the question. The right to interpret its powers had been given by the treaty to the Commission. He said further that, even if a local gendarmerie existed, it was necessary to know whether or not in a grave emergency the Governing Commission had the undoubted right to appeal to any force placed at its disposal. And Rault made it evident once more that he was not enthusiastic about the prospect of developing a local gendarmerie. Nevertheless, "at the moment," the Commission was continuing, in agreement with the Council, to develop such a force as far as possibilities of recruiting and finances allowed it.

Rault was also interrogated as to the importation and use of French troops during the miners' strike. He explained that the Mines Administration had requested him to have additional troops brought into the Saar, and he had complied without submitting the matter to the Governing Commission. As Minister of the Interior, in charge of public safety, he knew quite well what should be done. The total number of troops involved was between five and six thousand. Of these, four thousand had been needed to guard the mines. After he had called them in, he had notified the Governing Commission of his action. This explanation did not impress the British representative favorably. He reminded Chairman Rault that on more than one occasion the Council had stated that except for an emergency, keeping in the Saar French troops—paid by the French government, and in charge of French officers—was not a satisfactory system for maintaining order, and that the Council had repeatedly urged the establishment of a local gendarmerie. Lord Cecil gave voice to the hope, therefore, that Monsieur Rault could tell how soon he could carry out the Council's recommendation to dispense with the troops. Rault replied that he could not say at the moment; there was always danger of serious incidents, such as had occurred in the Saar in 1919; and the question was a very delicate one. In order to deal with any kind of emergency, in his estimate, at least four thousand men would be needed, and he doubted the possibility of increasing the local gendarmerie by more than two hundred men a year. There could be only one conclusion from Rault's appraisal, although he stopped short of drawing it in specific terms: French troops could not be dispensed with at all. For if the gendarmerie could only be increased by two hundred men a year, it would still be too small by 1935, the year of the plebiscite, to take care of "any incident." Presumably, then, the deficiency would be made up by the use of French troops.

When Richard Deans Waugh, the Canadian member of the Commission, was interrogated, the rift within the Commission, which had been rumored in various quarters but had never been indicated in Rault's quarterly reports to the League, was frankly revealed. Actually, Waugh had differed with the chairman and the majority of the Commission on several matters. On the question of the 20 percent coal tax, for example, he informed the Council that the local representatives of the people had unanimously favored retention of this tax. And he expressed the opinion that the procedure leading to the final reduction of the tax to 5 percent was "irregular." He asserted that Rault had gone to Paris, carried on negotiations with the French government concerning the reduction of the tax, and had concluded an agreement without previously consulting his colleagues and without asking the opinion of the member of the Governing Commission who was in charge of the Department of Finance. Waugh and Dr. Hector, who followed von Boch as Saar member on the Commission, considered the matter of such importance that they refused to acquiesce in the agreement, holding that the chairman should have consulted the Commission before an agreement with the French government had been concluded. Rault's version of the matter was quite different. He said that the French government had lodged a complaint against the coal-tax rate, and that he had submitted this matter to the Governing Commission, which had taken a stand on it.

Both Waugh and Dr. Hector had also opposed the views of the chairman in another matter. In reply to Lord Cecil's question, the circumstances were explained by Rault as follows: The Financial Committee of the French Senate paid a visit to the Saar to inquire into the establishment of an office of the French state mines. This committee believed that the coal tax was too high, and called in person on Chairman Rault to request a statement of the receipts and expenditures of the Governing Commission for the financial year 1920–1921. Rault, according to his statement, refused the request, but let the committee understand that if the French government asked the Governing Commission to communicate such information, the application might be granted. He undertook, then, in his capacity of "French commissioner," to present the question to the Governing Commission and received from it the authorization to communicate to the French government the desired information. Rault added that as the French government was the principal taxpayer in the Saar, its request could hardly be denied.

Waugh's explanation of the controversy differed somewhat from that of Rault. He said he had submitted the accounts for the fiscal year 1920–1921 to the Governing Commission in order that they might be forwarded to the Secretariat of the League of Nations. However, Chairman Rault informed the Commission that he had received instructions from a commission of the French Senate to send the accounts to the French government and contended that the latter had the right under the treaty to ask the Governing Commission directly for such accounts. Waugh, on the other hand, had contended that if the French government wished to receive the accounts, it should have addressed the request to the Council of the League of Nations or to the secretary general. In spite of his and Dr. Hector's protests, a decision was made to send the accounts first to the French government. And he had been informed that as late as April the Secretariat of the League had not received the accounts.

The Canadian member stated that he had also been opposed to the unpopular provisional decree of March 7. He had thought it unnecessary, in view of the orderly character of the strike and the absence of any occurrence that would have disturbed the public peace. Likewise, the decree on picketing, promulgated toward the end of the strike, contained provisions which he could not approve. He had observed no "reign of terror," such as had been described by Rault, and inasmuch as 75 percent of the officials under his orders were nationals of the Saar, he thought he would have known if any sign of terror had existed.

Waugh also testified to his dissatisfaction with the manner in which the official reports of the Governing Commission had been drafted. Although each department furnished a separate report dealing with its own administration, the conclusions of the report, treating matters of general policy, were formulated by the chairman alone. Nevertheless these were made to appear as if they expressed the opinion of all members of the Commission. At this point, Hanotaux came to the defense of Rault, commenting that under a majority rule there could be no minority opinion. Once the vote was taken, the opinion of the majority became that of the Commission as a whole. Lord Cecil was not ready to agree but held that this was a point the Council would have to examine before considering its acceptance. However, the matter was not pursued beyond this point.

The Inquiry of 1923 was not intended to destroy or embarrass the Governing Commission in the fulfillment of its responsibilities. Consequently, when the time came to draw up resolutions expressing the findings of the Council, care was taken to phrase them in moderate and conciliatory language which would not have the effect of undermining the authority of the Commission. Moreover, the findings must somehow seem to reconcile the positions of Hanotaux and Lord Cecil, at least to such an extent that they would both give their approval. Consequently, to one unfamiliar with the background and with the extreme care diplomats employ in phraseology when reducing spoken words to writing, the resolutions adopted may seem rather pale and anemic, possibly even worthless. To one familiar with these matters, the resolutions did point out certain facts that deserved emphasis and by inference suggested that the Governing Commission needed some reorientation of viewpoint. For example, it was pointed out that the Saar government was instituted "in order to assure the rights and well-being of the population and to guarantee to France complete freedom in working the French state mines, upon which the prosperity of the country depends." The significance of this statement lies in the fact that the French had habitually put the property guaranty first when they discussed the Saar, and Hanotaux had even emphasized during the inquiry that Article 45, which dealt with the transfer of the mines to France, came before Article 46, which provided the guaranties for the rights and welfare of the Saar population.

The chief purpose of the Inquiry of 1923 had been to expose policies and procedures of the Commission allegedly dictated by or in the interests of France and to emphasize that they were not consistent with the terms of the treaty. Now the Council declared that the Governing Commission was "responsible to the League of Nations for the execution of its duties in accordance with the Treaty of Versailles," and that the members of the Commission were "collectively responsible" for the execution of the duties assigned to individual members. In the opinion of Lord Cecil and of Branting this point was the most important of all. Lord Cecil emphasized that the Commission was responsible to the League, and to it alone, and owed no allegiance to any other body whatever. The perennial question of the maintenance of French troops was brought up once again, the longest paragraph in the resolutions reiterating that these troops should be dispensed with and the local gendarmerie built up.

The feeling in Geneva was quite generally that the inquiry had been helpful. And the Germans, in spite of the fact that they had not been formally heard, showed a tendency to think that it represented a moral victory for them and a blow to the Commission. The frank character of the inquiry and the publication in full of the minutes of the Council meeting indicated that the League was seeking to discharge its responsibilities in this matter with fairness and impartiality. But could it do so without some changes in the personnel of the Commission? It was rumored in Geneva that the next development would be the resignation of the Danish and Saar members of the Commission—that the British would insist on changes in the personnel at least in this respect. It was not generally expected that Rault, whose industry and efficiency had never been questioned, would be replaced. But there was a question in the minds of many as to whether he should be retained as chairman of the Governing Commission. The inquiry abundantly confirmed the growing impression in neutral quarters that it was not possible for Rault to be at one and the same time a faithful representative of France and French interests on the Commission and also the impartial chairman of that body. That he had utilized the opportunities afforded by the chairmanship to protect and advance what he honestly conceived to be the legitimate rights of his country under the treaty was apparent from his testimony at the inquiry and need occasion no surprise. The mistake was made by the Council in the first place, by giving the chairmanship of an international commission, with delicate and difficult tasks to perform in an atmosphere charged with international tension, to a person committed to the service of his country. The chairmanship should have gone to one of the three members of the Commission who were not avowedly appointed to represent special interests.

Within less than a month after the inquiry, the Canadian member, Waugh, placed his resignation in the hands of the secretary general of the League. This was quite unexpected, at any rate outside League circles. He had been an efficient member of the Commission, and strictly objective in his approach to the solution of the controversial problems that generated so much heat between the Commission and the Germans. But his frank testimony at the inquiry regarding his constant differences with the chairman and the "docile majority" made it evident that if Rault retained the chairmanship and a working majority on the Commission, Waugh would probably have to acquiesce in policies which he could not honestly support, or he would have to resign. When it became clear to him that Rault was apparently slated to remain, and that what the Canadian regarded as pro-French policy would continue to be in the ascendancy, Waugh chose the latter course. In bringing the matter before the Council, its *rapporteur* took occasion to compliment Waugh for his service on the Commission and to observe that he had "won from the population of the Territory general esteem, and . . . . been praised for his honesty of purpose and disinterested impartiality." Another Canadian was appointed to succeed him, Major George Washington Stephens, who had a knowledge of both French and German and several years' administrative experience gained as president of the Montreal Harbor

Commission. He arrived in the Territory in November 1923 and took over the Department of Finance.

The Inquiry of 1923 into the affairs of the Saar might never have taken place had the British Government not lost its attitude of acquiescence toward France as a result of Poincaré's policy on the Continent, culminating in the occupation of the Ruhr. Thus, for a moment the Saar was brought into the international spotlight and secured an international hearing, not for its own sake but in the course of the game of power politics, which on this occasion happened to serve the European community. The Saar's fortunes were also affected by the shifting of national policies, beginning in the following year, and the general improvement in European political relations. For in 1924, Edouard Herriot and the leftist groups displaced Raymond Poincaré and his rightist followers and announced the "program of liberal France." They refused to accept the thesis of the French nationalists that "the way to treat a Prussian is to stamp on his toes until he apologizes," and held that it was "stupid both from the moral and political point of view" to attempt to destroy Germany. It would be the task of liberal France to give encouragement and aid to democratic elements in Germany and to uphold the Weimar Republic against the forces of both Right and Left, which were attempting to destroy it. Moreover, the eloquent and influential Aristide Briand admitted that while the League of Nations was young and frail, it was nevertheless, in his conception, to serve as the instrument for reconciling France and the new Germany and achieving peace. For this and other tasks the League was to be strengthened through the Geneva Protocol, which had the support of the British Labor Government and liberal Continental opinion.

Although the succeeding British Conservative Government would not give its support to the protocol, it did sign in the following year the Treaty of Mutual Guarantee of the Franco-German frontier, which was intended to relieve both Germany and France of their fears of aggression. This treaty, along with other developments, brought a new confidence that the "spirit of Locarno," working through the agency of the League of Nations would guide the European rivals to an enduring peace. In the following year, as part of the understanding reached, Germany became a member of the League and was given a permanent seat on the Council along with the other principal powers. Now recognized once again as an equal among equals in the Council of the Great Powers, she was also in a position to protect her interests in the Saar and elsewhere. To be sure, the Treaty of Versailles still stood, and even Herriot insisted that Germany must pay her debts and live up to the treaty, but the French Left was prepared to make concessions which Raymond Poincaré and the French nationalists would never have considered. Thus Germany was able as early as 1926 to free herself from the Interallied Commission of Control, and by 1928 began negotiations which resulted in an agreement that all Allied troops of occupation in the Rhineland should be withdrawn by June 30, 1930. And, as we shall see, Aristide Briand and Gustav Stresemann, the French and German foreign ministers, were even to enter into discussions exploring the possibilities of returning the Saar to Germany without a plebiscite.

It is within the foregoing framework that events in the Saar during the next several years can be viewed most understandingly. Problems and difficulties did not disappear overnight, but the manner in which they were approached and settled was such as to reduce tensions and, during the period of the German Republic, at any rate, make the regime in the Territory at least tolerable to all parties concerned. It is significant in this connection that although Germany, especially from 1920 to 1924, had constantly lodged complaints against the Governing Commission with the League of Nations, she did not utilize her position later as a Council member to indulge in any criticisms of the Saar government. Moreover, the political leaders in the Saar all but discontinued the practice of bombarding the League with petitions of one kind or another. Contributing strongly to improved relations was the action of the Council in effecting changes in the Commission itself. Count de Moltke Hvitfeldt and Julius Land, the Danish and Saar members respectively, saw the handwriting on the wall and resigned before their terms expired on March 31, 1924. In the meantime, the Catholic deans of the Saar had petitioned the Council to appoint a Roman Catholic as a member of the Commission, to be put in charge of education and worship. About three-fourths of the Saar population was Roman Catholic, and this was undoubtedly a consideration when the Council selected Espinosa de los Monteros, a Spaniard and a Catholic, to take the place vacated by the Danish member.

The selection of a successor to Julius Land presented more of a problem, since Lord Parmoor (the former Sir Charles Alfred Cripps), new representative of the British Labor Government, and Hjalmar Branting of Sweden were of the opinion that the elected representatives of the Saar population should first be consulted, while Gabriel Hanotaux took the position that this would be contrary to the treaty. The candidate of the Saar was Dr. Franz Levacher, leader of the Center party, the strongest party in the Territory. Moreover, the leader of the second strongest political group, the Social Democratic party, came to Geneva to urge the appointment of Dr. Levacher. Still, Lord Cecil and Hanotaux had agreed several months earlier to support Dr. Bartholomäus Kossman, a former member of the Reichstag and president of the Advisory Council. Under the circumstances, the Labor Government in Great Britain felt compelled to honor the Cecil-Hanotaux understanding, and Kossman was selected by the Council to succeed Land. He proved to be quite diligent in the protection of the interests of the Territory and quite acceptable to the people.

More significant than any of these changes in Commission personnel was the resignation of Victor Rault in March 1926 and the appointment of Waugh's successor, the Canadian George Washington Stephens, as chairman of the Commission. This was calculated not only to dispel, or at least alleviate, German criticism but to give the Commission a moral standing among League of Nations supporters which it could never have commanded under a French chairman. Mr. Stevens proved to be most congenial to the Germans of the Saar. He spoke the language, liked the beer, and was not above mingling with the people in the cafes of Saarbrücken. He remained on the Commission little more than a year, and was succeeded as chairman by Sir Ernest Wilton of the British Foreign Office, who in turn was replaced by Geoffrey Knox, a British diplomat, in 1932. Thus the chairmanship continued in British hands, Knox holding the post until after the plebiscite, when the Territory was returned to Germany. However, it was not until 1928 that the French lost their preponderant influence on the Commission with the replacement of Major Lambert of Belgium by a Finn, von Ehrenrooth.

7

ECONOMICS, POLITICS, AND PROPAGANDA

The picture that has emerged from the preceding chapters is one of embattled Germans and French locked in an uncompromising struggle for the Saar, each determined to win the plebiscite in 1935. Both sides had tended to regard the Treaty of Versailles merely as a truce of longer or shorter duration to be followed, it was feared or hoped, by the "war after the war." Thus, although a much larger stake than the Saar was envisaged, the "cold war" of preparation for the eventual struggle was waged on every sector, and the Saar was by no means the least of these. Thus, the French commission sent into the Rhineland in 1922 to assess political conditions recommended a policy for the Saar on the basis of a careful sociological analysis. It was concluded that French policy should be "delicate, prudent, and sustained." Pan-German officials should be progressively replaced. The formula also included "the conquest of the school, alliance with this [the] clergy . . . . the utilization of the press, the organization of the working classes into trade unions with a defined tendency . . . ." These sentiments were shared in general by French conservatives, who frankly called for a policy which would utilize all the advantages possessed by France under the Saar provisions of the treaty, in order to convince the inhabitants that it would be in their interest to vote for France in 1935.

That all French groups were not in agreement with such a policy in the Saar became evident before many years. Certain economic groups, for example, advocated the termination of the new arrangements which they found prejudicial to their interests. These groups included the French steel manufacturers, who had to contend with Saar competition; the coal interests in the north of France, who had to compete with Saar coal; and certain French industrialists who regarded the elimination of the customs barrier between France and the Saar as inimical to their interests. But since influential French economic groups in the Saar and in France, including manufacturers and Lorraine agriculturists, desired to maintain the status quo, it is doubtful whether the influence of the dissidents was strong enough to make itself felt in French politics.

After 1924, for several years there was a disposition in the political sphere to consider returning the Saar to Germany in advance of the date of the plebiscite, provided Germany was willing to offer something in the way of a *quid pro quo*. By 1926 the French mines had been rehabilitated. It will be recalled that the French diplomats had argued at the Peace Conference that this rehabilitation would require ten or more years, and that therefore a special political regime must be set up in the Saar to insure that France would have Saar coal while her own mines were being repaired. Now, that argument was no longer relevant. Moreover, Aristide Briand and the party groups of the Left were anxious to remove obstacles to the reconciliation of the two peoples and, since it had become evident in the 'twenties that France probably could not win the plebiscite in 1935, it might be an act of prudent foresight as well as a gesture of friendship for her voluntarily to agree to the liquidation of the Saar regime. However, when in 1926 Briand and Stresemann were about to reach an agreement involving the immediate release of the Saar in return for economic concessions from Germany, public disapproval in France compelled the French statesman to defer negotiations. They were not resumed until the summer of 1929, when they were reopened apparently on the initiative of Stresemann. His death in October of the same year, and later the replacement of Briand by André Tardieu as French premier, did not immediately terminate the discussions. Briand remained foreign minister for a while after Stresemann's death, but it was eventually to become clear that the moment for a policy of conciliation and mutual concessions had passed.

Although Tardieu continued discussions with the Germans, it could not be expected that he would consent to the abandonment of the considerable rights which France had acquired in the Saar unless substantial compensation were secured. As Clemenceau's right-hand man he had fought at the Peace Conference for the economic position France was accorded there, and it was unthinkable that he would rate the doubtful prospect of winning German friendship higher than the "rights" of France. And although, as has been pointed out, there were French groups which had all along been opposed to this part of the treaty, there were others of greater influence quite as much determined to see the Saar regime maintained. French nationalists stressed the strategic and economic importance of the Saar to France and hoped that the plebiscite would at least result in the perpetuation of the League government; but even they were not hopeful of a favorable vote for France. Active to this end was the Association Française de la Sarre, organized in 1928. The many articles in Parisian and provincial publications for which it was responsible do not seem to have had a noticeable effect on French public opinion, although they served to substantiate German suspicions that France harbored annexationist ambitions in the Saar.

Considering the foregoing views, shared generally by members of the Right, and the uncompromising attitude adopted by the Germans, it is not astonishing that Tardieu's conversations with the latter centered around economic questions. The French wanted guaranties of Saar coal for the steel industry of Lorraine beyond 1935, as well as continued recognition of agreements which had been made by the Governing Commission and certain French coal companies, enabling the latter to mine Saar coal from pitheads in Lorraine. France also sought an extension of the customs arrangements for fifteen years after 1935. The Germans evidently thought this too high a price for the return of the Saar without a plebiscite, which they were confident of winning anyhow, for they refused to consider any economic compensation whatever. Thus the negotiations failed and were never again resumed.

From this time on, German propaganda to win the 1935 plebiscite with an overwhelming vote was revived and stepped up, reaching a crescendo under Hitler's rule, as the time for the vote drew near. The issue of French troops in the Saar was no longer of use to agitators after 1930, for in that year the last foreign soldiers were removed from the Territory. But there were other alleged grievances that could be exploited, especially after the effects of the world depression began to be felt in the Saar. Therefore, the political parties of the Territory were organized in a "united front" under the direction of the steel magnate Hermann Röchling, who enjoyed a subsidy from the Reich. The German government also contributed financial support to various propaganda organizations in the Saar, which carried on agitation through lectures and pamphlets, and through celebrations in which speakers sent from the Reich participated.

The world-wide depression furnished new ammunition to the Saar leaders. Previously it had been difficult to criticize the Governing Commission on economic grounds. The Territory had been forbidden the luxury of an armed establishment by the treaty, and it was also relieved from the payment of reparations and war debts. The Commission had therefore been able to spend money on internal improvements, develop educational facilities in the Territory, and at the same time build up a substantial surplus before the depression struck. Although the Saar was somewhat cushioned against the painful consequences of the economic breakdown, by reason of its beneficial trade relations with both France and Germany, it began to experience shutdowns in industry and consequent unemployment in the second half of 1930. As a result, the Governing Commission was not only compelled to deplete its surplus through outlays for unemployment relief and subsidies for the railroads but also had to increase taxation. This measure would have been unpopular in any event, for people have never liked tax collectors, but from a "foreign" government it was regarded as a new evidence of oppression, and the political leaders made the most of the situation. The people were told that in spite of the fact that the Commission did not have to meet reparation charges their taxes were higher than those of their kinsmen in Germany because their resources were being drained off by France. The charges were not true, but the leaders were organized to repeat them so often and so effectively that the people of the Saar, conditioned over a period of years to believe the worst of the Commission, thought "German" on the subject, and apparently in large numbers developed the "will to believe" everything their leaders told them.

As the depression grew acute in France, there was inevitably a lessened consumption of Saar coal. This, too, drew forth a denunciation of France and of the Commission. It was declared that considerations of politics had influenced the French, and that the Commission and the League of Nations itself must take responsibility for the restriction of coal output in the Saar, consequent to the shrinking market in France and elsewhere. And although the Mines Administration asserted that its earnings from the Saar mines were low, and much less than France had been able to make from the Moselle mines, the Germans challenged the truthfulness of this statement and suggested that some of the heavy profits of former years be used to maintain employment in the mines during the depression. A special grievance of the German government arose from the decision of the Governing Commission to limit the entry of workers, who had been coming in considerable numbers from adjacent areas in Germany. The decision was considered necessary because of the alarming increase of unemployed Saar residents, and was made only after an attempt to reach an agreement with the German government. Nevertheless the Commission was censured both in the Reich and in the Saar for the action it took in this emergency.

An examination of the record of labor-management relations in the Saar during the period of the Governing Commission would warrant the supposition that labor on the whole had been contented. The two miners' strikes over a fifteen-year period could be traced to political sources and to a desire of the political leaders to embarrass the Commission rather than to dissatisfaction with economic conditions on the part of the workers. More than a third of the miners owned their homes, which were scattered over the Territory and occasionally included small plots of arable land; and they even enjoyed a certain prestige in the industrial community. Moreover, the framers of the treaty sought to write in protective clauses on behalf of labor in general and the miners in particular. Under the German Republic, however, the workers and their unions had an assured status in the Reich and state recognition of collective bargaining, such as had not been accorded in the Saar. And although both management and labor in the Saar—including the largest employer of labor, the French Mines Administration—tended to follow the lead of the Reich and adopt collective bargaining in principle, the Saar leaders could point to the fact that the legal position of Saar workers was not as good as that of their brothers in the Reich. Moreover, the propagandists asserted that if the mines were under German exploitation, with German rather than foreign overseers and engineers, the miners would earn higher wages and enjoy better working conditions.

Contrary to the contentions of the Germans, the Governing Commission, favored by the circumstances arising from the special economic and political position of the Territory under the treaty, was able and willing to shield the Saar from the worst consequences of the depression suffered in Germany, France, and, in fact, throughout the world. Consequently, some Frenchmen reasoned that self-interest if not gratitude would suggest even to Germans living in the Saar that they would be better off in the future by supporting the continuance of the League regime. They could thus be free from the heavy taxes which the people of the Great Powers had to pay for armaments and for an illusory security. And they could remain at peace with France and at the same time retain their cultural ties with their kinsmen in Germany. These same Frenchmen realized nevertheless that the nationalistic Germans would not automatically respond to the promptings of economic self-interest. In fact their leaders and the German government were carrying on intense propaganda, as has been stated, to convince them that their economic as well as their spiritual interests demanded that they return to the Fatherland. Some Frenchmen and French sympathizers had believed from the first that propaganda must be met by counterpropaganda, pressure by counterpressure; and the French government was criticized for its failure to do what the Germans were doing so thoroughly. For instance, it was pointed out that France could have subsidized or bought up newspapers, encouraged public lectures "sounding the right note," distributed literature, or supported friendly candidates for office. French critics claimed that France did none of these things, and that if the Saar were lost it would be lost by default.

German propaganda, at any rate prior to the Nazi campaign, laid great emphasis on the economic advantages which would accrue to the Saar by voting for a resumption of the political connection with the Reich. Although there was apparently no fear that the people of the Territory would choose France at the plebiscite, there was some uneasiness among the Germans lest they vote for the maintenance of the status quo. For even before the League regime, close economic ties had developed between the Saar and Lorraine, and during the League rule the French market had largely displaced that formerly enjoyed in Germany. A referendum in favor of the League would result in the continuance of this economic relationship as well as of Commission rule, which, in the view of many observers, had on the whole been beneficial to the Saar. The Germans contended, however, that the Saar steel industry had remained largely dependent on the German market, and that with the return of the Territory to the Reich the people of the Saar would regain the German coal market and be accorded cheaper transportation facilities than ever before. And they declared that if Lorraine minette were withheld from Saar steel manufactures, as had been suggested, they could bring in iron ore from other sources in Germany and elsewhere without excessive cost. This was disputed by the French who, with the Saar mines in hand and a majority control in the metallurgical industries, as well as with other economic assets, hoped against hope that when the time came for the choice to be made in 1935, objective economics would carry the day against subjective politics.

It has been observed that the Treaty of Versailles was obnoxious to the Weimar Republic and that there was no enthusiasm for a policy of fulfillment. But it has also been pointed out that Germany was weak and impotent and, under Stresemann's guidance, sought by peaceful methods to obtain concessions from the Allies. This policy met with a considerable degree of success. Nevertheless, the substance of the Treaty of Versailles remained untouched, and the most that could be done, apparently, was to whittle it away gradually and depend upon time to erode its main supports. Of course it is an open question whether Stresemann, who had been an ardent imperialist before the defeat of the Reich, was not merely making the best of a bad situation until Germany could rearm.

With the rise of the National Socialists to power it was soon spelled out for all but the blind to see that although the Führer could on occasion utter soft words and indulge in beguiling blandishments, he and his followers were essentially international buccaneers, contemptuous of progress through compromise and the conventions of international intercourse. An intense chauvinism was skillfully cultivated by Adolf Hitler, Joseph Goebbels, and their unsavory associates. Pacifism and internationalism were derided and identified in particular with Jews and Communists. The bright German sword was out of the scabbard again, to be used now against traitors within as well as enemies without. Once more the German people had a *Führer,* and one who could evoke their most rhythmic and ecstatic *Heil*'s and inspire in them the desire to goose-step their way to glory.

It was inevitable that National Socialism, with its racial dogma and amoral dynamism, should cause widespread repercussions in the Saar. Prior to Hitler's elevation to power in Germany, all the political groups of any importance in the Territory were united in their determination to vote the Saar back into the Reich in 1935. After the Nazi triumph and the persecution of Jews, Socialists, Catholics, Communists, and in fact any dissenters who sought to oppose National Socialist dogma, groups not sympathetic to Nazism in the Saar began to have misgivings. The Saar Socialists and Communists foresaw their own probable fate when their counterparts were outlawed in Germany, and began to advocate a continuation of the League administration beyond 1935 and the deferment of the plebiscite until after the eclipse of the Nazi regime. The Roman Catholics, who formed a large majority of the population, soon became divided, the chief organ of the Center party, the *Landeszeitung,* going over to Hitler. This move was, no doubt, strongly influenced by the fact that the Holy See had struck a bargain with Hitler in the concordat of June 1933.

Prior to the victory of Hitler in Germany the Nazis had formed a National Socialist party in the Saar, but until the *Führer* and his supporters took over the Reich they were numerically small and lacking in prestige, although they did cause concern to the Governing Commission. Now they grew in number, strength, and arrogance. They merged all political groups which would join into a Saar Deutsche Front, under the immediate leadership of a fanatic Prussian, Alois Spaniol, and sought as far as possible to employ against their opponents the strong-arm tactics which were succeeding so well in the Reich. They stigmatized such adversaries as Max Braun, the editor of the Socialist *Volksstimme,* as traitors; and Spaniol is reported to have declared at a great public gathering that "the day will come when we will call these criminals to account, when we will slay these torturers of the soul of German children like mad dogs."

The Governing Commission was now confronted not only with

conspiracy but with the threat of a state within a state. Most of the twelve thousand officials serving under it were Germans and, reflecting the general opinion that the Saar would vote to return to the Reich in 1935, they were not disposed to jeopardize their future by placing their loyalty to the Governing Commission above allegiance to the Third Reich and refusing to be "co-ordinated." The Nazis let it be known that all officials, judges as well as police and other public servants of the Commission, would be dismissed after the return of the Saar to Germany, unless they had joined the National Socialist party and worked to further its aims.

As early as the autumn of 1933, according to Sarah Wambaugh, one of the members of the Plebiscite Commission, the measures of the Nazis to supplant and subvert the authority of the Governing Commission were most painstaking and thorough: "Police officials, even of the highest ranks, met secretly under the command of Spaniol, and the public services, posts, telegraph and telephone, tax collectors, municipal authorities, *Bürgermeister,* priests, pastors, and even judges and magistrates, were largely subservient to the Nazi leader. The complaint of a reign of terror made by non-Nazi inhabitants was echoed in the foreign press, the charges including intimidation and espionage, secret denunciations, kidnappings across the German frontier, threat of dismissal and loss of pensions to officials disregarding orders of the unofficial government, interception of letters and telegrams, listening-in to telephone conversations, leniency of police to Nazi offenders and severity to anti-Nazis."

This noxious growth came to full flower after Hitler, with the prestige, financial resources, and opportunity for maneuver afforded by a firm control of the Reich, had perfected his organization of subversion. But as early as 1928, before the Nazis had been regarded as a threat, the Governing Commission had had a foreshadowing of what was to develop. Nationalist organizations in the Reich had become increasingly active in the Saar, where they began to assume a military character. The Commission, therefore, found it necessary to forbid members of these organizations to wear military uniforms or insignia in public and had to dissolve them and seize their weapons when their military nature was revealed. As early as 1931, the National Socialist party was among the organizations whose members were forbidden to wear uniforms. By 1932, ordinances had become necessary prohibiting military marching and drilling at night and the manufacture or possession of explosives; and in November of the same year it was discovered that the Nazis had been engaging surreptitiously in military maneuvers and other forbidden activities.

Thereupon the Commission ordered their organizations dissolved and their weapons confiscated.

In May 1933, the Governing Commission was forced to take more drastic measures by promulgating several restrictive decrees for the maintenance of public order. Realizing the unreliability of the police because of the pressures to which they were subjected by the Nazis, the Commission sought to discourage disaffection in their ranks, or at least to lessen its effect, by decreeing that if the public safety demanded, the authority of the regular communal police officials might be withdrawn and vested in an official of the Commission; and furthermore, that any executive official of the police found guilty of serious dereliction of duty would be subject to summary dismissal. Further controls over public meetings and the press were established to prevent inflammatory and treasonable attacks on the Commission, and penalties were imposed to prevent acts of intimidation or violence aimed at hindering persons in the exercise of their civil rights or other rights guaranteed them under the treaty.

The foregoing measures were necessitated not only by the treasonable activities of the Nazis against the Governing Commission and their efforts to confuse and intimidate opponents, but because the Commission felt an obligation to give protection to those refugees from the Reich, Jews and gentiles alike, who were the objects of the most venomous attacks. Aided and abetted by the authorities of the Reich, who broadcast anti-Semitic tirades for the benefit of the Saar inhabitants and revealed the technique of persecution as it was being worked out in Germany, the Nazis in the Saar sought to incite the people to boycott Jewish merchants and professional men, and even attempted to impose, by stealth, anti-Jewish measures which had been adopted in the Reich. The *Saar-Front,* organ of the National Socialists, made such vehement and provocative attacks against the Jews that the Commission suspended it for several weeks; and it decided to ban altogether *Der Stürmer,* the obscene anti-Jewish weekly of Otto Strasser. Reluctantly, the Governing Commission came to the decision that the Jews should have a separate school for their children, since they themselves had requested it in view of the intolerable persecution to which Jewish children had been subjected in the regular schools of the Territory. In its report to the League, the Commission made the comment: "The very fact that that community has resigned itself, after centuries of freedom, to seeking for its children the segregation of the ghetto will suffice in itself to show the full extent of their persecution."

At the same time that Hitler and his associates were unleashing a typical Nazi campaign in which a mixture of cajolery and brutal pressure was used to make sure that "autonomists," "separatists," and other "traitors" should not woo the inhabitants away from the Fatherland, they were proposing to France that since the vote for Germany in the coming plebiscite was assured in any event, it would contribute to the friendship of the two nations if the Saar were returned immediately. Thus Hitler gave an interview to the correspondent of the *Nation* (London) on November 16, 1933, in which he claimed that once the Saar question was settled there would be nothing to disturb the good relations between France and Germany. In the following month a note was handed to the French ambassador in Berlin, specifically requesting that the Saar be returned to Germany at once and that the question of the disposition of the coal mines be made the subject of further negotiations. In his speech to the Reichstag on January 30, 1934, Adolf Hitler prepared a bait calculated to attract the nervous French. Once the Saar question was settled, he declared, the German government "would be prepared and determined not only to accept the letter but also the spirit of the Locarno Pact."

Prior to Hitler's speech, the French had indicated the stand which they were to maintain. On November 14, 1933, the French foreign minister, Joseph Paul-Boncour, declared in the Chamber of Deputies that his country had no right "to go contrary to an international regime which had given to the inhabitants of the Saar themselves the right to decide their own fate." Actually the French were concerned above all with the problems of armament and security. The Saar question was not unrelated to these, but its separate and isolated solution held little appeal to the logical French. Thus, except perhaps for certain members of the Right, who were predisposed to make a deal with the *Führer,* the disposition was to await the outcome of the plebiscite.

8

BACK TO THE FATHERLAND

The decision of the Peace Conference to hold a plebiscite in the Saar, but to defer it for fifteen years, was, as has been observed, part of the compromise President Wilson and the French agreed upon in order to avoid a stalemate which might wreck the conference and send the Americans home. Except for French opinion, there was a general conviction that the people of the Saar were thoroughly German and wanted to remain German. Certainly, this accounted for President Wilson's obduracy in refusing to consider the transfer of these Germans to France even for a term of years. He did not want to create another irredentist region. On the other hand, France undoubtedly had a good economic case for "reparation in kind," in view of the wanton damage inflicted by the retreating Germans to her coal mines. Could an arrangement be made, therefore, to give her for a prescribed period the coal under the ground, without at the same time affording her opportunities to control the population on the surface? And, at the end of the period, could the people be consulted under conditions which would enable them without fear or constraint to make their wishes felt? The framers of the treaty attempted to reach satisfactory answers to both questions.

The plebiscite was to be held at the end of fifteen years. During this period Germany was required to renounce the government of the Territory but not to relinquish her sovereignty. At the prescribed time the inhabitants of the Saar were by their votes to "indicate the sovereignty under which they desire to be placed." Eligibility for voting was also specified: "All persons without distinction of sex, more than twenty years old at the date of voting, resident in the territory at the date of the signature of the present Treaty . . . ." The ultimate decision, however, lay with the League of Nations, which "shall decide on the sovereignty under which the territory is to be placed, taking into account the wishes of the inhabitants as expressed by the voting." The people of the Saar had three choices. They could vote to have the German political connection restored, they could express a desire to be placed under French sovereignty, or they could ask to have the government of the League made definitive. However, the vote was to be taken by communes or districts, and conceivably certain communes might vote solidly for one alternative and others express themselves as strongly for a different solution. Would the League then decide to divide the territory, with the consequent destruction of economic unity and perhaps with other unhappy results? The treaty provisions seemed obscure on this point, and prior to the plebiscite there was a good deal of speculation on the matter.

As early as 1922, the Council of the League appointed a provisional records commissioner for the Saar Basin plebiscite. His task was to examine, classify, and recommend the preservation of such records and documents as would be required at the time of the plebiscite. These included voters' lists, census data, and lists of taxpayers for 1918–1919, as well as police registers, showing arrivals and departures. The League Council then acted to insure the safeguarding of these documents by establishing certain rules binding on the state and local authorities. The work was finally completed in 1926 and seems to have satisfied the Saar leaders, who had been fearful that fraudulent or inaccurate voters' lists would be prepared.

Eight years later, in January 1934, the time had come for the following item to be placed on the Council's agenda: "The Preparatory Measures to Be Taken with a View to the Plebiscite in the Saar Territory." Germany was still a member of the League and entitled to participate in the consideration of the matter, but the tenor of the disarmament discussions had displeased her and she had absented herself from the Council meetings. She was advised in advance that the question of the Saar plebiscite had been placed on the agenda and care was taken not to hold the meeting until she had time to send a representative. Nevertheless, Freiherr Konstantin von Neurath, the German foreign minister, replied to the Council's invitation that "the German Government regrets that, for reasons of principle, it must decline to take part in the discussions . . . ." Thus the Council had to proceed without German participation, and feared that the already delicate relations with the Reich would be aggravated. Its *rapporteur* on Saar questions was Baron Pompeo Aloisi of Italy, a country which certainly could not be regarded as particularly friendly to Britain or France. Aloisi was empowered by the Council to select two other members of that body to assist him in preparing a further report on the problems involved in the administration of the plebiscite.

The Committee of Three included in addition to the chairman, Baron Aloisi, the representatives of Spain and Argentina. Such a committee could hardly be expected to bring in recommendations prejudicial to German interests, and in fact the German government indicated its willingness to negotiate with it. Tension was further eased by an agreement between the German government and France, resulting in the issue of identical notes on June 2, 1934, in which both governments agreed: (1) to refrain from exercising pressure to affect the voting and to restrain or punish their nationals for conduct inconsistent with such undertakings; (2) to establish and maintain for "a transitional period of one year as from the establishment of the final regime" a Supreme Plebiscite Tribunal empowered to hear complaints regarding "pressure, persecution, reprisals or discrimination," and to prescribe "any appropriate reparation"; (3) to bring any dispute between Council members over these undertakings before the Permanent Court of International Justice. The Council of the League, meeting two days later, not only took note of and approved these plans but declared that it would see that they were carried out. Altogether it looked like the auspicious beginning of an attempt to substitute law for force in the ultimate disposal of the Saar question.

The foregoing undertakings were important, but they did not touch upon the question of the organization of the plebiscite. That was the responsibility of the Council. And in at least one respect it could rely upon precedent. Several plebiscites had been held following World War I to determine under what sovereignty particular national groups desired to live, and in each of these an international plebiscite commission had been entrusted with the administration of the territory and the supervision of the vote. In the Saar a commission, presumably neutral, was already functioning and was intended to govern the Saar until after the plebiscite. However, for various reasons, including the heavy burden this additional task would impose upon it, the Governing Commission was relieved of primary responsibilities for the plebiscite, and a decision was made to establish a special Plebiscite Commission, appointed by the Council of the League. This commission, acting under the authority of the Council, was intended to organize, direct, and supervise the plebiscite. Its three members were of Dutch, Swedish, and Swiss nationality; its technical expert and alternate member was an American citizen, Miss Sarah Wambaugh, who had had considerable firsthand experience in the conduct of international plebiscites and was perhaps the foremost authority on the subject.

In any plebiscite no question is of greater importance than how to provide ways and means whereby the campaign and the voting may be conducted in an orderly fashion and free from illicit activities and coercive tactics of partisan groups desiring to win at any cost. In all postwar plebiscites the need for neutral policing had been evident. But in the Saar, circumstances were such that even greater precautions seemed necessary. The inhabitants, though reputed to be a peaceful folk, had been subjected for the greater part of fifteen years to propaganda appeals designed to arouse hatred of France, of the Treaty of Versailles, and of the Governing Commission, in order that in 1935 they would "remember they were Germans." And, with the coming of Hitler, the Nazis exhorted them with the most frenzied appeals and tried surreptitiously to organize them for violent action. Under the circumstances, the small police force which the Governing Commission had at its disposal seemed totally inadequate.

In each of the postwar European plebiscites an international police force, free from the taint of partisanship and the temptations to which local police were subject, had been provided; and the reasons for the employment of such a force in the Saar plebiscite seemed compelling, even though the treaty had stipulated that "only a local gendarmerie for the maintenance of order" should be established. The Germans argued that this applied to the plebiscite phase as well as to the rest of the fifteen-year period. But it could be pointed out that the Council of the League was under special obligation to prescribe such arrangements for the plebiscite as would, in the words of the treaty, "secure the freedom, secrecy, and trustworthiness of the voting." If, as experience in other plebiscite situations indicated, an outside force seemed necessary, the Council was under an obligation to provide such a force.

In June 1934, when it became clear to the Governing Commission and the League Council that there was danger that the situation would get out of hand, the latter authorized the Commission to supplement the local gendarmerie by the recruitment of neutral volunteers. Geoffrey George Knox, the English chairman of the Commission, then appointed an Englishman, Captain Arthur C. Helmsley, as his chief of police; and in the following months a small number of British, Norwegian, and Czech officers were engaged, as well as additional recruits from the Saar itself. In the meantime, there were growing rumors that the Nazis were planning a *Putsch*. Whether true or not, the threats and extravagant utterances of certain of the Nazi leaders added to a general feeling of uneasiness, and forced a further consideration of the adequacy of the small existing forces at the disposal of the Commission.

At the Council meeting in September, when the Committee of Three made a report concerning the question of the maintenance of order, the French representative declared that France had special responsibilities in the Saar and was determined to discharge them. In 1926 the Council had approved the Governing Commission's position that in the event of an emergency it should be entitled to call upon

French troops stationed outside the Saar Territory. The French now indicated in the press that they were prepared to furnish such troops within a few hours, should Chairman Knox be confronted with an emergency. The Germans immediately interpreted this as an attempt to intimidate the voters, and feeling in Germany ran high. The Reich government circularized the Locarno powers with protests, after the German ambassador at Paris had made two calls at the Quai d'Orsay and failed to get satisfaction.

In November 1934, however, it became apparent that the German government had decided to change its tactics and tone down its belligerency as well as lay a restraining hand on its fanatical followers in the Saar. No doubt, its unaccustomed restraint about this time was actuated by the fear that it was overplaying its hand and that it might endanger its position in the Saar by precipitating armed intervention by France. When it suited him, Hitler could coo like a dove and be most distressed at the proclivities of eagles. It suited him now. There was also the plebiscite to consider, and in this connection the attitude of the Roman Catholics of the Saar was important. A papal emissary who called himself "the eyes and ears of the Holy Father, but not his mouth," was present in the Territory. And in the summer, a new Catholic paper, the *Neue Saarpost,* had come out for the maintenance of the status quo. It was apparent that this was not the time for a *Kulturkampf.* These considerations may well have motivated the order issued on November 2, 1934, by Hitler's commissioner for the Saar, Joseph Bürckel, prohibiting the wearing of uniforms between January 10 and February 10, 1935, within a twenty-five-mile zone along the Saar frontier, and likewise forbidding meetings, parades, and processions in this area. The next day the Nazi leader in the Saar, Pirro, ordered his followers to observe the strictest discipline and laid down stringent penalties for any infractions of the rules.

Pierre Laval of France now followed with a conciliatory statement intimating that his government did not desire to take unilateral military action in the Saar and, on December 5, specifically requested the participation of other countries, should military action be required. Anthony Eden, speaking for the British Government, immediately announced that the best way to deal with the situation in the Saar appeared to be the introduction "on the responsibility of the Council as a whole before the plebiscite took place of an international force, which should not include troops of either of the two parties concerned, for the purpose of keeping order." Moreover, he declared, if the Council decided to take such a step, and France and Germany assented to the arrangement, the United Kingdom would be prepared to "supply a suitable proportion of such an international force." The representatives of Italy, the USSR, and Czechoslovakia on the League Council immediately agreed to Eden's proposal—and the concurrence of Germany and France was likewise secured—paving the way for its adoption by the Council. This was followed on December 8 by a resolution of the Council inviting the British, Italian, Dutch, and Swedish governments to supply contingents, which would constitute a reserve for emergencies but not a regular police force. The strength of this force was fixed at slightly more than 3,000 men, the British furnishing 1,500, the Italians 1,300, the Swedes 250, and the Dutch 250. It was a happy solution and contributed considerably to the removal of fear and the stabilization of the situation in the Territory, although difficulties of another kind still had to be faced.

The bias of the members of the local courts in the Territory presented another problem. Under the treaty "the civil and criminal courts existing in the Territory of the Saar Basin shall continue." The judges were for the most part appointees of the Prussian and Bavarian governments and, as Germans, found it difficult to withstand the constantly mounting pressure on the part of the Nazi organization to deliver partisan judgments in the case of political offenders against the regime. Although the Saar Supreme Court, composed of international judges, could and did in a number of instances reverse the decisions of the local magistrates, this tended only to accentuate the cleavage between the two sets of courts and between the Commission and the population. To remedy the situation, the French member of the Governing Commission proposed the establishment of courts of neutral judges for political cases. The Saar member, however, pointed out that this would be a violation of the Saar statute, and the proposal was not adopted.

In the meantime, the Governing Commission was faced with the necessity of countering the action of the courts and of the municipal councils and officials. Thus in August 1934, after the Commission had raided the Deutsche Front headquarters and seized evidence of illegal activities on the part of the organization, a local court ordered the release of the incriminating documents, and the Commission had to reconfiscate them. The Deutsche Front attempted to get exclusive rights for the hiring of halls and for the holding of open-air meetings in the public squares of the various municipalities. The Commission advised the municipal councils that such permission could be granted only with the proviso that the squares should also be placed at the disposal of anti-Nazi groups. All but one of the municipal councils refused to accept the condition—an indication of the power and influence which the Nazis were exerting in the Territory.

For several months prior to this, the anti-Nazi groups of the Left, stigmatized by the National Socialists as traitors deserving of no consideration, had been petitioning the Council of the League to take drastic steps to insure freedom of opinion in the Territory, including, where necessary, the removal of judges, the dismissal of unreliable police officials and local authorities, and the supervision of teachers so that propaganda might be eliminated from the schools. They also demanded the protection of Saar inhabitants who were being arrested and imprisoned in Germany. The leaders of the Deutsche Front, on the other hand, insisted that the measures already taken by the Governing Commission were harsh and repressive and should be withdrawn. Thus rival delegations from the Landesrat were sent to urge their respective claims before the Council in Geneva: the Deutsche Front spokesmen protesting that the Commission was arbitrary and unfair and urging that the plebiscite should be held as early as possible under the terms of the treaty; the Social Democrats contending that unless the Council could insure a proper atmosphere, the vote should be postponed.

The struggle of the two groups also took the form of huge demonstrations. On August 26, 1934, the Deutsche Front staged a great meeting at Coblenz, at which Hitler spoke before a crowd of possibly half a million people. Special trains, busses, and motor cars came from the Saar bringing, according to Nazi statistics, as many as two hundred thousand persons. On this occasion the tactics of the Nazis were designed to instill general confidence rather than to emphasize the orthodox tenets of National Socialism. Catholics, Lutherans, and even the dissidents of the Left were wooed. Services of both faiths were held at the beginning of the meeting, and Hitler followed this gesture with a speech promising in substance that after the plebiscite all would be forgiven his political opponents. Nor was France forgotten. After the victorious plebiscite there would be no further issue dividing the two countries, and peace would be assured. Ten thousand white pigeons were pressed into service at this point, by being released above the mammoth gathering. What more assurances were needed that Hitler had come like that earlier Saviour, "to bring peace not a sword!"

On the same day the Freiheitsfront, representing the Socialists and Communists, held a counterdemonstration within the Saar, at Sulzbach. It attracted, according to the *Volksstimme,* about one hundred thousand persons, but according to unbiased sources this figure should be cut in half. In the opinion of officials of the Plebiscite Commission, which by this time was keeping a close watch on the situation in the Territory, most of those in attendance were workers who saluted with the closed fist and sang the "International." Max Braun and others spoke against allowing the "brown regime" of Germany to be extended to the Saar, and contrasted economic conditions in the Territory with those in the Reich. The note which the Freiheitsfront was sounding was expressed in the *Volksstimme:* "Let us hold fast to the small territory which is the last bit of Germany free from Hitler." The Socialists, who as Germans found it difficult to consider even an extension of League rule in the Saar, much less its perpetuation, evidently saw in National Socialism a menace that must be combated at all costs.

In the meantime, the French government revealed a certain shrewd foresight in an *aide-mémoire,* which it forwarded to the League Council in September 1934. It took the position, in the first place, that attention should not be directed merely to the holding of the plebiscite but likewise to anticipating the various contingencies which would follow the vote for one or the other of the three choices presented to the electorate. Whatever the verdict of the inhabitants and the subsequent decision of the Council, various adjustments requiring agreements between France and Germany as well as decisions by the League would have to be made. It is quite possible that the French were partly motivated by the belief that they would be in a better position to protect their interests by securing agreements before the plebiscite rather than by seeking them afterward. In any event, their statement of the case for advance exploration and agreements was persuasive: "To await the result of the plebiscite before beginning the study of these problems would be to run the risk of improperly prolonging the period between the plebiscite and the coming into force of the new regime—a course which might be not only inconvenient but even dangerous—or of adopting incomplete and inadequately considered solutions which would prejudice legitimate interests and, first of all, in many cases, the interests of the inhabitants of the Saar."

The French proceeded in the *aide-mémoire* to outline their views on the various legal, economic, and financial questions which would arise if the Territory voted either for the maintenance of the status quo or for return to Germany. If, as a result of the vote, the Council should decide on the retention of the League regime, they declared that France would be prepared to hand over to the Territory a large part of the mining deposits, currently owned by the French state, "on equitable terms." But prior to the plebiscite it was the duty of the

Council to fix the status quo as a definitive regime, in order that the voters would know whether they favored it or rather one of the other solutions. If the electorate voted to return the Territory to Germany, it must be remembered that the mines, which were French property, would under the treaty provision have to be redeemed by the Reich in gold. And France would not relinquish her ownership "without obtaining satisfactory settlement."

The treaty stipulated that the amount which Germany should pay was to be fixed by three experts, and that the Council of the League was to determine the time and method of payment. But the French contended that to follow such a procedure might mean either that there would be a delay before the Saar could be returned to Germany after the plebiscite, or that the Territory would have to be restored without the mines, for France would insist that her title to this property would not be given up until the mines had been paid for in full. Moreover, France had other claims in connection with the railway system and the customs stations. Thus the Council should assume responsibility for expediting a settlement, so that a Franco-German agreement might be concluded under its auspices before the plebiscite. There were various additional financial questions which should be taken up at once. For example, the French franc was the legal currency of the Territory. If the Saar reverted to Germany, arrangements would have to be worked out for the orderly substitution of the mark.

The Council of the League referred the questions raised in the *aide-mémoire* to the consideration of its Committee of Three, which met in Rome on November 5, 1934, for that purpose. In the meantime, certain features of the French memorandum aroused the apprehension of the political leaders of the Deutsche Front, and elicited strong protests from them and the local press, as well as from the Reich. The document had not explicitly envisaged a second plebiscite, but supporters of the status quo gave it that interpretation and aroused the Nazis to combat any such suggestion. It did promise, however, that if the status quo were perpetuated, France would cede a portion of the mines to the Territory. The Deutsche Front asserted that, far from benefiting the people of the Saar, such action would injure them, because they would have to shoulder part of the deficit incurred by the French state mines and would lose the contributions the German government had been making toward the support of persons wounded in the war and of other needy groups. And to vote for the status quo would mean approving the perpetuation of autocratic government by foreigners. Gauleiter Joseph Bürckel lent a note of authority to these arguments by proclaiming that an independent Saar was unthinkable, that it would provide a haven for *Emigranten* and Communists. As for a second plebiscite, it would be in violation of the Treaty of Versailles!

In the meantime, Premier Jean Louis Barthou, whose memorandum had caused such concern in the Reich and among the Saar Nazis, was murdered at Marseilles by assassins who, in the opinion of the leftist groups in the Saar, were probably in the pay of Germany. Although this occurrence led to more excitement and further recriminations in the Saar, fortunately it did not prevent the continued exploration at Rome of the questions which had been raised by the *aide-mémoire*. At these meetings, held under the auspices of the League's Committee of Three, not only were the French and German ambassadors to Italy present but also economic and financial experts of the two countries and from the League and the International Labor Organization. Members of the subcommittee of the League of Nations' Financial Committee were of the greatest assistance in working out the solutions adopted in connection with the French mines and railways in the Saar.

On December 5, 1934, only five weeks before the date of the plebiscite (January 13, 1935), Baron Aloisi, as chairman of the Committee of Three was able to present a report to the Council of the League, which included a direct agreement between France and Germany, specific guaranties from the two powers to the population, and certain recommendations concerning the future government of the Territory, which would require adoption by the Council. The Franco-German agreement provided that should the Saar be returned to Germany, the French government would cede its mines, railways, customs stations, and other immovable property in the Saar in return for the payment of a lump sum of nine hundred million francs. The payment was to be made by the transfer to Germany of 95 percent of Bank of France notes and other foreign means of payment circulating in the Saar, and by free deliveries of coal so spread as to ensure full payment in five years. In addition, Germany was to pay dues on the Warndt leases, averaging over two million tons per annum, for five years, or if the nine-hundred-million-franc payment had not by then been discharged in full, until such time as the payment might be completed.

All things considered, it was remarkable that the two governments were able to reach an agreement in such a short time on the amount and the method of payment by Germany for these French properties. For example, at the time of the Peace Conference the German estimate of the value of the Saar mines was very high—much higher than the estimates of the French experts—but by 1930 the Germans were claiming that the mines had lost much of their value because of the wasteful methods of exploitation employed by the French; and some German nationalists, among them Hermann Röchling, were quoted as declaring that Germany would not pay France anything for the return of the mines. Moreover, it was asserted that by 1925 the French government had fully recouped any losses sustained by France due to the damage to her mines during the World War. But the French stated officially that from 1920 to 1928 they had invested five hundred fifty million francs in the Saar mines and had introduced so many improvements that they were worth much more than in 1920.

The Committee of Three was also successful in obtaining specific guaranties from France and Germany on behalf of the Saar population. Among these was the pledge to respect the right of the individual to leave the territory and to retain or sell his property during the period of transition from the existing to the new regime. Quite important also was the German guaranty to refrain for one year after the change of regime from any discrimination against the inhabitants on grounds of race, language, or religion. It may be observed that the French government did not place a time limit on a similar promise. The two governments also pledged themselves to safeguard the rights to annuities, pensions, and other benefits which the inhabitants had acquired or were in the process of acquiring under arrangements made during the regime of the Governing Commission. And the agreement which had been reached on June 2, 1934, to refrain from pressure or reprisals affecting the voting in the plebiscite was now extended to cover nonvoters, including refugees from Germany.

The French government's desire, expressed in the *aide-mémoire,* that the Council should define the status quo, since it was one of the three choices for which the inhabitants might vote at the time of the plebiscite, led the Committee of Three to propose and the Council to adopt a clarifying statement. It pointed out that "though the Council could not now define the form of government to be established should the plebiscite result in a vote for the status quo, it could state that there would be a change of sovereignty, since this would pass to the League. This change would empower the League to make changes in the form of government, and, if it thought fit, later to dispose of that sovereignty (within the limits of the Versailles Treaty, i.e., to France, to Germany or to the Territory)." This statement seemed not to rule out a second plebiscite at some future time, and such a contingency was anticipated in the observations of several council members. Pierre Laval said that if the people of the Saar voted for the status quo and later desired a second plebiscite, "France would not oppose it." Maxim

Litvinov, the representative of the USSR in the Council, expressed the conviction that the Saar people would clearly be entitled to it under the right of self-determination, and Eduard Beneš concurred, declaring that this expressed the view of the Council as a whole.

In the meantime, on November 30, 1934, a number of Catholic priests founded the Deutscher Volksbund party. It announced that it was "for Christ and our Germany against National Socialism and neopaganism," and therefore supported the maintenance of the status quo for the time being. This drew the fire of spokesmen of the Deutsche Front, who declared that these supporters of the status quo had ranged themselves alongside the antichrist Communists and Marxists and therefore against Germany. Nor did they get aid and comfort in high places within the Roman Catholic hierarchy. The Bishops of Trier and Speyer even forbade the priests within their jurisdiction from attending public political meetings in the Saar and from "the bringing of politics into the Church and the care of souls." Nevertheless the Deutscher Volksbund organized meetings throughout the Territory every Sunday; and in spite of great counterdemonstrations by the Deutsche Front and the most bitter attacks of the Nazis, who feared it more than they did the Einheitsfront, it continued to proclaim, *"Christus ist unser Führer, nicht Hitler!"*

Late in December the International Force under a British commander in chief and equipped with armored cars and motor lorries, arrived in the Territory, prepared if called upon by the chairman of the Governing Commission to intervene and maintain or restore order. Following the technique developed elsewhere by the British in anticipating and dealing with mass disorders, the troops displayed their strength before the inhabitants and remained on the alert, ready to concentrate on any trouble spot—which they did with swiftness on several occasions. But they left the routine maintenance of order to the police. The Deutsche Front was strongly opposed to this force from the first and ordered its members not to watch or fraternize with this "army of occupation." However, the sport-loving and informal British had brought along footballs and eventually succeeded in scheduling some games with the local teams, thus breaking down whatever initial resistance the population as a whole may have had.

On January 12, 1935, the day before the plebiscite, the Council of the League emphasized the solemnity of the occasion by telegraphing to the Governing Commission a message for the population : "On the eve of the plebiscite, the Council desires to make a solemn appeal to the population of the Saar. It urges them to show by their calm and dignified attitude that they are conscious of the importance of the vote which they are called upon to record. It counts upon their preserving the same attitude after the vote and awaiting with confidence the decisions which the Council will take within as short an interval as possible following upon the vote." The injunction was strictly followed, owing partly to the strict discipline enforced by the Deutsche Front on its members and to the obvious preparations that had been made by the League, the Plebiscite Commission, and the International Force to deal promptly and effectively with disturbing elements.

The results of the plebiscite were unexpected and very disappointing to advocates of the continuance of the status quo. On the other hand, the event bore out the advance predictions of the Nazi leaders, who were themselves somewhat surprised, as were neutral observers, by the extent of their overwhelming victory. Of the 528,105 votes cast, 477,119 were for union with Germany, representing over 90 percent of the valid ballots. Only 46,613 voters cast ballots for the status quo and but 2,124 for union with France. The plebiscite was also remarkable in that the vote for Germany did not fall below 83 percent in any voting district—a circumstance, incidentally, which made easy the ensuing decision of the Council.

Within four days after the vote, the Plebiscite Commission made its official report to the Council of the League. Baron Aloisi, chairman of the Committee of Three, paid a special tribute to Chairman Geoffrey Knox of the Governing Commission, as one who had "earned the gratitude of all who had at heart the prestige of the League of Nations and the maintenance of peace." (During the plebiscite campaign the Nazis had tried unsuccessfully to shake Knox's imperturbable calm by constant charges of "gross partisanship.") At the conclusion of the committee's report, the Council decided on the union of the whole Territory with Germany, and fixed March 1, 1935, as the date when the transfer should take place. On the appointed day, the Territory was duly handed over to Dr. Wilhelm Frick, Reichsminister of the interior, and the League regime came to an end.

9

THE PRICE

The verdict of the plebiscite of 1935 demonstrated the power of nationalism over economics and over internationalism. From an economic standpoint the people of the Saar had been better off under an international governing commission than had their kinsmen in the Reich. They were legally removed from the arena of international politics and relieved of the burden of armaments, which citizens of the Great Powers must bear. Their taxes were lower, their incomes higher than those of their compatriots in Germany. The governing authority was efficient and, except for the first few years, was scrupulously honest and impartial. It maintained and developed an excellent school system, fostered public improvements, paid its officials well, and, at the end, handed over a treasury balance and no public debt. Moreover, except as the public security and the fulfillment of treaty obligations required temporary restrictions, the inhabitants enjoyed the civil rights prized in democratic communities and considerable political freedom as well.

On the other hand, for nearly two years before the plebiscite was held, Germans under the Third Reich had been subjected to a regimentation and loss of personal liberty that was in striking contrast to the civil and political rights enjoyed in democratic countries and was much more severe than the people of the Saar had ever experienced under the Governing Commission. On the economic side, the leaders of the Reich determined to pour the nation's energy into armaments, and frankly proclaimed "guns before butter." In the field of foreign policy, the *Führer* and his advisers had shown a cynical disregard for international commitments and a determination to blast their way to world power regardless of consequences. The controlled press of Germany told the people of the Reich only what Joseph Goebbels, the minister of propaganda and enlightenment, wanted them to know and think.

By contrast, the people of the Saar, though deluged with Nazi propaganda and exposed to the most thoroughgoing "enlightenment," were legally free to read anything they pleased and to listen to anyone whom they wished to hear. Moreover, the Governing Commission and the Plebiscite Commission took pains to see that the public platforms, auditoriums, and arenas were not monopolized by the Nazis, and that the inhabitants were not terrorized at the polls. But the over-whelming vote for union with Hitler's Reich was so impressive that only one conclusion could be drawn, namely, that the totalitarian German regime was not distasteful to most of the Saar inhabitants, and that they preferred it even to an efficient, economical, and benevolent international rule. To be sure, there were some who rgarded the Third Reich with so much aversion and fear that they fled over the border to France when the results of the plebiscite became known. But there were only about three thousand three hundred of these (in addition to the eight hundred refugees who had previously fled from the Reich) from a total population of about eight hundred thousand. Those who remained were to have the privilege, within less than five years, of fighting and dying to achieve the objectives of the *Führer*, and of seeing their homeland invaded and damaged in the course of Allied efforts at thwarting him.

It suited the convenience of the National Socialist government to avoid a complete change in the Saar's boundaries as they had been drawn at Versailles fifteen years before. The parts which had been carved from Prussia and Bavaria, on the decision of the Allies, were not returned to these states but were combined with the Bavarian Palatinate to form the Gau Westmark. And the Saar region was entitled again to send deputies to the Reichstag, although the procedure for their selection was changed. They were to be nominated by the chancellor's plenipotentiary for the Saar, Joseph Bürckel, and appointed by Hitler himself. Elections had become superfluous. The people had voted in overwhelming numbers for the Leader. He and his elite would henceforth free them from making further political decisions they were not thought competent to make.

Labor in particular felt the impact of the new order of things. The labor unions were dissolved, as they had been in the rest of the Reich after Hitler came to power, and were incorporated into the Deutsche Arbeitsfront. Prior to Hitler, the unions had developed considerable strength throughout Germany and had been instrumental, directly or indirectly, in improving the lot of the German masses in various ways. But for those very reasons they could not be tolerated by the *Führer* and his lieutenants, who had other goals in mind than social security for the masses.

The character of the Saar economy insured the attention of Hitler and his associates, who were feverishly preparing for war. To this end they acted to double the amount of vital materials marketed within Germany and halve that exported to France. The mining and steel industries were greatly stimulated as a result of war preparations, which were carried forward without regard to cost. For example, the natural source of iron ore was the nearby Lorraine field, but the German government now began to import the more costly Swedish ore—partly displacing that from Lorraine—since war with France would shut off the Lorraine imports, and the Nazis wanted to be prepared.

It was well understood that the industrial character of the Saar, with its heavy war industries and its location adjacent to French Lorraine, would sooner or later make it an object of enemy attack. Accordingly, secret military preparations were pushed forward. Over two thousand carefully camouflaged ferroconcrete bunkers were constructed along the Saar river and in the hills to the north and east. And in the central part of the Saar, belts of steel and concrete antitank barricades were thrown up. These "dragon's teeth" became part of the Siegfried line of defense, which Hitler began to build in 1937, the year after he had marched into the Rhineland and two years after his entry into the Saar.

After Hitler had launched the war, further precautionary measures were taken by large-scale evacuation of civilians from the Saar to other parts of Germany. These people were returned when the armistice with France apparently had removed the danger of an Allied attack. However, after the invasion of the Continent by General Dwight Eisenhower's forces, the nonessential civilian population was again evacuated. Henceforth the Saar was to experience heavy bombing, followed by attacks of the Third and Seventh Armies of the United States in December 1944. Military operations were continued on a devastating scale until March 1945, when German resistance was completely broken.

The war brought hardship and suffering everywhere in the Reich. For the Saar its consequences were appalling. From a population of about 800,000 in 1939, over 200,000 men were mobilized; nearly 50,000 were killed; and about 30,000 were disabled. In addition to these incapacitated soldiers, 60,000 women and children had to be cared for. The fortified industrial areas of Saarbrücken and Saarlouis were about 80 percent destroyed, and other lesser cities also felt the effects of the bombing. More than 60,000 houses were totally or partially destroyed. This proportion of a total of about 127,000 houses in the Saar resulted in such acute housing shortage that many families were forced to live in air-raid shelters for months after the war ended. The chief targets of the bombers had of course been military installations, industrial plants, transportation facilities, and communications. Nevertheless, great damage to houses, churches, schools, and hospitals was inevitable. But the German gods must have been guarding the great steelworks of the notorious Hermann Röchling at Völklingen. They seem to have escaped unscathed.

The American Fifteenth Army first occupied the Saar in May 1945, and the alert French sent in economic and mining missions to reopen the mines and in general to prepare the way for later French occupation. The region was turned over to French forces in July of the same year and, in accordance with the decision of the Potsdam Conference, was henceforth to be included in the French zone of occupation. No time was lost by the French authorities in setting up a military administration under Colonel Gilbert Grandval. Moreover, they set about energetically to restore the Saar as far and as fast as possible, by providing housing facilities, repairing factories, rebuilding railroads, and bringing in food supplies for the undernourished population.

Although the French policy from the first was to show special solicitude for the Saar Germans in contrast to Germans in the remainder of their occupation zone, they did not hesitate to deal vigorously with notorious Nazis and other troublemakers. Consequently, denazification proceedings were instituted in the Saar as in the rest of Germany, but at the same time the French tried to avoid obvious mistakes and any action that would alienate Saar public opinion. Thus, there was no wholesale purge of persons merely because they were known to be anti-French. Special commissions were appointed to investigate charges against former Nazi party officials, members of the SS, and "persons who left at liberty might constitute a hindrance to the realization of the aims pursued by the Military Government or, again, a danger to the security of the Allied Forces." Eventually the military government approved and ordered the expulsion of about 580 families. The heads of many of these were Nazi party officials of non-Saar origin, who had made trouble for the French before and who were regarded as likely to form centers of resistance in the future. Be that as it may, among the deported were also persons catalogued as "suspects judged undesirable in the Saar." These deportations met with such universal protest from all political groups that the French military governor was obliged to give assurance that no further expulsions would be ordered.

Other measures, less drastic but also anticipating trouble, were designed to smooth the way for the collaboration of the *sarrois* and the French in the development of French Saar policy. German refugees from the east were not allowed to enter the Saar, publications from Germany were banned, censorship of Saar publications was undertaken, and, except for students, travel between Germany and the Saar was placed under restrictions, while movement between the Saar and Western European countries was unlimited.

In 1919, André Tardieu and other French spokesmen had confidently asserted that the free exposure of the *sarrois* for fifteen years to French culture would incline them toward France. But methods of persuasion such as the French were able to use in 1945 were not available to them under the government of the Saar by the League of Nations. These measures, as shown above, were restrictive and preventive and were designed to give constructive French policy an opportunity to succeed. The French were convinced that they were necessary but by no means a final solution. Nor does it appear that the French intended to make over Saar Germans into the likeness of Frenchmen, with French as distinguished from German culture. The intent rather seems to have been to foster an indigenous Saar culture as a merger of the two, and to have the Saar serve as a bridge rather than as a bridgehead between the two powers. It is true that early in the French occupation Colonel Grandval placed a somewhat different emphasis on the intentions of France when he declared that she would exert "all possible efforts to bring the Saar culturally into the orbit of French political, intellectual, and artistic effulgence . . . ." However, it is to be observed that although the French have established and heavily subsidized a Saar University at Homburg, it is a bilingual institution, with a Franco-German teaching staff. Students from Germany are admitted, and it seems not to have been set up as a French propaganda agency.

Fear of a resurgent Germany has dictated the political policy of the French with regard to the status of the Rhineland, the Ruhr, and the Saar; and most French leaders, and the groups for which they spoke, have differed, if at all, on matters of strategy and detail rather than on substance. When the French took control of the Saar, the provisional government of the French Republic was under the leadership of General Charles de Gaulle, who set the tone in most questions of foreign policy. As to the reconstitution of Germany, he was adamantly opposed to a Fourth Reich "with power to do harm." France, he reminded foreign statesmen, had been invaded three times within the experience of living Frenchmen. Drastic steps must be taken to see that it happened no more. France, therefore, must permanently control not only the Saar but the entire Rhineland, from Cologne to Switzerland. And in the area north of Cologne, a region of concern not only to France but to Belgium, the Netherlands, and Britain, international control should be established. The entire Rhineland should be integrated into the Western European rather than the Central European complex.

Support for the de Gaulle program, except as it involved the Saar and international control of other key areas, was not forthcoming in France outside the ranks of de Gaulle's own political followers. In a debate in the Constituent Assembly on January 16, 1946, the Socialists declared their opposition to the annexation of German territory, although they favored a prolonged period of occupation and international control. President Félix Gouin, who had succeeded de Gaulle, spoke in favor of international control of the Ruhr but was opposed to the separation of the Rhineland from Germany. In the following April, at the Moscow Conference of the Council of Foreign Ministers, Foreign Minister Georges Bidault declared that France did not desire to annex the Ruhr, but he insisted that in the interest of French security it must not remain under German control.

As regards the Saar, Bidault declared that France needed Saar coal and then added: "This benefit is enhanced on the security plane by the corresponding diminution of the German war potential." The mines, therefore, should again become the property of the French state, and the Saar Territory should be included in the economic and monetary system of France. Under these circumstances, France would be prepared to have her reparations from Germany scaled down. Finally Bidault asked that the Saar be removed immediately from the authority of the Allied Control Council. Britain and the United States were unwilling to agree to the French demands as long as France opposed the creation of centralized agencies for Germany permitting the attainment of economic unity. France finally agreed to the other powers' proposals on condition that such agencies would have no jurisdiction over the Saar, and in this the Western Powers acquiesced. But Vyacheslav M. Molotov, speaking for the USSR, insisted that the French were not entitled to detach any German territory in the absence of agreement by the Allied Control Council and that the Saar must be considered a part of German territory until the Big Four could agree on new frontiers.

The Russian rebuff did not deter the French, and although the Potsdam Conference recognized the boundaries of the Saar as those existing at the date of the plebiscite in 1935, French authorities now proceeded to redraw them by unilateral action. In May 1946, Lieutenant General Joseph Marie Pierre Koenig, in a speech at Saarlouis, foreshadowed an extension of the Saar boundaries by stating that the delimitation of 1919 had been "imperfect," and that a modification was now necessary in order to bring in certain areas indispensable to the welfare of the region. On July 18, 1946, the French commander in chief in Germany increased the area of the Saar by about 48 percent. Explaining this move at the Moscow meeting of the Conference of Foreign Ministers, Bidault stated that the boundaries drawn in 1919 were "arbitrary from the administrative and economic points of view." He declared that the Saar had needed a larger agricultural base and that the added territory was economically dependent upon the Saar.

The official attitude of the United States toward French aspirations in the Saar was stated by Secretary of State James F. Byrnes in September 1946, in an important speech at Stuttgart, and by his successor, General George Marshall, in April 1947. Byrnes declared that the government of the United States did not feel that it could deny to France, which had been invaded three times by Germany in the short span of seventy years, its claims in the Saar. Confirming Byrnes' position a few months later, Secretary of State Marshall agreed that the region should be detached politically from Germany and integrated economically and financially with France. France should also be entitled to defend the Saar from attack, but its political autonomy and the right of the inhabitants to manage their local affairs should be safeguarded. And he added that, except for minor rectifications, the boundaries of the Saar should be those of 1935, the time of the plebiscite. The Secretary of State also made it clear that this would be the attitude and the policy of the American government when the time came to draw up a German peace settlement. But he pointed out that "the definitive detachment of the Saar from Germany and the definitive determination of its boundaries" were decisions which could only be made at the peace conference.

Although the American Secretary of State did not purport to speak for any other governments, actually he was unequivocally supported by Ernest Bevin, the British foreign secretary. Both were apparently motivated by a disinclination to approve any action that might jeopardize the prosperity of Western Germany and by a fear of creating a new and politically dangerous irredentism. It has also been suggested that they were likewise moved by the apprehension that the severance of any sizable and important area from Western Germany might afford the expanding USSR a plausible excuse for proceeding to act in the same manner in the eastern part of the Reich.

The apparent unanimity of the American and British governments as regards the Saar convinced the French that they had gone too far, and they proceeded, possibly with some reluctance, to redraw the Saar frontier. Actually, they extended the boundary in the northeast, but gave up a much larger area in the northwest, so that the new area, though still about 33 percent greater than the Saar in 1945, was reduced from 1,106 to 987.7 square miles. However, when in April 1948 the question of the boundaries of the Saar was given consideration at a conference of the representatives of the United Kingdom, France, the United States, and the Benelux countries, the French indicated that they were still dissatisfied. They now contended that certain further extensions of the Saar boundaries were necessary in order to alleviate hardships to the population arising from the configuration of the existing frontier. Accordingly, conference representatives were appointed to make an on-the-spot investigation. Following this exploration, in March 1949 a recommendation was made to the six powers—the United States, Great Britain, France, the Netherlands, Belgium, and Luxemburg—and tacitly accepted, that certain changes in the Saar boundary be approved, bringing its total area to 990.9 square miles. Thus, as of January 1950, the *de facto* area of the Saar, though smaller than that claimed by France in 1946, was considerably larger than that of the Versailles settlement of 1919.

At the moment there seems to be a tacit understanding among the Western Powers that they will support the present boundaries of the Saar and its relationship with France when a future peace conference shall undertake to reach definitive decisions as regards the status and boundaries of Germany. But the Soviet government, whose attitude must be taken into account on this as on other European questions, has refused to commit itself. Whether it will eventually accept the *de facto* situation brought about by the French will undoubtedly depend upon the price France and the other Western Powers are willing to pay, for Soviet foreign policy is capable of great elasticity.

During the period under review the French have shown remarkable speed, energy, and skill in taking measures to insure the rapid economic recovery of the Saar. These naturally have centered on the revival of the coal industry. The French Mines Administration had taken great pride in its accomplishments during the period of 1920–1935, and the French were prepared to capitalize upon the experience acquired during these fifteen years. They knew precisely what they wanted to do and, understanding the German mentality, they made their intentions clear and executed their decisions with firmness. Their managers, technicians, and foremen were experienced and they spoke German. New recruits were trained at the Nancy School of Mines in French methods. Discipline was strict, and the co-operation of miners' delegates was enlisted against absentees, slackers, and agitators. On the other hand, the miners were made a favored class. The repatriation of German war prisoners was expedited if they had formerly been coal miners, and it seems that the latter received priority for rehousing, increased rations, special allocation of scarce gasoline, and other preferential treatment.

Up to the present it appears that this combination of efficiency, firmness, and benevolence has yielded good results. The output per man of the Saar mines has reached a level higher than that of the Ruhr mines, and absenteeism has been considerably less. Figures indicate a coal production of about fourteen million tons for 1949, or the equivalent of the maximum output in the years before the war. This is a very good record, especially in view of the fact that the Nazis during the war had allowed much of the mining machinery to deteriorate, and the French have had to renew or replace it. At the moment the workers seem contented—unmoved by Communist agitators and untroubled by pressure from Reich politicians. It is only fair to add that while the French should be given credit for this relatively happy situation, the general circumstances under which the Saar miners live have always been more favorable than those confronting the miners of the Ruhr and of other European coal fields.

It has already been observed that the iron and steel industry suffered heavy war damage caused by physical destruction. But the wasteful wartime exploitation which it endured under the Nazis was also a factor contributing to its deterioration. These industries now presented a problem to the French. Competing industrial interests in France had never been quite reconciled to the Saar's economic union with France, and it is possible that the government wanted to avoid disturbing them. At any rate, they seem to have been favored over the Saar industries in the allocation of coal and coke after the war. It also appears that modernization of iron and steel plants in the Saar has not been undertaken with the energy shown by the French in rehabilitating the coal industry. On the other hand, they have exempted the Saar from the dismantling policy carried out in the regular occupation zones, and by other positive measures had succeeded by the end of 1949 in bringing iron and steel production to about 70 percent of the prewar figure.

One unorthodox measure of the French, connected with their policy of weakening Germany and building up the Saar, was the dismantling of factories in the French zone of occupation and transferring them to the Saar. This met with an immediate protest from the United States. The latter charged that this unilateral act was a violation of the Potsdam Agreement, since such transfers affected the level of German industrial capacity and was thus a matter for Four

Power consideration. General Lucius Clay, United States commander in chief in Germany, contended specifically that since France had isolated the Saar from the rest of her occupied territory and was giving it a preferred status, the effect of French action was to transfer the plants to France outside the reparations agreements. However, the French representative on the Allied Control Council declared that "France does not feel obliged to report to other occupying powers on the removal of a factory from one place to another in our zone," and that her action in this instance was no concern of the Control Council. In view of the French attitude, the United States announced that she might have to regard any further removals as part of future French reparations.

As early as December 1946, the French declared that "in view of the future integration of the Saar, France, beginning now, is undertaking economic measures to ensure that the Saar is in as good condition as possible when that moment comes." They have therefore worked at the business of "integration" on several fronts. They established control over Saar radio facilities, primarily to prevent them from becoming a propaganda agency in the hands of Germans hostile to French policy. Other measures were taken, designed, as far as possible, to sever the ties of the Territory with Germany. The German railways in the area were reorganized into a separate unit, and communications in general were organized along French lines. A separate social security system, divorced from that of the Reich, was instituted; and a "reformed" monetary system—involving at first the introduction of a new currency, the Saarmark, and the elimination of the German mark—was introduced. However, a few months later, in November 1947, the franc was made legal tender, and in January 1948 it became the sole currency in the Territory.

Perhaps the most drastic step was the immediate erection of a customs barrier between the Saar and the rest of occupied Germany. This was occasioned, according to the French authorities, by the desire to prevent French food supplies intended for the Saar from being diverted to the German black market, as well as to allow the French to proceed without embarrassment in the introduction of the monetary reforms already mentioned. It is clear, however—and the French did not deny it—that the reimposition of the customs frontier was not intended merely as an emergency measure, but was vitally connected with long-range French policy for the Saar.

In nearly everything they have done in the economic sphere, the French have sought to explain and justify the steps they have taken as in the interests of the *Sarrois* themselves. They have given assurances that French protection will not mean French exploitation and political serfdom. For example, in 1947, the French High Commissioner declared that France was not seeking to substitute its own imperialism for that of Prussia and make the Saarland "the poor relation of the French economy." Apparently these assurances are accepted in the Saar as made in good faith. At any rate, there are positive indications that the political leaders and chief party organizations support the French program and are prepared at present to work with the French on the main points.

IO

PEACE AND POLITICS

During the period of American occupation in the Saar no political parties were authorized. However, soon after the French took over, on October 27, 1945, leaders of the three principal political organizations, anticipating revival, addressed a public political meeting in Saarbrücken. The French presently lifted the ban, and the Christian Peoples party (CVP), the Social Democratic party (SPS), and the Communist party (KP) began to function. With the coming of the French, there also developed the Mouvement pour le Rattachement de la Sarre à la France (MRS), which, though not itself a political party, began to exert a strong influence on behalf of France in the ranks of the principal party organizations.

The liberality with which the French greeted and encouraged the growth of indigenous political institutions in the Saar was well calculated to convince the *Sarrois* that France had no desire or intention to impose on them her own system. However, it was equally clear that the French authorities were determined that the parties they authorized should be distinctively and exclusively Saar parties. Experience under the League of Nations regime had convinced the French that political organizations in the Saar should not be allowed to have official connections with their counterparts in Germany. The latter could be assumed to be automatically opposed to French policy in the Saar, as they had been under the League administration; and to allow an organic connection between them and the political parties of the Saar would certainly invite trouble as well as be inconsistent with the over-all policy of France. That policy was to sever once and for all the political and economic ties which had hitherto bound the Saar to Germany.

Apparently the foregoing decisions of the French have been accepted in the Saar by the major political parties without protest and without expressed regret. Whether they were making a virtue out of necessity or had been convinced by the French that they would have a happier and more secure existence under the new orientation is perhaps not altogether clear. Nevertheless, there is considerable evidence that although they were not satisfied with all elements of French policy, they approved it on the whole. As early as April 1946, the Christian Peoples party expressed appreciation of the efforts of Colonel Gilbert Grandval to relieve suffering in the Saar and approved economic integration with France. At the same time this party called attention to France's declaration that she did not seek to annex the Saar and expressed the hope that the French authorities would respect the German language and the German Christian schools. A few days later the presidents of the two leading parties sent a telegram to the Conference of Foreign Ministers, meeting in Paris, strongly endorsing on behalf of the Saar people the French proposals for the economic attachment of the Saar to France and asserting that "it is not a question of a part of the Saar people with an opportunistic attitude."

The municipal elections held in September 1946, and apparently free from pressure by the French, seemed to confirm the impressions given by the political leaders that the population was prepared to cooperate with the Saar policy of France in the political and economic spheres. Over 90 percent of the registered voters participated in these elections, and the candidates of the CVP and the SPS, which favored the French program, received over 90 percent of the votes. The Communists, who were avowedly anti-French, were supported by less than 9 percent of the voters. The outcome of the elections, which showed an almost unanimous public opinion behind the stated objectives of France, undoubtedly convinced her that the time was ripe for the political implementation of these objectives.

A few months later (February 1947), the French Ministry of Foreign Affairs instructed Grandval, now French High Commissioner to the Saar, to initiate studies to serve as a basis for the drafting of a constitution for the *Sarrois*. Accordingly, Grandval consulted with the Administrative Commission of seven members, which had been established by the French in the month following the municipal elections. The Commission was chosen from and reflected in its membership the relative strength of the political parties; and the French had reason, therefore, to believe that it would be co-operative. Following this consultation, a Constitutional Commission of twenty members was appointed in agreement with the heads of the political parties. The membership of this commission was weighted to reflect the comparative strength of the political parties, as revealed in the 1946 municipal elections, and care was also taken to see that the views of the MRS were represented. Dr. Johannes Hoffman, head of the CVP, the strongest party, was made president of the Commission.

Within a few days after the constitution had been completed and made public, elections to the Landtag, or Saar Assembly, were held. There was some criticism, chiefly by the Communists, that the electorate had not been afforded the opportunity to pass directly on the constitution by means of a referendum. The election had centered on domestic issues, and it was argued that the merit of the proposed fundamental law was scarcely mentioned by the candidates. However, the French apparently felt that the constitutional issue was too complex and that no good result could be expected were it to be thrown into a general election. Possibly they had become fearful of plebiscites and the inflammatory appeals that too often accompanied them. Probably, too, they felt confident of the results derived from a reasoned consideration of the issues by a body of political leaders known to be favorably disposed toward the French point of view.

In the elections the Christian People's party captured 28 seats and the Social Democrats, 17. Since the total membership of the Landtag was 50, the party of the Catholics had a clear majority and the Socialists were in second place. Only 2 Communists were elected. This was the body to which the constitution was submitted. However, it was not to have the last word. Any action which it might take was subject to the final approval of France. That matters were well in hand, however, was indicated by the fact that on December 15, 1947, the Landtag voted its approval of the proposed constitution by the overwhelming majority of 48 to 1. And the French blessing followed shortly. But it is not recorded that there was rejoicing in Western Germany.

That France had reason to be pleased with the result can be seen from the provisions of the constitution as they related to her own position. The Preamble records certain basic decisions. The Saar was to be politically independent of Germany and was to be economically attached to France by a monetary and customs union. Its defense and external relations were likewise to be entrusted to the French Republic. Up to this point the resemblance seems to be close to the regime provided in the Treaty of Versailles, except that under the Saar constitution France assumes responsibility for the defense of the Territory, whereas formerly such defense was entrusted to the Governing Commission. But here the resemblance practically ends. While before, the general supervision of the Governing Commission was in the hands of the Council of the League of Nations, now a representative of the French Republic is given extensive powers to issue decrees safeguarding the Saar's economic union with France, and he is also given general powers of control to guarantee observance of the constitution. Thus France has become not only military guardian of the Saar but the ultimate judge in the interpretation of the fundamental law of the country and her own powers in relation to it. It may also be observed that although the Landtag may adopt an amendment to the constitution by a three-fourths vote, no such amendment is valid if it is contrary to the fundamental principles contained in the constitution, and those fundamental principles are in essence French policy. Finally, under the League regime the German legal system was retained, but the Preamble of the Saar constitution as well as recent measures of implementation indicate that French law may be employed in a number of fields.

The first part of the constitution lays down the rights and obligations of the individual and of religious, economic, and other groups in the community. The civil rights customarily guaranteed in modern constitutions are included, with safeguarding provisions designed to enable the government to maintain order and security and to protect the public interest. It may be noted that equality before the law is guaranteed for all, without distinction of sex, race, origin, or religious or political conviction. Men and women are to have the same rights and the same civic obligations. All men and women are to have the right to express their thoughts freely, to form associations, and to propagate scientific and artistic works, unless, in doing so, they attack or imperil the constitution. But political groups or organizations resorting to suppression by violence of the liberties and rights guaranteed in the constitution are declared illegal. In view of the expulsions that had taken place under the French military administration, and the resultant universal protest in the Saar, it is also of interest that the constitution states that no *Sarrois* may be expelled from the Territory. Likewise, it is significant that persons outside the Saar are allowed the right of asylum if they suffer from persecution for holding principles embodied in the Saar constitution.

In its attention to the subject of economic and social rights and obligations, the constitution reflects recent progressive trends in economic and political thought, and at the same time indirectly rules out a Communist order. The right to work according to individual ability is protected by the state, and, without prejudice to personal liberty, each individual has also the obligation to work. Social insurance, covering sickness, accident, old age, and death, is to be provided on a broad scale. The system is to be under control of the state and administered by the insured themselves, together with employers. The principle is set forth that conditions of work should be such as to guarantee material existence, the dignity of the individual and of family life, and the cultural aspirations of the workers. Freedom of association to guarantee and ameliorate conditions of work is recognized; and the right to strike is permitted within the framework of the law. As regards property rights, they may only be restricted by law and in cases where the general interest is involved. The coal mines and other industries of basic importance to the economy of the entire community, or having the character of monopolies, may not be appropriated by private interests. Any economic enterprise which by its methods or practices menaces the public welfare can be expropriated by law and made part of the public domain. It may be added that the constitution enjoins the protection and encouragement of the middle classes concerned in business, industry, and commerce; and that agriculture as the source of the national food supply is particularly encouraged. Furthermore, it is stipulated that all appropriate means should be employed to assure the maintenance of an independent peasant class.

Whatever the political regime, the Saar remains a region made up predominantly of people of the Roman Catholic faith. That the constitution reflects this fact is understandable, and that the French have been careful to tread lightly with respect to its ecclesiastical provisions, in order to avoid giving offense to Saar Catholics, was to be expected. Since the French Revolution, when the Church as one of the privileged orders of the *ancien régime* lost her favored position in France and had to face anticlerical legislation, the relations between the Holy See and the French state have never been altogether satisfactory to the Vatican. It will be recalled that under the League of Nations regime the Governing Commission's effort to establish direct relations between the Saar Catholics and Rome failed, and that, consequently, the immediate superiors of the Saar Catholic clergy remained the German archbishops of Trier and Speyer. It will also be recalled that prior to the plebiscite of 1935, these archbishops openly exhorted Saar Catholics to vote for the return of the Saar to Germany.

That at least one of the German archbishops was still of the same political faith twelve years later is indicated in a pastoral letter from the Archbishop of Trier to the faithful in March 1947, in which he explicitly indicated the political path which, as Christians, they should follow. In this letter the Saar Catholics were admonished that "to abandon one's country for purely selfish reasons in order to avoid the sacrifices it demands of us, is contrary to the Christian spirit which holds that sacrifice is superior to physical possessions." (Apparently by rendering unto Caesar the things which are Caesar's the people of the Saar were at the same time following Peter.) Two months later the Pope appointed a native of the Saar as "Apostolic Visitor" for the Saarland, but what immediate political significance is to be attached to this move is not altogether clear. No doubt, the Holy See will view the somewhat anomalous situation in the Saar in relation to the long-range objectives as well as the immediate interests of the Church.

These interests, apparently with the ready concurrence of the French, have received full recognition in the constitution.

The Church has always insisted that in Roman Catholic countries the education of the youth should be regarded as an ecclesiastical prerogative. The Saar constitution accepts this principle. It does not give the Roman Catholic Church a monopoly of religious instruction, since other confessions are equally recognized, but it is apparent that the Church has no reason to be disturbed by this. The constitution stipulates that the public schools of primary grade are to be confessional schools in which moral and religious principles are inculcated. Moreover, religious instruction is to be included in the programs of the secondary and professional schools. Finally, the churches are to have complete liberty within their domains without interference from the state, and are to continue to be entitled to such subventions as they have enjoyed in the past. Finally, it may be remarked that these provisions have little more than nominal significance except for Roman Catholics, since other faiths have very few followers in the Saar.

As regards the structure and distribution of powers, a parliamentary type of government is provided. The supreme power is declared to emanate from the *peuple sarrois,* acting through their elected representatives and in certain circumstances by way of a referendum. A single assembly of fifty deputies, elected for six years, exercises the legislative power and oversees the execution of the laws. A parliamentary system is provided in which the ministers originally approved by the assembly exercise the executive power as long as they retain the confidence of that body. The cabinet, in turn, has the appointive power as regards judges and other officials. In the constitutional system the assembly is supreme. A parliamentary constitutional committee, elected at the beginning of each legislature, has the sole competence in interpreting the constitution.

In the final analysis it would appear that France has the last word as to the character of the constitutional regime in the Saar and has taken care to insure that the implementation of the fundamental law shall accord with her interests and long-term objectives. Grandval, the military governor, became French high commissioner to the Saar immediately after the termination of the military regime in December 1947. As such he was empowered by decree to supervise the execution of the Saar constitution, of all conventions between France and the Saar, and also of applicable international obligations. Moreover, should he at any time believe the new relationship to be in jeopardy, he was empowered as stated in the Preamble of the constitution to take all steps deemed necessary to maintain public order.

Even under normal conditions his powers are sweeping and apparently without recourse. Thus, he has the power of absolute veto over all laws and enactments of the government of the Saar, over all appointments to high offices in the Territory, and even over grants of Saar citizenship. In addition to the power of veto over legislation, which is itself in the nature of a legislative power, the high commissioner may issue decrees designed to implement the economic union of France and the Saar, and thus act in a legislative capacity on matters which otherwise would fall under the jurisdiction of the Saar Parliament. Finally, by being vested with control of all French civil servants in the Saar, whose numbers are inevitably increasing, he exercises direct authority over part of the civil service.

To some Frenchmen, and possibly a very small number of Saar Germans, logic and expediency suggest that what the German Social Democrats have characterized as a "protectorate" should become politically a part of France. It should then have political representation in French national assemblies. But it does not appear that there is much support in France at present for such a development. If a considerable majority of the Saar Germans should unmistakably express a desire to belong to France, they would probably be welcomed. Otherwise, most informed Frenchmen are likely to look askance at any proposal to bring into the republic nearly a million "indigestible" Germans who have no enthusiasm for France but quite possibly an abiding nostalgia for the German Fatherland.

As regards the relations of the Saar with Western Europe, certain events must be recorded. In May 1949 the Council of Europe came into existence. The member countries included Belgium, Denmark, France, Eire, Italy, Luxembourg, Holland, Norway, Sweden, and the United Kingdom. They came together in response to the "need of a closer unity between all like-minded countries of Europe . . . ." (Preamble to the Statute of the Council of Europe). The Statute excluded questions related to national defense, being intended to further discussion and common action on "economic, social, cultural, scientific, legal, and administrative matters" as well as to advance "human rights and fundamental freedoms." The chief organ of the Council of Europe was the Committee of Ministers. The deliberative organ was the Consultative Assembly, which was an advisory body having power only to make recommendations to the ministers.

Neither the German Federal Republic, now functioning in Western Germany, nor the Saar was included in the new organization, but membership in it was not frozen; and geographic, political, and economic considerations might well be advanced for the admission of both. In these circumstances the chief political parties of the Saar realized that there might be certain advantages attached to membership in an organization which would associate them with the West against communism. It may well be that they also calculated that such membership would serve as a safeguard against political absorption by France at some future time when French policy might not be satisfied with the present relationship. Moreover, they may have speculated that when the German Federal Republic became a member, as was contemplated by the Western Powers, their own entry would bring them into association with the Fatherland—at present denied to them—in a form acceptable to the French.

The meeting of the Consultative Assembly of the Council of Europe in September 1949 at Strasbourg afforded an opportunity to the Saar political leaders to advocate in person the admission of the Saar to that body. The Saar Landtag armed them with authority to take this step by a vote of 49 to 1. Thus, the chief government officials as well as the heads of the two main political parties were able to come to Strasbourg and declare that they were speaking for the vast majority of the Saar people. In the face of a certain amount of skepticism as to whether the Saar could possibly serve as a "bridge" between France and Germany, in view of the sentiments indicated in the plebiscite of 1935, they declared that the vote of that year was held under Nazi pressure, terrorism, and fraud, and did not reflect the true feelings of the people. They now wanted it understood that they were neither a German nor a French state, but rather a European political entity of a new type, desiring to live in freedom and peace within the framework of a European federation, working for the welfare of the European community rather than lending themselves to the power interests or ambitions of any state.

The position of the French on the admission of the Saar, and of Germany also, to the Council of Europe was stated on July 9, 1949, in the National Assembly, in the course of the discussion of a bill authorizing the president of the republic to ratify the statute of the Council of Europe. Robert Schuman, the French foreign minister, after stating that in principle Germany should be admitted to the Council of Europe, pointed out that she could not become a full-fledged member until the peace treaty had been signed and ratified. In the meantime, if it were found that she was capable of conforming to the provisions of Article 3 of the proposed statute, including the acceptance of "the principles of the rule of law and of the enjoyment by all persons within its [her] jurisdiction of human rights and fundamental freedoms," she might be invited to become an associate member. After this cautious hedging as regards the admission of

Germany, Schuman made the following succinct and categorical declaration with respect to the Saar: "There is also the Saar. It already fulfills the juridical conditions for admission, since it has a democratically elected government and parliament."

The French government, in initiating and presenting the candidacy of the Saar for associate membership in the Council of Europe, which would allow it to be represented in the Consultative Assembly of the European organization, pointed out that under the Saar constitution France was "responsible for the defense of the Saar territory and its external relations with foreign states." However, it was made plain that in this instance France was acting after having received the complete endorsement and collaboration of the Saar authorities. Nevertheless, the Saar constitution reveals that France took care to retain in her own hands the responsibility for conducting the relations of the Saar with "foreign states," which would seem to include Germany, and that she is free to accept or reject advice in this sphere tendered by the political leaders of the Territory.

In the following months it appeared that not only the Saar but the German federal government would probably be welcomed by France into the Consultative Assembly. It was also evident that the Adenauer government at Bonn was disposed to seek admission. Apparently all that remained was for the Council of Europe to extend it an official invitation. This was forthcoming in April 1950. But in the meantime the French and Saar governments had concluded several agreements whereby France, among other things, was granted a fifty-year lease on the Saar coal mines. These mines, which the Germans had always insisted were the property of the German state, now seemed to be slipping away to France.

The Adenauer government, always facing criticism from opposing political groups for being too compliant toward the occupation powers, was now confronted with the necessity of strongly protesting these new arrangements. It would probably have been inclined to do so in any event since Germans were chronically suspicious of every French move which seemed to be designed to attract the Saar away from Germany. In these circumstances the Bonn government indicated that it could not accept an associate membership in the Council of Europe. Strong opposition to such membership came not only from elements of the extreme Right and from the Communists, but from Kurt Schumacher, influential leader of the Social Democrats, who regarded the March agreements as leading to virtual annexation of the Saar to France.

But Adenauer had to take account not only of the internal political situation but of the wishes of the occupying powers. And apparently it suited Allied policy to have Germany apply for associate membership in the Council of Europe. That Adenauer gave way on the issue may have been due to pressure from the occupying powers, but another consideration may also have played a part. The French foreign minister, Robert Schuman, arrested the attention of Western Europe with a bold proposal to merge the coal and steel industries of France, including those of the Saar, with the same industries of Western Germany. Thus when the question of German acceptance of associate membership in the Council of Europe was brought before the Bonn parliament in May 1950 the opposition of the Social Democrats and others was eventually overcome, and the Adenauer forces won, though not by an impressive majority.

The acceptance of associate membership in the Council of Europe on June fifteenth was followed in July by similar action of the Saar. Shortly thereafter the foreign ministers of the Council indicated that it was their hope that in the future they would be able to deal directly with both governments instead of routing their communications through channels of the occupying powers. Moreover, the new associate members understood that their representatives would henceforth be privileged to meet with the ministers in a consultative capacity whenever the discussion of specific problems might seem to warrant it. And henceforth nationals of the German Federal Republic and Saar nationals were to be eligible for employment on the Council's permanent Secretariat.

The several conventions signed at Paris on March 3, 1950, by Saar Premier Johannes Hoffman and the French minister of foreign affairs, Robert Schuman, have been mentioned in connection with the discussion of the Bonn government's candidacy for associate membership in the Council of Europe. As was pointed out, the Convention for a fifty-year lease of the Saar coal mines to France caused the greatest concern in German circles. To be sure, in this Convention France agreed to a mixed board of directors for the mines in which the Saar was to have equal representation with France. Moreover, France offered to support the Saar's claims to ownership at the time of the peace settlement with Germany. With these French pledges the Hoffman government was apparently satisfied, but German critics outside the Saar saw in this and the other Conventions and Accords concluded at this time another move in the process of alienating the Saar from Germany.

There was also a railway convention integrating the Saar railway system with that of France, and providing in general for identical rates. And, as in the case of the mining convention, the directing board was to include Saarlanders as well as Frenchmen. Politics aside, these arrangements made a great deal of sense. But again Germans, unreconciled to the permanent detachment of the Saar from the Fatherland, saw in them evidences of the determination of France to take advantage of German impotence, as well as Western fears of communism, and swallow the Saar on the installment plan.

The other agreements contracted at this time confirmed the suspicions of German nationalists, and apparently also of Socialists such as Kurt Schumacher. These included measures to attain complete economic union of France and the Saar, and those looking forward to eventual freedom of French and Saar citizens to live and conduct businesses as if there were no boundary line between the two countries. These and other measures, the more hostile critics seemed to think, were analogous to the bland and deliberate tactics of absorption and assimilation practiced by boa constrictors. They were quick to point out that important matters which might have been included in the several conventions were avoided. For example, they asserted that the French had appropriated valuable properties in the Saar. Were the latter going to make no restitution to the Territory for these acts? As regards trade relations, were the French interested only in freer commerce between France and the Saar? In particular, when would they relax their restrictions on trade and travel between Germany and the Saar?

The foregoing criticisms testify not only to German suspicions as to the political objectives of France, but also to the continuing determination of German nationalists to carry on the struggle against her and keep the Saar question open. As for the Conventions of March, an objective appraisal might conclude that they registered some immediate gains of substance for the Saar. For example, its legislative and administrative autonomy were formally confirmed. Henceforth the Saar police were to have the responsibility of maintaining order in the Territory, and their competence was to extend to all persons domiciled or resident there. However, French officials in the Saar had jurisdiction in cases involving the security of France or of French troops in the Saar. And the fact that France considered it necessary to continue to have her troops stationed there is eloquent testimony to the fact that she regards Saar Germans as yet not altogether trustworthy, in the absence of concrete evidences of French power. On the other hand, at less vital points France was ready to make concessions. For example, the High Commissioner's status was now acknowledged to be that of a diplomatic representative of France, and the Saar was to be allowed to send representatives with diplomatic rank and privileges to Paris, as well as having agents in French consulates where special Saar interests could be served.

From the point of view of West German officials the fundamental objection to the Conventions of March 3 was that through them the French sought to prepare new *faits accomplis* which would be difficult or impossible to repudiate at the time of the future German peace settlement. Although the French government points out that it is understood and plainly stated that the arrangements are subject to review when the time comes for a definitive peace, this carries no conviction to the critics. In the words of one of their spokesmen the agreement of March 3, 1950, consisting of the Conventions mentioned and several additional Accords, "solidifies an accomplished fact and sets out to establish a *de jure* status of separation from Germany by contract with a government whose authority for such a transaction . . . . is highly debatable."

The policy of the French in relation to the Saar may be regarded by the critics as highhanded, coldly opportunistic, even cynically Machiavellian. Whatever may be thought of it, there can be no doubt that its chief motivation is the desire for French security against Germany. The French are sufficiently imaginative, however, to realize that the mere subtraction of territory and resources from a temporarily prostrate Reich, with the resultant diminution of German power, guarantees no safety for the future; and happily they realize that other, broader solutions must be attempted.

On May 9, 1950, the French Foreign Minister made a statement which suggests that the French government is capable of approaching the Saar problem as one of many to be viewed in a wider perspective, and solved within a larger framework than would seem to be apparent from the examination of French policy revealed in the preceding discussion. In words reminiscent of his distinguished predecessor Aristide Briand, who worked with courage and vision to achieve a lasting peace between France and Germany, M. Schuman declared for the eventual federation of Europe, and, as a necessary condition of its realization, that "the age-old enmity of France and Germany be eliminated." As a first step in that direction, and toward the realization of the broader objective, he proposed that all French and German steel production, including the steel industry of the Saar, should be pooled and placed under a supranational common high authority. Moreover, other European nations would be welcome to join the organization which would then constitute the first step toward European federation.

The Schuman Plan has been accepted in principle not only by the Adenauer government, but also by Italy and the Benelux countries. On the other hand, Kurt Schumacher and the Social Democrats of Western Germany seem to be fearful that it would block the way to the socialization of basic industries and open the way to the formation of private cartels. Whether M. Schuman's reassurances on these matters will dissolve their skepticism, and in any event whether acceptance in principle by the various countries will be followed by ratification, can only be conjectured at the present time.

As for the Saar, it would seem to have a stake in the ultimate decision. If the principles of the Schuman Plan should be written into a treaty, the political status of the Saar presumably would still be a question to be decided by a future German peace treaty. In the meantime in the economic sphere it would seem that France necessarily would lose some of the controls over Saar life that she retains at present; and such economic benefits as are expected to accrue to the participating states should be shared by the Saar as well. Moreover, in operation the Plan should remove French fears of the use of the great German Ruhr military potential for the purposes of a new war of aggression. For the intent of the French is, perhaps chiefly, to divert German energy into peaceful economic channels. The ultimate goal of European federation, as envisaged by M. Schuman, is, of course, an ideal which, if it should eventually be realized, would free the Saarlanders, as well as the French and other European peoples joining it, of new conflicts destructive of their peace and well-being.

In the over-all economic picture, French policy at the moment is not altogether clear, in spite of official pronouncements designed to quiet fears in the Saar. There are large iron and steel industries in France, reported to be fearful of Saar competition now that the customs frontier has been eliminated and the Saar has become the object of special solicitude on the part of the French state. On the other hand, the Saar steel industry, fearful of its competitive position because much-needed modernization has been delayed, is at present reported to be dissatisfied. These are problems involving both economics and politics and will require careful handling by the French. Should the Schuman Plan be realized, however, their solution might be possible.

With respect to their fundamental political status, as provided in the constitution, there seems to be no open dissatisfaction among the people of the Saar. In fact, if the declarations of their leaders conceal no reservations, they welcome it. But it is also evident that they want to extract the maximum of freedom from it and are sensitive to any act of the French which might be interpreted as placing the Saar in the category of occupied territories. Thus, they resented having the French representative—whom they seem to like personally—called "high commissioner," a designation applied to the Allied heads of the occupied zones. When a change of name was adopted for the French representative, more appropriate for an envoy to an "autonomous" state, one grievance was removed with no cost.

The foregoing observations seem to reflect the attitude of the orthodox political leaders in the Saar and may, therefore, be regarded as indicating the views accepted by the population in general. They do not portray the uncompromising attitude of the small Communist minority. This fact is worth recording, although the comparative prosperity and even greater expectations of the Saar workers make most of them, for the time being, immune to the gospel of Marx and Stalin. Nevertheless, the Saar Communists, perhaps in response to the dictates of the party line, have shed the coat of class consciousness and attired themselves in the garb of staunch German nationalism. They denounce French policy in the Saar as imperialistic and darkly calculated to lead to the political annexation of the Saar to France. Under the circumstances, the dictum of the Communist Manifesto of Marx and Engels that "working men have no country" does not seem to answer the tactical needs of the Communists. They now have adopted an authentic bourgeois slogan, "Back to the Fatherland." But at the moment this cry seems to have lost its appeal in the Saar. Perhaps it does not sound as genuine uttered by Communists as when it was shouted by bona fide nationalists. At any rate, the workers do not seem to be impressed. Their spokesmen accept the inclusion of the Saar within the French economic orbit and declare that this precludes political connection with Germany.

At the present time political circumstances favor the announced objectives of France in the Saar. By contrast with the sharp and protracted struggle which she had to wage on behalf of her Saar policy with the Allies in 1919, she now seems, if we except the USSR, to have received the benediction of the Great Powers. Until there is a German peace settlement she does not have to account to any international body—except perhaps the Allied Control Council for Germany—or seek the satisfaction of her claims, or the protection of her interests through an international commission, as she did at the end of World War I. And in the meantime, it is conceivable that by her own moderation and firmness, and a favorable concatenation of circumstances, she may be permitted to continue the relationship with the Saar without the intrusion of any embarrassing outside circumscriptions.

The "cold war" at present is providing France with opportunities for unilateral action that normally she could not expect to be afforded; for it is holding up the peace settlement, which in its German aspects is crucial for Europe, and it is checkmating the Russians. Moreover, as long as the settlement is delayed, there can be no resurgent Reich, capable of making trouble for France in the Saar or elsewhere. In one way or another, France can be expected to insist on a "weak" Germany, incapable of physical aggression and unable to threaten the policies of France in Europe.

The present political attitude of the *Sarrois* under the new order of things has been recounted, but for the future it can only be conjectured in relation to different sets of circumstances which may conceivably develop. There are imponderables, the force of which cannot be assessed or altogether anticipated; and the future alignments and complications of international politics cannot be charted. At present Germany and German organizations are not permitted, as they were during the League regime, to carry on anti-French propaganda, and this may very well be an important factor in the existing outlook of the inhabitants of the Saar. Their attitude may perhaps be described as one of watchful waiting, infused with hope for a more secure if less glorious future.

Left to themselves, it may well be surmised that the *Sarrois* will continue to exhibit the qualities of a solid, thrifty, hard-working people, expending their energies in making a living, rearing children, caring for their homes, and seeking spiritual solace through their Christian faith. Like Germans in general, they love order, are habituated to authority, and accustomed to a firm hand, though always by preference a German hand. Unlike the French, they are not individualists and do not fret under discipline. In fact, they prefer it and are lost without it. They have been through two wars disastrous to Germany and the German people. For the last one they were psychologically conditioned by the Nazi leaders as well as prepared by the warlike tradition of modern Germany, and they marched to the voice of authority as Germans had marched in the past.

Have they been sobered by these tragic events? Undoubtedly they have. Have they been made immune to the siren calls of untrustworthy leaders who would snare them into new wars on behalf of the German *Volk?* Apparently so, under present conditions—but will the immunization prove to be permanent? The test may come in the not far distant future. For already Reich Germans are beginning to assert themselves and, in the West at least, to make demands rather than voice requests. And, as was to be expected, they seem to be ready to exploit the dissensions between East and West whenever possible.

Programs designed to instill democratic ideas into the Germans have been undertaken with more or less enthusiasm in the Western zones. But many observers are coming to the conclusion that these evangelistic endeavors have not succeeded to date, and that, except for a minority, Germans are still susceptible to appeals on behalf of the political and social values taught by the National Socialists during Hitler's ascendancy. Whether or not this is an accurate assessment of the situation, it can hardly be doubted that as a defeated and humiliated people the Germans will seize opportunities to play the East against the West, in order to extort concessions from both sides and so regain their status as a great power.

What bearing have these considerations on the subject of the present inquiry? It is not to be expected that once a restored Reich is able to command attention by renewed strength and influence it will reconcile itself to the loss of the "German brothers" in the Saar. The latter will almost certainly be regarded as an irredentist territory torn from the body of Germany and to be redeemed by one means or another at the first opportunity. In fact, this point of view is already foreshadowed by the position taken by the officials of the new state of Western Germany, sponsored by the Western Powers. They reiterate and stress the fact that the unilateral action taken by France in the Saar endows her with no legal rights, and that the definitive status of the Territory can only be determined in a future German peace treaty. This is not open to dispute, but they do not let the case rest at this point. Apparently anticipating that a future peace conference might ratify the French *fait accompli,* they are already beginning to demand that the people of the Saar should be accorded the privilege of a plebiscite, and that their political status should depend upon its outcome. Needless to say, this proposal is repugnant to the French, and they can be expected to hold to their present position with characteristic tenacity. From the French point of view, the people of the Saar, uncoerced and unafraid, have unmistakably expressed their approval of the new arrangements, and at the proper time this should be formally ratified by the powers.

One must regretfully close this study with a painful observation. In the final analysis, the political future of the inhabitants will not be determined by the *Sarrois* themselves, nor by France, nor by Germany. In the game of international politics, as it is still played, it is to be expected that the Saar will have significance not as a community of human beings, interested primarily in life, liberty, and the pursuit of happiness, but chiefly as a certain place of strategic importance on the political map.

APPENDIX

EXTRACT FROM THE TREATY OF VERSAILLES

SECTION IV. SAAR BASIN

ARTICLE 45

As compensation for the destruction of the coal-mines in the north of France and as part payment towards the total reparation due from Germany for the damage resulting from the war, Germany cedes to France in full and absolute possession, with exclusive rights of exploitation, unencumbered and free from all debts and charges of any kind, the coal-mines situated in the Saar Basin as defined in Article 48.

ARTICLE 46

In order to assure the rights and welfare of the population and to guarantee to France complete freedom in working the mines, Germany agrees to the provisions of Chapters I and II of the Annex hereto.

ARTICLE 47

In order to make in due time permanent provision for the government of the Saar Basin in accordance with the wishes of the populations, France and Germany agree to the provisions of Chapter III of the Annex hereto.

ARTICLE 48

The boundaries of the territory of the Saar Basin, as dealt with in the present stipulations, will be fixed as follows:

On the south and south-west: by the frontier of France as fixed by the present Treaty.

On the north-west and north: by a line following the northern administrative boundary of the *Kreis* of Merzig from the point where it leaves the French frontier to the point where it meets the administrative boundary separating the commune of Saar-Hölzbach from the commune of Britten; following this communal boundary southwards and reaching the administrative boundary of the canton of Merzig so as to include in the territory of the Saar Basin the canton of Mettlach, with the exception of the commune of Britten; following successively the northern boundaries of the cantons of Merzig and Haustedt, which are incorporated in the aforesaid Saar Basin, then successively the administrative boundaries separating the *Kreise* of Sarrelouis, Ottweiler, and Saint-Wendel from the *Kreise* of Merzig, Trèves (Trier), and the Principality of Birkenfeld as far as a point situated about 500 metres north of the village of Furschweiler (*viz.*, the highest point of the Metzelberg).

On the north-east and east: from the last point defined above to a point about 3½ kilometres east-north-east of Saint-Wendel:

a line to be fixed on the ground passing east of Furschweiler, west of Roschberg, east of points 418, 329 (south of Roschberg), west of Leitersweiler, north-east of point 464, and following the line of the crest southwards to its junction with the administrative boundary of the *Kreis* of Kusel;

133

thence in a southerly direction the boundary of the *Kreis* of Kusel, then the boundary of the *Kreis* of Homburg towards the south-south-east to a point situated about 1,000 metres west of Dunzweiler;

thence to a point about 1 kilometre south of Hornbach:

a line to be fixed on the ground passing through point 424 (about 1,000 metres south-east of Dunzweiler), point 363 (Fuchs-Berg), point 322 (south-west of Waldmohr), then east of Jägersburg and Erbach, then encircling Homburg, passing through the points 361 (about 2½ kilometres north-east by east of that town), 342 (about 2 kilometres south-east of that town), 347 (Schreiners-Berg), 356, 350 (about 1½ kilometres south-east of Schwarzen-bach), then passing east of Einöd, south-east of points 322 and 333, about 2 kilometres east of Webenheim, about 2 kilometres east of Mimbach, passing east of the plateau which is traversed by the road from Mimbach to Böckweiler (so as to include this road in the territory of the Saar Basin), passing immediately north of the junction of the roads from Böckweiler and Altheim situated about 2 kilometres north of Altheim, then passing south of Ringweilerhof and north of point 322, rejoining the frontier of France at the angle which it makes about 1 kilometre south of Hornbach (see Map No. 2 scale 1/100,000 annexed to the present Treaty).

A Commission composed of five members, one appointed by France, one by Germany, and three by the Council of the League of Nations, which will select nationals of other Powers, will be constituted within fifteen days from the coming into force of the present Treaty, to trace on the spot the frontier line described above.

In those parts of the preceding line which do not coincide with administrative boundaries, the Commission will endeavor to keep to the line indicated, while taking into consideration, so far as is possible, local economic interests and existing communal boundaries.

The decisions of this Commission will be taken by a majority and will be binding on the parties concerned.

ARTICLE 49

Germany renounces in favour of the League of Nations, in the capacity of trustee, the government of the territory defined above.

At the end of fifteen years from the coming into force of the present Treaty the inhabitants of the said territory shall be called upon to indicate the sovereignty under which they desire to be placed.

ARTICLE 50

The stipulations under which the cession of the mines in the Saar Basin shall be carried out, together with the measures intended to guarantee the rights and the well-being of the inhabitants and the government of the territory, as well as the conditions in accordance with which the plebiscite hereinbefore provided for is to be made, are laid down in the Annex hereto. This Annex shall be considered as an integral part of the present Treaty, and Germany declares her adherence to it.

ANNEX

In accordance with the provisions of Articles 45 to 50 of the present Treaty, the stipulations under which the cession by Germany to France of the mines of the Saar Basin will be effected, as well as the measures intended to ensure respect for the rights and well-being of the population and the government of the territory, and the conditions in which the inhabitants will be called upon to indicate the sovereignty under which they may wish to be placed, have been laid down as follows:

CHAPTER I

CESSION AND EXPLOITATION OF MINING PROPERTY

1

From the date of the coming into force of the present Treaty, all the deposits of coal situated within the Saar Basin as defined in Article 48 of the said Treaty, become the complete and absolute property of the French State.

The French State will have the right of working or not working the said mines, or of transferring to a third party the right of working them, without having to obtain any previous authorisation or to fulfil any formalities.

The French State may always require that the German mining laws and regulations referred to below shall be applied in order to ensure the determination of its rights.

2

The right of ownership of the French State will apply not only to the deposits which are free and for which concessions have not yet been granted, but also to the deposits for which concessions have already been granted, whoever may be the present proprietors, irrespective of whether they belong to the Prussian State, to the Bavarian State, to other States or bodies, to companies or to individuals, whether they have been worked or not, or whether a right of exploitation distinct from the right of the owners of the surface of the soil has or has not been recognised.

3

As far as concerns the mines which are being worked, the transfer of the ownership to the French State will apply to all the accessories and subsidiaries of the said mines, in particular to their plant and equipment both on and below the surface, to their extracting machinery, their plants for transforming coal into electric power, coke and by-products, their workshops, means of communication, electric lines, plant for catching and distributing water, land, buildings such as offices, managers', employees' and workmen's dwellings, schools, hospitals and dispensaries, their stocks and supplies of every description, their archives and plans, and in general everything which those who own or exploit the mines possess or enjoy for the purpose of exploiting the mines and their accessories and subsidiaries.

The transfer will apply also to the debts owing for products delivered before the entry into possession by the French State, and after the signature of the present Treaty, and to deposits of money made by customers, whose rights will be guaranteed by the French State.

4

The French State will acquire the property free and clear of all debts and charges. Nevertheless, the rights acquired, or in course of being acquired, by the employees of the mines and their accessories and subsidiaries at the date of the coming into force of the present Treaty, in connection with pensions for old age or disability, will not be affected. In return, Germany must pay over to the French State a sum representing the actuarial amounts to which the said employees are entitled.

5

The value of the property thus ceded to the French State will be determined by the Reparation Commission referred to in Article 233 of Part VIII (Reparation) of the present Treaty.

This value shall be credited to Germany in part payment of the amount due for reparation.

It will be for Germany to indemnify the proprietors or parties concerned, whoever they may be.

6

No tariff shall be established on the German railways and canals which may directly or indirectly discriminate to the prejudice of the transport of the personnel or products of the mines and their accessories or subsidiaries, or of the material necessary to their exploitation. Such transport shall enjoy all the rights and privileges which any international railway conventions may guarantee to similar products of French origin.

7

The equipment and personnel necessary to ensure the despatch and transport of the products of the mines and their accessories and subsidiaries, as well as the carriage of workmen and employees, will be provided by the local railway administration of the Basin.

8

No obstacles shall be placed in the way of such improvements of railways or waterways as the French State may judge necessary to assure the despatch and the transport of the products of the mines and their accessories and subsidiaries, such as double trackage, enlargement of stations, and construction of yards and appurtenances. The distribution of expenses will, in the event of disagreement, be submitted to arbitration.

The French State may also establish any new means of communication, such as roads, electric lines, and telephone connections, which it may consider necessary for the exploitation of the mines.

It may exploit freely and without any restrictions the means of communication of which it may become the owner, particularly those connecting the mines and their accessories and subsidiaries with the means of communication situated in French territory.

9

The French State shall always be entitled to demand the application of the German mining laws and regulations in force on November 11, 1918, excepting provisions adopted exclusively in view of the state of war, with a view to the acquisition of such land as it may judge necessary for the exploitation of the mines and their accessories and subsidiaries.

The payment for damage caused to immovable property by the working of the said mines and their accessories and subsidiaries shall be made in accordance with the German mining laws and regulations above referred to.

10

Every person whom the French State may substitute for itself as regards the whole or part of its rights to the exploitation of the mines and their accessories and subsidiaries shall enjoy the benefit of the privileges provided in this Annex.

11

The mines and other immovable property which become the property of the French State may never be made the subject of measures of forfeiture, forced sale, expropriation or requisition, nor of any other measure affecting the right of property.

The personnel and the plant connected with the exploitation of these mines or their accessories and subsidiaries, as well as the product extracted from the mines or manufactured in their accessories and subsidiaries, may not at any time be made the subject of any measures of requisition.

12

The exploitation of the mines and their accessories and subsidiaries, which become the property of the French State, will continue, subject to the provisions of paragraph 23 below, to be subject to the régime established by the German laws and regulations in force on November 11, 1918, excepting provisions adopted exclusively in view of the state of war.

The rights of the workmen shall similarly be maintained, subject to the provisions of the said paragraph 23, as established on November 11, 1918, by the German laws and regulations above referred to.

No impediment shall be placed in the way of the introduction or employment in the mines and their accessories and subsidiaries of workmen from without the Basin.

The employees and workmen of French nationality shall have the right to belong to French labour unions.

13

The amount contributed by the mines and their accessories and subsidiaries, either to the local budget of the territory of the Saar Basin or to the communal funds, shall be fixed with due regard to the ratio of the value of the mines to the total taxable wealth of the Basin.

14

The French State shall always have the right of establishing and maintaining, as incidental to the mines, primary or technical schools for its employees and their children, and of causing instruction therein to be given in the French language, in accordance with such curriculum and by such teachers as it may select.

It shall also have the right to establish and maintain hospitals, dispensaries, workmen's houses and gardens and other charitable and social institutions.

15

The French State shall enjoy complete liberty with respect to the distribution, despatch and sale prices of the products of the mines and their accessories and subsidiaries.

Nevertheless, whatever may be the total product of the mines, the French Government undertakes that the requirements of local consumption for industrial and domestic purposes shall always be satisfied in the proportion existing in 1913 between the amount consumed locally and the total output of the Saar Basin.

CHAPTER II

GOVERNMENT OF THE TERRITORY OF THE SAAR BASIN

16

The Government of the territory of the Saar Basin shall be entrusted to a Commission representing the League of Nations. The Commission shall sit in the territory of the Saar Basin.

17

The Governing Commission provided for by paragraph 16 shall consist of five members chosen by the Council of the League of Nations, and will include one citizen of France, one native inhabitant of the Saar Basin, not a citizen of France, and three members belonging to three countries other than France or Germany.

The members of the Governing Commission shall be appointed for one year and may be re-appointed. They can be removed by the Council of the League of Nations, which will provide for their replacement.

The members of the Governing Commission will be entitled to a salary which will be fixed by the Council of the League of Nations, and charged on the local revenues.

18

The Chairman of the Governing Commission shall be appointed for one year from among the members of the Commission by the Council of the League of Nations and may be re-appointed.

The Chairman will act as the executive of the Commission.

19

Within the territory of the Saar Basin the Governing Commission shall have all the powers of government hitherto belonging to the German Empire, Prussia, or Bavaria, including the appointment and dismissal of officials, and the creation of such administrative and representative bodies as it may deem necessary.

It shall have full powers to administer and operate the railways, canals, and the different public services.

Its decisions shall be taken by a majority.

20

Germany will place at the disposal of the Governing Commission all official documents and archives under the control of Germany, of any German State, or of any local authority, which relate to the territory of the Saar Basin or to the rights of the inhabitants thereof.

21

It will be the duty of the Governing Commission to ensure, by such means and under such conditions as it may deem suitable, the protection abroad of the interests of the inhabitants of the territory of the Saar Basin.

22

The Governing Commission shall have the full right of user of all property, other than mines, belonging, either in public or in private domain, to the Government of the German Empire, or the Government of any German State, in the territory of the Saar Basin.

As regards the railways an equitable apportionment of rolling stock shall be made by a mixed Commission on which the Government of the territory of the Saar Basin and the German railways will be represented.

Persons, goods, vessels, carriages, wagons and mails coming from or going to the Saar Basin shall enjoy all the rights and privileges relating to transit and transport which are specified in the provisions of Part XII (Ports, Waterways and Railways) of the present Treaty.

23

The laws and regulations in force on November 11, 1918, in the territory of the Saar Basin (except those enacted in consequence of the state of war) shall continue to apply.

If for general reasons or to bring these laws and regulations into accord with the provisions of the present Treaty, it is necessary to introduce modifications, these shall be decided on, and put into effect by the Governing Commission, after consultation with the elected representatives of the inhabitants in such a manner as the Commission may determine.

No modification may be made in the legal régime for the exploitation of the mines, provided for in paragraph 12, without the French State being previously consulted, unless such modification results from a general regulation respecting labour adopted by the League of Nations.

In fixing the conditions and hours of labour for men, women and children, the Governing Commission is to take into consideration the wishes expressed by the local labour organisations, as well as the principles adopted by the League of Nations.

24

Subject to the provisions of paragraph 4, no rights of the inhabitants of the Saar Basin acquired or in process of acquisition at the date of the coming into force of this Treaty, in respect of any insurance system of Germany or in respect of any pension of any kind, are affected by any of the provisions of the present Treaty.

Germany and the Government of the territory of the Saar Basin will preserve and continue all of the aforesaid rights.

25

The civil and criminal courts existing in the territory of the Saar Basin shall continue.

A civil and criminal court will be established by the Governing Commission to hear appeals from the decisions of the said courts and to decide matters for which these courts are not competent.

The Governing Commission will be responsible for settling the organisation and jurisdiction of the said court.

Justice will be rendered in the name of the Governing Commission.

26

The Governing Commission will alone have the power of levying taxes and dues in the territory of the Saar Basin.

These taxes and dues will be exclusively applied to the needs of the territory.

The fiscal system existing on November 11, 1918, will be maintaind as far as possible, and no new tax except customs duties may be imposed without previously consulting the elected representatives of the inhabitants.

27

The present stipulation will not affect the existing nationality of the inhabitants of the territory of the Saar Basin.

No hindrance shall be placed in the way of those who wish to acquire a different nationality, but in such case the acquisition of the new nationality will involve the loss of any other.

28

Under the control of the Governing Commission the inhabitants will retain their local assemblies, their religious liberties, their schools and their language.

The right of voting will not be exercised for any assemblies other than the local assemblies, and will belong to every inhabitant over the age of twenty years, without distinction of sex.

29

Any of the inhabitants of the Saar Basin who may desire to leave the territory will have full liberty to retain in it their immovable property or to sell it at fair prices, and to remove their movable property free of any charges.

30

There will be no military service, whether compulsory or voluntary, in the territory of the Saar Basin, and the construction of fortifications therein is forbidden.

Only a local gendarmerie for the maintenance of order may be established.

It will be the duty of the Governing Commission to provide in all cases for the protection of persons and property in the Saar Basin.

31

The territory of the Saar Basin as defined by Article 48 of the present Treaty shall be subjected to the French customs régime. The receipts from the customs duties on goods intended for local consumption shall be included in the budget of the said territory after deduction of all costs of collection.

No export tax shall be imposed upon metallurgical products or coal exported from the said territory to Germany, nor upon German exports for the use of the industries of the territory of the Saar Basin.

Natural or manufactured products originating in the Basin in transit over German territory and, similarly, German products in transit over the territory of the Basin shall be free of all customs duties.

Products which both originate in and pass from the Basin into Germany shall be free of import duties for a period of five years from the date of the coming into force of the present Treaty, and during the same period articles imported from Germany into the territory of the Basin for local consumption shall likewise be free of import duties.

During these five years the French Government reserves to itself the right of limiting to the annual average of the quantities imported into Alsace-Lorraine and France in the years 1911 to 1913 the quantities which may be sent into France of all articles coming from the Basin which include raw materials and semi-manufactured goods imported duty free from Germany. Such average shall be determined after reference to all available official information and statistics.

32

No prohibition or restriction shall be imposed upon the circulation of French money in the territory of the Saar Basin.

The French State shall have the right to use French money in all purchases, payments, and contracts connected with the exploitation of the mines or their accessories and subsidiaries.

33

The Governing Commission shall have power to decide all questions arising from the interpretation of the preceding provisions.

France and Germany agree that any dispute involving a difference of opinion as to the interpretation of the said provisions shall in the same way be submitted to the Governing Commission, and the decision of a majority of the Commission shall be binding on both countries.

CHAPTER III

PLEBISCITE

34

At the termination of a period of fifteen years from the coming into force of the present Treaty, the population of the territory of the Saar Basin will be called upon to indicate their desires in the following manner:

A vote will take place by communes or districts, on the three following alternatives: (a) maintenance of the régime established by the present Treaty and by this Annex; (b) union with France; (c) union with Germany.

All persons without distinction of sex, more than twenty years old at the date of the voting, resident in the territory at the date of the signature of the present Treaty, will have the right to vote.

The other conditions, methods, and the date of the voting shall be fixed by the Council of the League of Nations in such a way as to secure the freedom, secrecy and trustworthiness of the voting.

35

The League of Nations shall decide on the sovereignty under which the territory is to be placed, taking into account the wishes of the inhabitants as expressed by the voting.

(a) If, for the whole or part of the territory, the League of Nations decides in favour of the maintenance of the régime established by the present Treaty and this Annex, Germany hereby agrees to make such renunciation of her sovereignty in favour of the League of Nations as the latter shall deem necessary. It will be the duty of the League of Nations to take appropriate steps to adapt the régime definitively adopted to the permanent welfare of the territory and the general interest.

(b) If, for the whole or part of the territory, the League of Nations decides in favour of union with France, Germany hereby agrees to cede to France, in accordance with the decision of the League of Nations, all rights and title over the territory specified by the League.

(c) If, for the whole or part of the territory, the League of Nations decides in favour of union with Germany, it will be the duty of the League of Nations to cause the German Government to be re-established in the government of the territory specified by the League.

36

If the League of Nations decides in favour of the union of the whole or part of the territory of the Saar Basin with Germany, France's rights of ownership in the mines situated in such part of the territory will be repurchased by Germany in their entirety at a price payable in gold. The price to be paid will be fixed by three experts, one nominated by Germany, one by France, and one, who shall be neither a Frenchman nor a German, by the Council of the League of Nations; the decision of the experts will be given by a majority.

The obligation of Germany to make such payment shall be taken into account by the Reparation Commission, and for the purpose of this payment Germany may create a prior charge upon her assets or revenues upon such detailed terms as shall be agreed to by the Reparation Commission.

If, nevertheless, Germany after a period of one year from the date on which the payment becomes due shall not have effected the said payment, the Reparation Commission shall do so in accordance with such instructions as may be given by the League of Nations, and, if necessary, by liquidating that part of the mines which is in question.

37

If, in consequence of the repurchase provided for in paragraph 36, the ownership of the mines or any part of them is transferred to Germany, the French State and French nationals shall have the right to purchase such amount of coal of the Saar Basin as their industrial and domestic needs are found at that time to require. An equitable arrangement regarding amounts of coal, duration of contract, and prices will be fixed in due time by the Council of the League of Nations.

38

It is understood that France and Germany may, by special agreements concluded before the time fixed for the payment of the price for the repurchase of the mines, modify the provisions of paragraphs 36 and 37.

39

The Council of the League of Nations shall make such provisions as may be necessary for the establishment of the régime which is to take effect after the decisions of the League of Nations mentioned in paragraph 35 have become operative, including an equitable apportionment of any obligations of the Government of the territory of the Saar Basin arising from loans raised by the Commission or from other causes.

From the coming into force of the new régime, the powers of the Governing Commission will terminate, except in the case provided for in paragraph 35(a).

40

In all matters dealt with in the present Annex, the decisions of the Council of the League of Nations will be taken by a majority.

REPORT ON THE SAAR BASIN*

In accordance with the instructions of the Council, I have the honour to submit to your approval the following considerations concerning the government of the Saar Basin, the appointment of the Commission to which this Government is entrusted and the petition of certain German inhabitants of regions adjacent to the Saar Basin.

By the terms of Article 49 of the Treaty of Versailles, Germany has renounced in favour of the League of Nations, in the capacity of trustee, the government of the territory of the Saar Basin, whose boundaries are established by Article 48 of the same Treaty.

The government of this territory is to be entrusted, according to Part 3, Section 4, Annex, Paragraphs 16–19 of the Treaty, to a Commission representing the League of Nations, consisting of five members:—

One citizen of France.

One native inhabitant of the Saar Basin, not a citizen of France.

And three members belonging to three countries other than France or Germany.

The five members will be appointed for one year by the Council of the League of Nations, and may be reappointed. They may be removed by the Council, which will provide for their replacement.

They will be entitled to a salary fixed by the Council of the League, and charged on the local revenues. (Paragraph 17.)

The Chairman of the Governing Commission will be appointed for one year from among the members of the Commission by the Council of the League of Nations and may be reappointed.

The Chairman will act as the executive of the Commission. (Paragraph 18.)

It seems to me that the Chairmanship of this Commission should fall to the French member of the Governing Commission. The economic development, and in general the prosperity of the population of the Saar Basin, depend largely on the assistance that the French Government may give them. In fact, by the stipulations of the Peace Treaty itself (Part 3, Section 4, Article 45 of the Treaty) the whole and absolute possession of the mines situated in the Saar Basin falls to France, who may exploit them without restriction. Moreover, Part 3, Section 4, Annex, Paragraph 31, stipulates that the territory of the Saar Basin shall be subjected to the French Customs régime. By ensuring to the French State the possession and exploitation of the mines of the Saar on the one hand, and on the other by entrusting it with the administration of the Customs, the Peace Treaty has granted to France rights on which the French Government is not required to consult the Governing Commission.

* Presented by Demetrius Caclamanos, representative of Greece, at the Third Public Meeting of the Council of the League of Nations, held February 13, 1920. *League of Nations Official Journal*, March 1920.

It is, however, important that these rights should be exercised in complete accord with the aforesaid Commission as far as the method of their application is concerned. Such are for example the right to construct and exploit the ways of communication for the service of the mines, the right to use French money for all payments or expenses connected with the mines, and so forth. This latter right means nothing less than the introduction of the French franc as currency in the State of the Saar by payments made there in connection with the exploitation of the mines.

It must not be forgotten that the metallurgic industry of the Saar, which has increased considerably during the war, cannot exist and develop without the iron ore of Lorraine, and that the railway system of the Saar, the administration of which is entrusted by the Treaty to the Governing Commission, cannot be organised or work effectively without the help of material from the neighbouring system of Alsace-Lorraine.

The welfare of the population of the Saar and the necessity of maintaining order in this region require a close collaboration between the French Government, which by the Treaty controls a very important part of the economic life of the Basin, and the Governing Commission, to which the Council entrusts its administration. This collaboration cannot be better ensured than by the relations which a French Chairman of the Commission would maintain with the French Government, by his knowledge of the details of French administration, which, like every other, is a delicate and complicated mechanism, and by the guarantee of a good understanding with France which, as a Frenchman, he would naturally possess.

I am of the opinion that the French member of the Commission alone among his colleagues would be fitted to fulfil these essential conditions, and so it is the French member that I have the honour to propose to the Council of the League as Chairman of the Governing Commission, which it will have to appoint in conformity with the stipulations of Part 3, Section 4, Annex, paragraph 18, of the Treaty.

The duties of the Commission are defined by paragraphs 19 and following of the Annex quoted above.

Within the territory of the Saar Basin it will have all the powers of government hitherto belonging to the German Empire, Prussia or Bavaria, including the appointment and dismissal of officials, and the creation of such administrative and representative bodies as it may deem necessary. It will have full power to administer and operate the railways, canals and the different public services. Its decisions will be taken by a majority. (Paragraph 19.)

It will be its duty to ensure, by such means and under such conditions as it may deem suitable, the protection abroad of the interests of the inhabitants of the territory of the Saar Basin. (Paragraph 21.)

It will have the full right of use of all property, other than mines, belonging, either in public or in private domain, to the Government of the German Empire, or the Government of any German State, in the territory of the Saar Basin. (Paragraph 22.)

It may modify the laws and regulations in force on November 11, 1918, under the conditions stipulated in paragraph 23.

It will establish, in conformity with paragraph 25, a civil and criminal court to hear appeals from the decisions of the courts existing in the territory, and justice will be rendered in its name.

It alone will have the power to levy taxes and dues under the conditions laid down in paragraph 26, and shall apply them exclusively to the needs of the territory.

It will be its duty, by the terms of paragraph 30, to provide in all cases for the protection of persons and property in the Saar Basin. Consequently it will have the power to demand the maintenance or return of all or a part of the troops called up to preserve order, if necessary, till the establishment of a gendarmerie of the Saar, as provided for in paragraph 30.

Finally paragraph 33 gives to the Governing Commission the power to interpret the provisions of the Treaty in case of a dispute on the subject between France and Germany, and the right to arbitrate by the decision of a majority.

After having thus recalled to the Council the principal stipulations of the Treaty concerning the composition and functions of the Governing Commission, I have the honour to submit to your approval the draft resolution relative to this Commission, which our Secretary General has drawn up and which seems to me to be excellent in every particular, but in which I have introduced a slight alteration as regards extra pay to be granted to the Chairman of the Commission for purposes of entertainment.

The rights and duties of the Commission in question are defined in the Treaty of Versailles, Part 3, Section 4, Annex, Chapter 2. Nevertheless I intend to formulate, in an annex to the aforesaid resolution, certain instructions and suggestions of a general nature for the use of the members of the Commission.

In this connection I have the honour to give you the following explanations :—

In paragraph 5 of the draft annex it is laid down that it is the duty of the Commission to decide whether, in case of necessity, and to what degree, its decisions shall be valid if they have been adopted in the absence of one or two of its members. In fact, the right to interpret the provisions of this part of the Treaty is granted to it by paragraph 33. The rule should be established that no member may be absent from the meetings except in case of absolute necessity, or for a good and sufficient reason; it would, however, be just to allow that decisions adopted in the absence of one or two of its members should be valid, since according to paragraph 19 the decisions of the Commission are to be adopted by a majority vote. Otherwise the temporary absence of one of the members would seriously hamper the labour of the Commission.

But, when it is a question of decisions of special importance, it would seem necessary that these decisions should be taken only when all members are present.

No mention is made in the Treaty of the possible nomination of substitutes for the members of the Commission; the nomination, under those conditions, will be made by the Council of the League of Nations. There should, however, be an exception in the cases of the French member and the native citizen of the Saar, who must be authorised, in case of urgency, to nominate temporary substitutes, so that as far as possible the Commission may not be incomplete. None the less the procedure proposed in paragraph 6 of the draft annex would have to be carried out, and, for a more secure guarantee, no decision should be taken in application of paragraph 33 of the annex to the Treaty, giving to the

Commission the right to interpret the provisions of this part of the Treaty and to arbitrate in any dispute implying a difference of opinion between France and Germany, except when the regular members of the Commission are present.

By the terms of paragraph 17 of the Annex to Section IV of Part III of the Treaty, the members of the Governing Commission will be entitled to salaries fixed by the Council of the League of Nations and charged on the local revenues. I have the honour to propose in paragraph VII of the draft annex that this salary be fixed, for each member, at 100,000 francs per annum, to date from his appointment. It would seem obvious that the Chairman of the Commission should receive at the same time an extra sum for entertainment, which might be set at 50,000 francs per annum.

Although the Peace Treaty contains no stipulation relative to the duty of the Commission to submit reports to the Council of the League of Nations, the draft annex that I have the honour to submit to your approval includes a provision to this effect. (Paragraph VIII.) Since the Commission in question is, by the terms of Paragraph 16 of the Annex to Section IV of Part III of the Treaty, the representative of the League of Nations, it seems essential that the League should be kept informed of the actions of the Commission, since the responsibility is involved. This control certainly should be very wide, and as much power as possible should be granted to the Governing Commission of the Saar. This is shown by the following considerations:—

(1) The authors of the Treaty admitted that the Governing Commission should have the maximum power of appeal and judgment, and be as closely in touch as possible with affairs and people in an essentially industrial country.

(2) It must be observed that the League of Nations always possesses, as a guarantee that its responsibility shall not be involved against its will, the power of annual appointment and of replacement of the members of the Commission.

(3) Finally, it must not be forgotten that the League of Nations, which will have so many different responsibilities, should not go too deeply into details; it would run the risk of becoming too material and of compromising the lofty moral authority which it should preserve as the Supreme Court of Appeal.

A petition has been addressed to the League of Nations by the Mayor and the Municipality of Sarrelouis, requesting that the city of Sarrelouis, on account of its importance and its situation, be chosen as the capital of the territory of the Saar Basin.

Since the provisions of the Annex relative to the Saar Basin grant to the Commission the right to choose its seat, I have the honour to propose that this petition be submitted for consideration to the Governing Commission of the Saar Basin.

Another petition has been addressed to the League of Nations by the inhabitants of the cantons of Wadern, Weisskirchen, Losheim and Britten, situated outside the territory of the Saar Basin, in which they ask to be attached to the said territory.

These petitions are, according to information in my possession, supported by the signatures of three-fourths of the inhabitants of the canton of Wadern and four-fifths of those of Weisskirchen and of Losheim.

It is not the duty of the Council of the League of Nations to modify the frontiers of the Saar Basin as fixed by the Treaty of Versailles, but I am sure that I express the feelings of the Council when I propose that this document also be transmitted to the Governing Commission in order that they may see whether it will not be possible, while keeping strictly within the terms of the Treaty, to remedy, by economic measures, the difficulties that the above cantons seem to fear as a result of their separation from the Saar Basin.

These are the conclusions of my report.

The appointment of a Governing Commission of a state created under the auspices of the League of Nations will be the first characteristic act of the League after leaving its theoretic existence to enter upon its practical life. It constitutes, so to speak, the incarnation of the lofty principles that inspired its creation and which are to guide its work of pacification and later of organisation and adjustment. It will therefore be the object of special care on the part of the Council of the League, which will desire, by its selection of the members of this Commission, not only to create an effective body for this special task, but at the same time to furnish positive proof of the practical application of the rights with which the League has been invested by the various Treaties signed by the Powers that brought the League into being, and by those that have already adhered to it.

I therefore submit the following resolution:—

Whereas, Germany has renounced in favour of the League of Nations, in the capacity of Trustee, the government of the territory of the Saar Basin and

Whereas, this government shall be entrusted to a Commission representing the League of Nations,

THE COUNCIL OF THE LEAGUE OF NATIONS HEREBY RESOLVE THAT—

(1) M. Rault, State Councillor (French), Mr. Alfred von Boch, Landrath de Sarrelouis (Sarrois), Major Lambert (Belgian), The Count de Moltke Hvitfeldt (Dane), be appointed to be Members of the Saar Basin Governing Commission, for a period of one year as from the date of this Resolution.

(The name of the fifth Member of the Commission will be announced later, when the answer to an invitation sent has been received.)

M. Rault to be Chairman of the Commission.

(2) The attached instructions for the Commission be hereby agreed to.

(3) Copies of the present Resolution and of the attached directions be forwarded to the Members of the Governing Commission by the Secretary General of the League of Nations.

ANNEX TO RESOLUTION OF THE COUNCIL OF THE LEAGUE OF NATIONS OF FEBRUARY 13TH, 1920, CONCERNING THE GOVERNING COMMISSION OF THE TERRITORY OF THE SAAR BASIN

DIRECTIONS FOR THE GOVERNING COMMISSION OF THE TERRITORY OF THE SAAR BASIN, ADOPTED BY THE COUNCIL OF THE LEAGUE OF NATIONS

I

The duties of the Governing Commission of the Territory of the Saar Basin are defined in the Annex to Section IV of Part III of the Treaty of Peace between the Allied and Associated Powers and Germany, signed at Versailles on 28th June, 1919. The Governing Commission will be responsible to the League of Nations for the execution of these duties in accordance with the stipulations of the Annex. Until experience has been gained, the Council of the League of Nations deems it unnecessary and inadvisable to lay down in advance detailed directions for the Commission, other than those given in the Annex.

II

The Governing Commission will select its own seat, which shall be within the territory of the Saar Basin. The Commission will endeavour to secure a place which presents the best conditions for easy and rapid dealing with the problems of government, due regard being paid to the facilities of internal and external communications. In this connection the Commission will bear in mind the stipulation of paragraph 22 of the Annex, that it shall have the full right of user of all property, other than mines, belonging either in public or in private domain to the Government of the German Empire or to the Government of any German State, in the territory of the Saar Basin.

III

The Governing Commission will have no occupation and no interest except the welfare of the people of the territory of the Saar Basin.

IV

The Governing Commission will determine its own Rules of Procedure, including rules for the execution of those duties which the Commission on its own responsibility may assign to its individual members in order to promote easy and rapid dealing with the problems of government. The Chairman of the Commission will act as its executive.

V

The Governing Commission will meet in permanent though not necessarily continuous session. The Commission will settle whether, and eventually to what extent, its decisions are valid if taken in the absence of one or more members. If the Commission decides that valid decisions may be taken in the absence of one or even of two of the five members, it should, nevertheless, be laid down that no member should be absent from the meetings unless by reason of *force majeure,* or for other adequate reason. In the event of one of the members being absent, the Commission will consider the advisability of postponing its final decisions until the absent member can again attend the meetings.

Decisions of particular importance, such as those under paragraph 33 of the Annex, must not be taken except in the presence of all the members of the Commission.

VI

Should it be necessary to appoint a substitute for any member of the Governing Commission, the appointment shall be made by the Council of the League of Nations. Nevertheless, the French member of the Governing Commission and the native inhabitant of the Saar Basin, members of the Commission, are authorised to appoint, in case of urgency, their own temporary substitutes. A substitute thus appointed shall be entitled to sit and vote as a member of the Commission immediately on appointment, except in the case of decisions taken under paragraph 33 of the Annex. This procedure is, however, conditional on the remaining members of the Commission expressly agreeing that the absence of the member concerned is satisfactorily accounted for. Further, the appointment of such substitutes shall, on each occasion, be reported, by telegram, to the Secretary General of the League of Nations, who shall inform the Council of the League of Nations. The Council shall decide whether the appointment shall be confirmed. On the same conditions, and in conformity with the stipulations of paragraph 5, the Chairman of the Commission is authorised to appoint as his temporary substitute another member of the Commission.

VII

The original members of the Commission will each be entitled from the date of their appointment to a salary at the rate of 100,000 francs a year (the President will receive in addition "frais de représentation" amounting to 50,000 francs per annum), which will be charged by the Governing Commission on the local revenues of the territory of the Saar Basin. The local revenues will also bear all expenses incurred in the execution of the official duties of the Commission and of the members thereof (office accommodation, travelling expenses, wages of staff, telegraphic expenses, &c.).

The Secretary General of the League of Nations will advance temporarily the requisite sums to meet the above expenses from the general fund of the League, making the necessary settlement of account with the Commission when it has taken over the funds and revenues of the Saar Basin.

VIII

The Governing Commission will report to the Council of the League of Nations, through the Secretary General, in order to keep the League informed on all questions of interest. The Commission will submit to the Council of the League of Nations proposals with regard to the form and extent of its reports to the Council.

CONSTITUTION DE LA SARRE*

PRÉAMBULE

Le Peuple Sarrois,

Appelé, après l'effondrement du Reich, à rénover les principes de sa vie culturelle, politique, économique et sociale;

Pénétré de la conviction que son existence et son développement peuvent être assurés par l'intégration organique de la Sarre dans la sphère économique de la République Française;

Confiant en un statut international, qui fixera la base garantissant sa vie propre et son relèvement;

fonde

son avenir sur le rattachement économique et sur l'union monétaire et douanière de la Sarre à la République Française, d'où découlent:

L'indépendance politique de la Sarre vis-à-vis du Reich allemand;

L'exercice par la République Française de la défense du Territoire et des relations extérieures du Territoire avec les Etats étrangers;

L'application en Sarre des lois françaises relatives au statut monétaire et douanier;

L'attribution à un représentant du Gouvernement de la République Française d'un pouvoir de réglementation en vue de garantir l'unité douanière et monétaire ainsi que d'un droit général de contrôle en vue de garantir le respect du statut.

Une organisation judiciaire établie de manière à assurer l'unité de jurisprudence nécessaire dans le cadre du statut.

En conséquence, l'Asemblée Sarroise librement élue par le peuple,

afin de donner à cette volonté une expression qui soit un engagement;

Afin d'établir solidement—après extirpation d'un système qui déshonorait et asservissait la personnalité humaine—la liberté, l'humanité, le droit et la morale comme fondements de l'Etat nouveau, dont la mission est d'établir un lien pour un rapprochement des peuples et de servir, dans le respect de Dieu, la cause de la paix du monde;

A adopté la Constitution suivante:

PREMIERE PARTIE

Droits et Devoirs Fondamentaux

TITRE PREMIER
L'individu

Article premier.—Tout homme a droit au respect de sa personnalité individuelle. Le droit à la vie, à la liberté, au respect de la dignité humaine

* Ministère des Affaires Etrangères, *Notes Documentaires et Etudes*, No. 773 (Série Textes et Documents—CLXXIV), Paris: Direction de la Documentation, 6 décembre 1947.

constitue, dans les limites posées par l'intérét public, le fondement de l'organisation sociale.

Article 2.—L'homme est libre et ne peut être contraint à faire, à ne pas faire ou tolérer une chose, s'il n'y est tenu par l'effet d'une loi.

Article 3.—La liberté de la personne est inviolable. Elle ne peut être restreinte que par une loi.

Article 4.—Les croyances, la conscience et les opinions sont libres.

Les droits et les devoirs civils et politiques ne sont ni conditionnés ni limités par cette liberté.

Article 5.—Chacun a le droit, dans les limites posées par la loi, d'exprimer son opinion par la parole, par les écrits manuscrits ou imprimés, par l'image ou de toute autre manière.

Les arts, les sciences et leur enseignements sont libres.

La censure de la presse n'est pas autorisée.

Toute autre restriction à ces libertés n'est autorisée que dans le cadre des lois.

Article 6.—Tous les Sarrois ont le droit, sans déclaration préalabl ni autorisation particulière, de tenir des réunions pacifiques et sans armes.

Les réunions en plein air pourront être soumises par la loi à l'obligation de la déclaration préalable et, en cas de péril imminent pour la sécurité publique, elles pourront être interdites.

Article 7.—Tous les Sarrois ont le droit de constituer des groupements et des associations.

Peuvent être interdits les groupements et associations dont les buts sont contraires aux bonnes mœurs ou aux lois.

Article 8.—Les groupements politiques de combat sont interdits, de même que les partis politiques ou autres organisations tendant à supprimer ou à saper par la violence ou par abus de compétence les libertés et les droits garantis par la Constitution.

Article 9.—Tous les Sarrois ont le droit d'émigrer.

Ce droit ne peut être restreint que par une loi.

Tous les Sarrois ont l'entière liberté du choix de leur résidence.

Article 10.—Le droit d'exprimer librement sa pensée, le droit de réunion et d'association, non plus que le droit de propagation des œuvres scientifiques et artistiques ne peuvent être invoqués par quiconque attaque ou met en péril l'ordre constitutionnel démocratique.

Le Tribunal Constitutionnel décidera par voie de recours, si ces conditions existent.

Article 11.—Aucun Sarrois ne peut être livré à une puissance étrangère, sauf en vertu d'accords de réciprocité; aucun Sarrois ne doit être expulsé du Territoire de la Sarre.

Les étrangers jouissent du droit d'asile si, victimes en dehors du Territoire Sarrois de persécutions contraires aux principes reconnus dans la présente Constitution, ils viennent chercher refuge dans le Territoire Sarrois.

Les détails à ce sujet seront réglés par une loi.

Article 12.—Tous les individus sont égaux devant la loi, sans distinction de sexe, de race, d'origine ni de conviction religieuse ou politique.

Hommes et femmes ont mêmes droits et mêmes obligations civiques.

Article 13.—Nul ne peut être poursuivi, arrêté ou détenu, si ce n'est dans les cas prévus par la loi et dans les formes prescrites par celle-ci.

Nul ne peut être maintenu en détention sans être cité devant un juge, au plus tard le lendemain de son arrestation. Possibilité doit être donnée à tout détenu de protester contre son arrestation. Si la détention dure plus d'un mois, sa prolongation doit être justifiée périodiquement aux intervalles prévus par la loi par une décision motivée du juge.

Article 14.—Nul ne doit être soustrait à son juge légal.

Tour inculpé doit être considéré comme innocent tant qu'un jugement rendu par un tribunal ordinaire et ayant acquis la force de la chose jugée ne l'aura pas déclaré coupable.

Au cours d'une instance devant une autorité publique, tout inculpé a le droit de recourir à l'assistance d'un conseil judiciaire.

Article 15.—Une peine ne peut être prononcée que sur la base des lois en vigeur à la date où a été commis le délit.

Article 16.—Le domicile est inviolable. Les exceptions ne peuvent être faites qu'en vertu d'une loi.

Article 17.—Le secret des correspondances, des communications postales, télégraphiques et téléphoniques est garanti. Toute exception doit être autorisée par une loi.

Article 18.—Le droit de propriété est garanti dans le cadre de la loi.

Le même principe s'applique aux droits successoraux.

Article 19.—Chacun est tenu, dans la mesure édictée par la loi, d'assumer une activité à titre honorifique, et de participer aux organisations de secours en cas de détresse.

L'obligation d'effectuer certaines prestations personnelles au profit de l'Etat ou des communes ne peut résulter que d'une décision prise à la majorité requise pour les modifications à la Constitution.

Article 20.—Un pourvoi ou recours administratif est ouvert à quiconque se croit lésé par les pouvoirs publics sarrois dans l'exercice de ses droits.

Article 21.—Les droits fondamentaux sont intangibles par essence. Ils lient le législateur, le juge et l'Administration.

TITRE II
Le mariage et la famille

Article 22.—Le mariage et la famille, en tant que fondements naturels de la vie en communauté, jouissent de la protection particulière de l'Etat et sont encouragés par lui.

Le mariage repose sur l'égalité des deux sexes.

Article 23.—La mère a droit à la protection et à l'assistance de l'Etat.

Article 24.—L'éducation des enfants, leur formation physique, intellectuelle, morale et aussi sociale sont le premier devoir et le droit naturel des parents. Seule une décision judiciaire peut les priver de tout ou partie de ce droit.

Les enfants légitimes et naturels sont égaux en droit.

Article 25.—La jeunesse doit être protégée contre ceux qui l'exploitent ou qui la laissent dans un état d'abandon physique, intellectuel et moral. C'est aux communes et à l'Etat qu'il incombe de créer les établissements nécessaires. Cette tâche pourra être confiée à des Associations charitables privées reconnues d'utilité publique.

Les mesures de protection de la jeunesse ne peuvent avoir caractère comminatoire que sur la base d'une loi.

TITRE III

Education—Enseignement
Education publique—Vie culturelle

Article 26.—L'enseignement et l'éducation ont pour but de préparer l'enfant à l'accomplissement de ses devoirs familiaux et sociaux.

Sur la base de la loi morale naturelle et chrétienne c'est aux parents qu'appartient en premier lieu le droit de déterminer la formation et l'éducation de leurs enfants.

Les Eglises et Communautés religieuses sont reconnues comme des agents culturels.

Article 27.—La formation de la jeunesse est assurée par des écoles publiques et des écoles privées. Tous les établissements d'enseignement sont soumis à la surveillance de l'Etat. Cette surveillance est exercée par des fonctionnaires titularisés et spécialisés.

Les écoles primaires publiques sont des écoles confessionnelles. Les élèves y sont instruits et formés par des instituteurs de même confession qu'eux. Education et instruction sont empreintes des principes moraux et religieux de ladite confession.

S'il y a dans une commune des élèves appartenant à une minorité confessionnelle pour laquelle il ne peut être créé d'école de leur confession, étant donné que le petit nombre des élèves ne garantirait pas un fonctionnement régulier de l'école, ces élèves ont le droit de se faire admettre dans une école d'une autre confession. Il faut tenir compte à ce propos que le fonctionnement régulier d'une école est garanti même par le système de la classe unique. Des mesures devront être prises pour faire donner à ces minorités confessionnelles l'instruction religieuse prévue dans les programmes par des éducateurs de ladite confession.

Les écoles primaires supérieures, les écoles professionnelles et les Etablissements secondaires sont des écoles chrétiennes simultanées.

La seule condition d'admission dans une école déterminée est l'aptitude du requérant. L'accès aux écoles primaires supérieures et secondaires doit être facilité aux sujets bien doués et peu fortunés par l'octroi de bourses prises sur les fonds publics.

Article 28.—Les écoles privées doivent être agréées par l'Etat. L'autorisation de l'Etat doit être accordée, si les écoles privées ne sont d'un niveau inférieur à celui des écoles publiques, ni par le but éducatif qu'elles poursuivent, ni part leur organisation, ni par la formation scientifique de leur personnel enseignant.

L'autorisation doit être refusée, si la situation économique et juridique du personnel enseignant n'est pas suffisamment assurée.

Article 29.—L'instruction religieuse fait partie du programme de toutes les écoles primaires, professionnelles, primaires supérieures et secondaires, ainsi que de toutes les Ecoles Normales. Elle est donnée au nom des Eglises et Communautés religieuses respectives et en conformité avec leurs dogmes et règlements. Les Eglises et les Communautés religieuses ont le droit, en accord avec les autorités de contrôle de l'Etat, de surveiller la façon dont est donnée l'instruction religieuse. Le programme et les livres concernant l'instruction religieuse sont à soumettre à l'approbation de l'Etat.

Les parents peuvent refuser de laisser participer leurs enfants aux cours de religion sans qu'il en résulte un préjudice pour les enfants. Ce refus peut également atteint l'âge de dix-huit ans révolus. Les élèves qui ne participent pas aux cours d'instruction religieuse reçoivent un enseignement spécial relatif aux vérités universellement reconnues de la morale naturelle.

Article 30.—L'histoire de la Sarre et son évolution politique font l'obligation à toutes les écoles de développer l'esprit de réconciliation entre les peuples. Elles enseignent, dans le cadre de la culture chrétienne et européenne, la culture allemande et contribuent, par l'enseignement de la langue française, au développement des relations culturelles entre la France et le Territoire de la Sarre.

Article 31.—La formation des instituteurs est assurée par des Ecoles normales confessionnelles.

Article 32.—Les communes et l'Etat encouragent l'éducation du peuple, y compris les bibliothèques et les universités populaires, conformément à l'esprit de l'article 30.

Article 33.—La création et l'extension de Facultés sarroises sont le but poursuivi.

Les Universités ont le droit d'administration autonome. La liberté des recherches et des doctrines est garantie. Les étudiants participent de façon démocratique au règlement des affaires qui leur sont propres.

L'accès aux Universités est ouvert à tous. Des mesures devront être prises pour permettre aux sujects bien doués, mais exerçant une activité professionnelle et non titulaires du baccalauréat, de fréquenter les Universités. Les modalités seront fixées par une loi.

Article 34.—L'Etat encourage les travaux artistiques et culturels.

Les monuments artistiques et historiques, les chefs-d'œuvre de la nature et les paysages jouissent de la protection et de la sollicitude de l'Etat.

La participation aux biens culturels doit être accessibles à toutes les charges sociales.

TITRE IV

Eglises et communautés religieuses

Article 35.—Le libre exercice de la religion est garanti et jouit de la protection de l'Etat. Les manifestations religieuses publiques sont autorisées.

L'Etat reconnait les conventions et contrats existant en droit avec les Eglises.

Les Eglises jouissent dans leur domaine propre d'une totale indépendance ; elles confèrent leurs charges sans le concours de l'Etat ou des communes, sous réserve de dispositions ou conventions légales pouvant exister par ailleurs.

Elles ont complète liberté d'enseignement et de direction spirituelle. Leurs rapports avec les prêtres et les fidèles, au moyen de lettres pastorales, bulletins officiels, arrêtés et instructions, ne sont soumis à aucun contrôle ni aucune limitation de l'Etat. Elles ont le droit de créer et d'entretenir des Associations et des organismes qui servent leurs buts religieux et charitables, sociaux et éducatifs. Les devoirs résultant des principes fondamentaux de la Constitution pour l'individu, les personnes morales et les personnes de droit public restent intangibles.

Article 36.—La formation des prêtres et des serviteurs de l'Eglise est le droit exclusif des Eglises et des Communautés religieuses. Dans ce but, elles jouissent d'une liberté complète dans l'organisation de leur enseignement, la direction et la gestion de leurs propres Universités, séminaires et pensions. L'Eglise peut, en accord avec l'Etat, créer des Facultés de Théologie.

Article 37.—Les Eglises et Communautés religieuses acquièrent la personnalité juridique selon les prescriptions de droit commun.

Les Eglises et les Communautés religieuses restent des personnes morales de droit public, dans la mesure où elles l'étaient jusqu'à maintenant. D'autres Communautés religieuses ou Fondations peuvent acquérir cette qualité aprés en avoir fait la demande et si leurs statuts ainsi que le nombre de leurs adhérents en garantisse la durée. Au cas où plusieurs Communautés religieuses s'uniraient en une Association, celle-ci serait également une personne morale de droit public. Les Eglises et Communautés religieuses, les personnes morales de droit public ont le droit, pour couvrir leurs dépenses en Sarre, de percevoir des impôts sur la base des rôles d'impôts ordinaires.

Article 38.—La propriété et autres droits des Eglises, des Communautés religieuses et de leurs organisations concernant les biens affectés au culte, à l'enseignement et aux œuvres de bienfaisance, sont garantis.

Article 39.—Les subventions que l'Etat ou les communes ont accordées jusqu'à ce jour—sur la base des lois, contrats ou autres titres légaux—aux Eglises, Communautés religieuses, de même qu'à leurs Etablissements, Fondations, Biens d'Eglises ou groupements sont maintenus.

Article 40.—Les institutions sociales et de bienfaisance entretenues par les Eglises ou Communautés religieuses, ainsi que les Ecoles, seront reconnues d'utilité publique.

Article 41.—Les dimanches et jours de fête religieuse reconnus par l'Etat sont réservés à l'édification religieuse, à l'élévation spirituelle et au repos et, comme tels, ils sont sous la protection de la loi.

Article 42.—Dans les hôpitaux et les établissements pénitentiaires et autres établissements publics, possibilité est donnée aux Eglises et Communautés religieuses de célébrer les offices et d'exercer leur action spirituelle.

TITRE V
Economie et organisation sociale

Article 43.—Le rôle de l'Economie est de servir au bien-être public et à la satisfaction de ses besoins.

Une loi doit prescrire les mesures capables d'influencer utilement la production, la fabrication et la répartition des richesses économiques, pour assurer à chacun une participation équitable au rendement économique et le protéger contre toute exploitation.

Article 44.—La liberté des contrats et des professions, sont garanties dans la mesure autorisée par les lois. Tout abus de la puissance économique est interdit.

Article 45.—La capacité de travail des individus jouit de la protection de l'Etat. Chacun a droit au travail dans la mesure de ses possibilités, et sans préjudice des libertés personnelles, chacun a l'obligation de travailler.

Article 46.—La conservation et le rétablissement de la santé et de l'aptitude au travail, la protection de la maternité, les assurances contre les conséquences économiques de la naissance, de la maladie, des accidents, de l'incapacité de travail, de la vieillesse, de l'invalidité et de la mort, la protection contre les vicissitudes du sort et contre les répercussions d'un chômage pour lesquel le travailleur n'est pas responsable, sont confiées à une Caisse d'Assurances sociales et d'Assurance-Chômage, ouverte à toutes les classes de la population et placée sous le controle de l'Etat. Cette Caisse est administrée de façon autonome par les assurés eux-mêmes, avec le concours des employeurs et possède en outre une juridiction particulière. Les modalités de détail seront réglées par la loi.

Article 47.—Une législation du travail, uniforme pour tous les travailleurs et sanctionnée par une juridiction particulière, devra réglementer la procédure d'apaisement des conflits ainsi que l'établissement des conventions collectives entre organisations patronales et syndicats.

Les conditions du travail doivent être telles qu'elles garantissent l'existence matérielle, la dignité, la vie familiale et les aspirations culturelles du travailleur. Les femmes et les adolescents doivent faire l'objet de la protection particulière de la loi. Pour le même rendement dans le même travail, hommes et femmes ont droit à un salaire égal.

Article 48.—La durée du travail doit être réglementée par la loi. Les jours fériés légaux doivent être payés. En outre, tout travailleur a droit à un congé payé.

Article 49.—Toute personne en service ou engagée par un contrat de travail a droit aux heures de liberté nécessaires pour exercer ses droits civiques ou s'acquitter des fonctions publiques qui lui ont été confiées, à titre gratuit, et elle a droit, en outre, au paiement des heures de travail perdues de ce fait. Les détails seront réglés par la loi.

Article 50.—La planification générale en la réalisation de la reconstruction économique et sociale du pays incombent à l'Etat dans la mesure édictée par les lois et dans le cadre du statut du pays.

Obéissant aux exigences de la justice sociale, l'Etat doit assurer par une loi la confiscation sans indemnité de tous bénéfices de guerre.

Article 51.—La propriété comporte des obligations à l'égard du peuple. L'usage qui en est fait ne doit pas être contraire à l'intérêt général.

Les restrictions du droit de propriété ou le retrait de celui-ci ne sont autorisés qu'en vertu d'une loi, dans le cas où l'exige l'intérêt général. Ceci s'applique également aux droits d'auteur et aux brevets d'invention.

L'expropriation ne peut avoir lieu que contre indemnité correspondante, à moins que la loi n'en décide autrement. Est acceptable toute indemnité dont la nature et le montant tiennent compte à la fois des intérêts des particuliers en jeu et les exigences de l'intérêt général.

En cas de contestation, un recours est ouvert aux intéressés devant les tribunaux ordinaires.

Article 52.—Les entreprises-clés, mines de charbon, potasse, minerais et autres ressources du sous-sol, production de l'énergie, communications et transports, ne peuvent, en raison de leur importance primordiale pour l'économie du pays ou de leur caractère monopoliste, faire l'objet d'appropriation privée et doivent être gérées dans l'intérêt public.

Toutes les entreprises économiques importantes peuvent être expropriées par une loi et remises dans le domaine public lorsque, par leur politique économique, leur administration et leurs méthodes d'exploitation, elles menacent le bien public. Lorsqu'il existe pour cela de bons motifs, lesdites entreprises peuvent être placées sous le contrôle de l'autorité publique, en vertu d'une loi édictée spécialement.

Les entreprises tombées dans le domaine public doivent, se cela est conforme à leur destination, être exploitées dans les formes propres à l'entreprise privée ou à l'entreprise mixte.

Lors du transfert d'entreprises dans le domaine public, les communes, associations de communes ou toutes autres organisations communales devront veiller à empêcher une concentration excessive de la puissance économique en intéressant les employés à la gestion de l'entreprise.

Article 53.—Le contrôle exercé par l'Etat sur les banques, institutions financières ou compagnies d'assurances sera réglementé par une loi.

L'Etat doit, avec le concours d'associations économiques, prendre les mesures nécessaires pour assurer le placement favorable des fonds publics.

Les modalités de détail seront fixées par une loi.

Article 54.—Les classes moyennes indépendantes devront être protégées dans l'industrie, dans les métiers et le commerce, et leur développement encouragé. Le régime coopératif devra être encouragé de la même façon.

Article 55.—L'agriculture étant le fondement du ravitaillement national, l'Etat a le devoir de l'encourager par tous les moyens appropriés et d'assurer le maintien d'une classe paysanne indépendante.

La mise en culture du sol est un devoir du propriétaire vis-à-vis de la communauté.

Toute acquisition ou cession de propriété agricole ou forestière par voie de contrat sera soumise à l'autorisation dans les termes édictés par la loi, si l'ensemble des biens fonciers du propriétaire excède un maximum qui reste encore à déterminer.

Article 56.—La liberté d'association en vue de garantir et d'améliorer les conditions de travail et d'exploitation est une liberté reconnue à tous les particuliers et dans toutes les professions.

Le droit de grève des travailleurs est reconnu dans le cadre des lois. La grève ne devra être déclenchée qu'après échec de toutes les tentatives d'accord et de négociations.

Article 57.—Les organisations patronales et les syndicats officiellement reconnus collaborent sur pied d'égalité à la défense des intérêts généraux dans le domaine social et le domaine économique.

Les organisations professionnelles reconnues d'employeurs et de salariés sont exclusivement appelées à la défense de leurs intérêts professionnels, économiques et sociaux. Seuls sont reconnus les syndicats qui sont indépendants vis-à-vis des employeurs. La loi règle les modalités de détail.

Article 58.—Les groupements d'employeurs et de salariés collaborent sur pied d'égalité dans les associations économiques. Elles ont à traiter les affaires communes concernant leur champ d'activité ; elles sont chargées de la défense des intérêts de leur branche dans le cadre de l'économie générale ; elles doivent être entendues par le Gouvernement sur toutes les mesures économiques et sociales d'importance essentielle.

Une direction de l'économie par l'Etat ne peut s'opérer que par le truchement des associations économiques. Les détails seront réglés par la loi.

Dans un but de représentation au sein des entreprises et pour la sauvegarde de leurs intérêts économiques et sociaux, les employés élisent un conseil d'entreprise. Une loi sur les conseils d'entreprise en règle les détails.

Article 59.—Toutes les entreprises sarroises sont juridiquement représentées soit par la Chambre de commerce et d'industrie, soit par la Chambre artisanale, soit par la Chambre d'agriculture et la Chambre du travail, auxquelles seront adjointes les Associations économiques.

Ces prescriptions s'appliquent également aux coopératives et aux entreprises publiques.

IIe PARTIE

ORGANISATION ET MISSION DES POUVOIRS PUBLICS

TITRE PREMIER

Prescriptions générales

Article 60.—La Sarre est un Territoire organisé de manière autonome, démocratique et sociale, et économiquement rattachée à la France.

Article 61.—La drapeau du Territoire se compose d'une croix blanche sur fond bleu et rouge.

Une loi en règlera les détails ainsi que la question des armes du Pays.

Article 62.—Le pouvoir suprême émane du peuple sarrois.

Le peuple exerce ce pouvoir par l'intermédiaire de représentants élus par lui et, conformément à l'article 101, par voie de référendum.

Article 63.—Les liens découlant de l'intégration de la Sarre dans la sphère économique française et dans le système monétaire et douanier français, les règles du droit international et les conventions présentes et à venir, sont partie intégrante du droit du Pays et l'emportent sur le droit interne de l'Etat.

Article 64.—La séparation constitutionnelle des pouvoirs législatif, exécutif et judiciaire est intangible.

TITRE II

Elections et référendums

Article 65.—Les élections et les référendums reposent sur le suffrage universel, égal et direct. Le vote est libre et secret.

Les opérations de scrutin ont obligatoirement lieu un dimanche ou un jour officiellement férié.

Article 66.—Le droit de vote appartient à tout Sarrois de l'un ou de l'autre sexe, âgé de plus de 20 ans, ayant son domicile en Sarre et non exclu des droits électoraux. Las modalités d'application seront fixées par une loi.

Les conditions d'acquisition et de perte de la nationalité sarroise seront déterminées par la loi.

TITRE III

Les organes de la volonté populaire

CHAPITRE PREMIER

L'Assemblée

Article 67.—L'Assemblée est la Chambre des représentants élus par le peuple. Elle exerce le pouvoir législatif dans la mesure où celui-ci n'est pas réservé directement au peuple par la Constitution. L'Assemblée ne peut pas déléguer le pouvoir législatif.

Elle surveille l'exécution des lois.

Article 68.—L'Assemblée se compose de 50 députés. Ceux-ci sont les représentants du peuple tout entier. Ils ne sont soumis qu'à leur conscience et ne peuvent être liés par des mandats.

Article 69.—Les députés sont élus dans les circonscriptions électorales d'après les principes de la représentation proportionnelle.

Est éligible tout titulaire du droit de vote âgé de 25 ans révolus.

L'Assemblée, après expiration de la première législature, fixée à 5 ans, est élue par circonscriptions. De cette manière, à la fin de chaque période de deux ans, de nouvelles élections pour 6 ans ont lieu respectivement dans chacune des trois circonscriptions.

L'Assemblée se réunit au plus tard le 15e jour après les élections.

La loi électorale fixera les modalités.

Article 70.—L'Assemblée se réunit en général au siège du Gouvernement. Chaque année comprend deux sessions ordinaires, du premier mercredi de novembre jusqu'à la fin de décembre au plus tard, et du premier mercredi de mars jusqu'à la fin du mois de mai au plus tard.

Le Président de l'Assemblée doit en outre convoquer celle-ci au cours d'une année à deux sessions extraordinaires d'un mois chacune sur la demande du Gouvernement ou d'un tiers des membres de l'Assemblée.

Dans les cas exceptionnels, il peut convoquer l'Assemblée en session extraordinaire, à la demande du Gouvernement.

L'Assemblée décide de la clôture de la session.

Article 71.—L'Assemblée peut prononcer sa propre dissolution par une décision prise à la majorité des deux tiers de ses membres.

Le Président de l'Assemblée doit procéder à la dissolution de l'Assemblée, si celle-ci a retiré sa confiance au Gouvernement par un vote et n'a pas pu, dans un délai de quatre semaines, aboutir à la constitution d'un nouveau Gouvernement jouissant de sa confiance.

Le renouvellement doit avoir lieu au plus tard le 6e dimanche après la dissolution.

Article 72.—L'Assemblée arrête son propre règlement.

Elle élit son Président, ses vice-présidents et les secrétaires en tenant compte de l'importance respective des différents groupes.

La Présidence expédie les affaires courantes jusqu'à la réunion d'une nouvelle Assemblée.

Article 73.—Le Président assure la gestion des locaux de l'Assemblée, et exerce dans ceux-ci les pouvoirs de police. Il est chargé de l'Administration de l'Assemblée, dispose des recettes et des dépenses dans la mesure prévue par le budget de l'Etat. Il représente l'Etat dans tous les actes juridiques et contestations de droit intéressant son administration.

Article 74.—Les débats de l'Assemblée sont publics.

A la demande du Gouvernement ou de dix membres de l'Assemblée, cette dernière peut décider, à la majorité des deux tiers de ses membres présents, que certaines questions particulières inscrites á l'ordre du jour, ne seront pas débattues en séance publique. Les débats et la décision relatifs à la demande d'huis clos ont lieu en séance secrète.

L'Assemblée décide si l'opinion publique doit être informée de ces débats et de quelle manière.

Article 75.—Les comptes rendus véridiques des débats en séance publique de l'Assemblée ou de ses Commissions n'entraînent aucune responsabilité pour leur auteur.

Article 76.—L'Assemblée prend ses décisions á la majorité simple dans la mesure où la Constitution ne prescrit pas une autre proportion des suffrages. Les décisions de l'Assemblée sont valables, lorsque plus de la moitié de ses membres sont présents.

Article 77.—L'Assemblée procède à la vérification des pouvoirs. Elle décide également si un député doit être déclaré déchu de sa qualité de membre de l'Assemblée.

Article 78.—Les membres du Gouvernement et les Commissaires du Gouvernement ont accès à tout moment aux séances de l'Assemblée, et s'ils le demandent, ils doivent être entendus également sur des questions qui ne sont pas inscrites à l'ordre du jour.

A la demande de l'Assemblée les membres du Gouvernement ou les Commissaires du Gouvernement doivent assister aux séances et fournir toutes explications requises.

Article 79.—L'Assemblée peut transmettre au Gouvernement les requêtes qui lui sont adressées et demander des explications au sujet des demandes et des plaintes reçues.

Article 80.—L'Assemblée peut constituer des Commissions selon les besoins ; la composition de celles-ci doit tenir compte de l'importance respective des groupes.

Article 81.—L'Assemblée a le droit et à la demande du tiers de ses membres, l'obligation d'instituer des commissions d'enquête. Les commissions mènent l'enquête en séance publique. L'huis clos peut être prononcé par la commission d'enquête à la majorité des deux tiers.

Le réglement de l'Assemblée fixe la procédure de la commission et détermine le nombre de ses membres.

Les tribunaux et les autorités administratives ont le devoir de donner suite aux requêtes des commissions concernant l'établissement des preuves; les dossiers administratifs doivent être communiqués aux commissions sur leur demande.

Les dispositions de la procédure pénale s'appliquent par analogie aux enquêtes menées par les commissions ou par les autorités requises par ces dernières.

Toutefois, le secret des correspondances et des communications postales, téléphoniques et télégraphiques est maintenu.

Article 82.—Nul député ne doit, en quelque moment que ce soit, faire l'objet de poursuites judiciaires ou disciplinaires ou être pris à partie d'une manière quelconque en dehors de l'Assemblée en raison de ses votes ou de déclarations faites dans l'exercise de son mandat.

Article 83.—Pendant toute la durée de la session parlementaire, nul député ne peut, sans l'autorisation de l'Assemblée, faire l'objet d'une enquête ou d'une arrestation, pour un acte réprimé par la justice légale, à moins toutefois qu'il n'ait été pris en flagrant délit ou arrêté au plus tard dans la journée du lendemain.

La même autorisation est nécessaire pour toute autre restriction de la liberté personnelle, qui porte préjudice à l'exercice du mandat parlementaire.

Tout procédure pénale contre un député, toute arrestation ou autre restriction à sa liberté personnelle, doit, si l'Assemblée le demande, être différée jusqu'à la fin de la session parlementaire.

Article 84.—Les députés ont le droit de refuser le témoigner lorsqu'il s'agit de personnes qui leur ont confié certains faits et auxquelles ils ont confié certains faits dans l'exercice de leur mandat parlementaire, ou bien lorsqu'il s'agit de ces faits eux-mêmes. En ce qui concerne la saisie de documents, les députés sont assimilés aux personnes, qui ont le droit légal de refuser témoigner.

Perquisitions et saisies ne peuvent être effectuées dans les locaux de L'Assemblée sans l'autorisation de son Président.

Article 85.—Les députés n'ont pas à solliciter de congés pour l'exercice de leur mandat. Le congé nécessaire à la préparation de leur campagne électorale doit être accordé à toute personne qui pose sa candidature.

Article 86.—Les dispositions des articles 81, 82, 83, 84 et 86 s'appliquent également à la présidence pour le temps qui s'écoule entre deux sessions et entre la dissolution de l'Assemblée jusqu'à la réunion de la nouvelle Assemblée.

Article 87.—Un député peut être mis en accusation devant le tribunal constitutionnel dans les deux cas suivants :

1) Si, dans une intention de lucre, il abuse de son influence ou de ses connaissances en tant que député, d'une façon qui compromette gravement le prestige de l'Assemblée.

2) S'il communique volontairement à autrui ses informations pour lesquelles le secret a été décidé dans une séance de l'Assemblée ou de l'une des Commissions, dans l'intention préméditée que ces informations soient portées à la connaissance du public.

CHAPITRE II

Le Gouvernement

Article 88.—Le gouvernement exerce le pouvoir exécutif en tant qu'autorité supérieure de l'Administration. Il se compose du Président du Conseil et des Ministres.

Article 89.—Le Président du Conseil est élu à la majorité du nombre légal de ses membres par l'Assemblée. Il nomme et révoque les Ministres, avec l'approbation de l'Assemblée.

Après expiration de la première législature le Président du Conseil nouvellement élu ne peut rester plus de trois ans en fonction. Il ne peut être réélu qu'après un délai d'un an au moins.

Article 90.—La confiance de l'Assemblée est nécessaire aux Ministres et au Président du Conseil pour l'exercice de leurs fonctions. Ils sont tenus de donner leur démission, si l'Assemblée leur retire sa confiance à la majorité du nombre légal de ses membres. La question de confiance ne peut être posée que par la totalité des membres du Gouvernement.

Le vote sur la question de confiance doit avoir lieu deux jours au plus tôt, et au plus tard sept jours, après la clôture des débats verbaux. Le vote est nominal.

Si le Président du Conseil, le Gouvernement ou l'un des Ministres perdent la confiance de l'Assemblée, ils continuent à expédier les affaires courantes jusqu'à l'entrée en fonction de leurs successeurs.

Article 91.—Lors de leur entrée en fonction, le Président du Conseil et les Ministres prêtent serment devant l'Assemblée, d'exercer leurs fonctions sans esprit de parti, dans le respect de la Constitution et des lois et conformément à l'intérêt général.

Article 92.—Le Presidént du Conseil préside les séances du Conseil des Ministres et dirige les affaires.

Le Gouvernement arrête un règlement de ses travaux.

Article 93.—Le Président du Conseil fixe les directives générales de la politique du Gouvernement. Dans le cadre de ces directives, chaque Ministre est indépendant dans son propre département.

Le Gouvernement, dans son ensemble, est responsable devant l'Assemblée pour sa politique générale et chaque Ministre en particulier est responsable personnellement de sa politique dans son département.

Article 94.—Le Gouvernement nomme et révoque les fonctionnaires d'Etat sauf dispositions contraires d'une Loi ou d'un statut. Il peut déléguer ce droit à d'autres services.

Article 95.—Aucune exécution capitale ne peut avoir lieu, sans le consentement unanime des membres du Gouvernement. L'exercice du droit de grâce est réglementé par la loi.

L'amnistie ne peut être prononcée que par la Loi.

Article 96.—L'Assemblée a le droit de mettre le Président du Conseil ou l'un quelconque des Ministres en accusation devant le Tribunal Constitutionnel pour violation de la Constitution ou des lois. La demande de mise en accusation doit être signée d'un tiers au moins des membres de l'Assemblée, et doit être approuvée par la majorité prescrite pour les modifications de la Constitution.

Les modalités d'application en sont réglées par la loi relative au Tribunal constitutionnel.

Article 97.—Les conventions et accords conclus dans le cadre du statut du Territoire par le Gouvernement ou par l'un des Ministres commis par lui à cet effet, ne sont valables qu'après leur ratification par l'Assemblée.

CHAPITRE III
Le Tribunal Constitutionnel

Article 98.—Il est créé un Tribunal Constitutionnel ayant son siège à Sarrebrück. Dans la mesure où ses attributions ne sont pas fixées par la Constitution, elles seront, ainsi que son organisation, réglées par voie législative.

Article 99.—La Commission de la Constitution à l'Assemblée, élue au début de chaque législature, est seule compétente dans l'interprétation de la constitution, des détails à ce sujet seront réglés par une loi.

TITRE IV
Le législation

Article 100.—Les projets de lois sont présentés, soit par le Président du Conseil au nom du Gouvernement, soit par un ou plusieurs membres de l'Assemblée.

Article 101.—Lorsqu'une loi aura été présentée à l'Assemblée selon les prescriptions de l'article 100, elle devra être soumise au référendum si plus d'un tiers des députés le demande et si un tiers des électeurs appuie cette proposition.

Les lois modifiant la Constitution ne peuvent être soumises à un référendum.

Il n'y a pas lieu à référendum si l'Assemblée adopte ensuite la loi. Les détails à ce sujet seront réglés par une loi.

Article 102.—La procédure de référendum est fixée par la loi. La loi budgétaire, les lois fiscales et le tableau des traitements ne peuvent être soumis au référendum populaire.

Article 103.—La Constitution ne peut être modifiée que par la voie législative. Tout projet de modification doit être repoussé s'il est contraire aux principes fondamentaux contenus dans la Constitution.

Les modifications de la Constitution s'effectuent par une décision de l'Assemblée prise à la majorité des $3/4$ du nombre légal de ses membres.

Article 104.—Les lois votées et approuvées conformément au statut du Territoire et à la Constitution, doivent être contresignés par le Président du Conseil et les Ministres compétents. e Président du Conseil en assure la publication au Journal officiel de la Sarre dans un délai de quinze jours.

Les lois, qui modifient la Constitution, doivent être contresignées par tous les membres du Gouvernement.

Article 105.—Les lois entrent en vigueur le lendemain de leur publication, au Journal officiel de la Sarre dans la mesure toutefois où elles ne contiennent pas à ce sujet de dispositions spéciales.

Article 106.—Les décrets et ordonnances nécessaires à l'application des lois sont rendus par le Gouvernement dans la mesure où les lois ou le statut du Territoire n'en disposent pas autrement.

TITRE V
Finances

Article 107.—Toutes les recettes et les dépenses de l'Etat doivent être évaluées pour chaque exercice et inscrites dans le budget. Le budget est établi par une loi avant le commencement de chaque exercice.

Si la loi budgétaire d'un nouvel exercice n'est pas votée en temps voulu, le Gouvernement peut établir le nouveau budget sur la base mensuelle de 1/12e des recettes et des dépenses du budget de l'année précédente, ceci à titre provisoire et jusqu'au vote définitif du budget ordinaire de l'exercice en cours.

Les dépenses de l'Etat sont en général votées pour un seul exercice; dans certains cas particuliers, elles peuvent également être consenties pour une durée plus longue.

La loi budgétaire ne doit contenir que des dispositions d'ordre financier.

Article 108.—Sous réserve des dispositions du rattachement économique, taxes et impôts ne peuvent être perçus qu'en vertu de dispositions légales.

Leur montant doit être proportionné à la puissance contributive de la population et calculé de façon progressive en tenant compte des conditions sociales.

Article 109.—A l'expiration de l'Exercice, le Ministre des Finances rend compte à l'Assemblée de l'emploi de toutes les recettes publiques, afin d'obtenir décharge pour le Gouvernement.

La procédure de vérification des comptes fera l'objet d'une loi particulière.

Article 110.—Toute dépense excédant les prévisions de la loi budgétaire doit être consentie par l'Assemblée.

Aucune dépense excédant le montant proposé et consenti par le Gouvernement ne peut être votée par l'Assemblée, à moins que la couverture financière n'en soit garantie.

Article 111.—Aucun crédit ne sera consenti, si ce n'est en cas de besoins extraordinaires ou pour des dépenses à but lucratif.

Le consentement de l'Assemblée est nécessaire pour lever un emprunt d'Etat ou accorder des garanties aux frais de l'Etat.

Le Gouvernement n'est pas tenu à la ratification par l'Assemblée des dépenses comprises dans les limites des crédits budgétaires.

TITRE VI
Justice

Article 112.—Le pouvoir judiciaire est exercé exclusivement par les tribunaux institués par la loi.

Les tribunaux d'exception sont interdits.

Des tribunaux spéciaux pourront être constitués pour certaines questions particulières.

Article 113.—Les juges sont indépendants et ne sont soumis qu'aux lois.

Article 114.—Les juges professionnels sont nommés à vie.

Après une mise en fonctions provisoire, les juges sont nommés à vie si, par leur qualités personnelles et leur activité en tant que magistrats, ils offrent la garantie d'exercer leurs fonctions dans l'esprit de la démocratie et de la compréhension sociale.

Le Gouvernement est compétent pour décider la mise en fonctions provisoire et de la nomination à vie.

Les juges ne peuvent pas être, contre leur volonté, ni mutés, ni mis à la retraite, ni relevés de leurs fonctions à titre temporaire ou définitif, si ce n'est en vertu d'une décision juridictionnelle, et seulement pour les motifs et dans les formes prévues par la Loi.

La Loi pourra fixer une limite d'âge, à partir de laquelle les juges seront mis à la retraite. La présente disposition ne concerne pas la suspension provisoire intervenant en vertu d'une Loi.

En cas de modification dans l'organisation des tribunaux ou de leurs ressorts respectifs, l'Administration de la Justice peut ordonner des mutations forcées ou des suspensions d'emploi, sans toutefois que le traitement du juge en puisse être affecté.

Les dispositions des paragraphes ci-dessus ne s'appliquent pas aux juges non professionnels.

Les détails seront réglés par une loi.

Article 115.—Les litiges administratifs sont de la compétence des Tribunaux administratifs institués par la loi.

TITRE VII
Administration et fonctionnaires

Article 116.—L'organisation de l'Administration générale de l'Etat et la détermination des compétences feront l'objet de lois. L'organisation de l'administration dans ses détails incombe au Gouvernement et aux différents ministères, auxquels il délègue ses pouvoirs.

Article 117.—Les fonctionnaires sont chargés d'exécuter les tâches que comporte l'administration publique. Ces tâches peuvent être confiées à des employés.

Article 118.—Les fondements de statut des fonctionnaires seront posés par la loi, le fonctionnariat de carrière est maintenu en principe.

Article 119.—Les fonctionnaires sont les serviteurs du peuple tout entier et non d'un parti politique. Le fonctionnaire doit, à tout instant, dans son service et dans sa vie privée, se conformer aux principes de l'Etat démocratique et constitutionnel.

Les fonctionnaires sont nommés à vie, à moins que la loi n'en dispose autrement. Le montant de leur retraite et de la pension de leurs ayants-droit est fixé par la loi.

Les droits justement acquis des fonctionnaires sont inviolables. Les fonctionnaires peuvent porter leurs revendications pécuniaires devant les tribunaux.

Les fonctionnaires ne peuvent être relevés temporairement de leurs fonctions, mis à la retraite à titre provisoire ou définitif ou rétrogradés, si ce n'est dans les cas et dans les formes prévus par la loi.

En cas de sanction administrative, le fonctionnaire doit avoir une voie de recours et la possibilité de demander sa réintégration. Aucune observation défavorable ne doit être portée au dossier personnel d'un fonctionnaire avant qu'il n'ait eu l'occasion de s'expliquer à ce sujet. Le fonctionnaire a le droit de prendre connaissance de son dossier personnel. La position du fonctionnaire vis-à-vis de l'Etat exclut le droit de grève.

Article 120.—Lorsqu'un fonctionnaire ou un employé de l'Etat dans l'exercice de l'autorité publique qui lui est déléguée, manque à ses obligations professionnelles à l'égard d'un tiers, la responsabilité des conséquences de sa faute est supportée par l'Etat ou par le Service public dont relève le fonctionnaire ou l'employé coupable. Toutefois l'Etat et les Services publics ont le droit de se retourner contre le fonctionnaire ou l'employé coupable. Le recours aux Tribunaux ordinaires est admis. Les modalités d'application seront fixées par la loi.

Article 121.—Les fonctionnaires ou employés des Services publics de l'Etat doivent prêter serment à la Constitution. Le serment comporte l'engagement d'exercer les fonctions confiées en toute équité et sans esprit de parti, de respecter la Constitution démocratique et les lois de l'Etat, de s'y conformer et le cas échéant, de les défendre.

TITRE VIII

Administration autonome des communes

Article 122.—Les communes ou associations de communes ont le droit d'administration autonome dans le cadre des limites posées par la loi.

Article 123.—Dans le cadre des compétences que leur donne la loi, les Communes et Associations de communes décident de toutes les questions qui concernent la vie économique, sociale et culturelle des populations de leur ressort.

Article 124.—La loi peut confier aux communes et associations de communes l'exécution de tâches qui incombent normalement à l'Etat.

Article 125.—Les prérogatives financières des Communes sont garanties dans le cadre des lois.

L'Etat doit assurer aux communes et associations de communes les moyens financiers nécessaires à l'exécution des tâches qu'il leur confie, par le moyen d'un compromis fiscal et d'une juste répartition des charges.

Article 126.—Les Assemblées représentatives doivent être élues dans les communes et associations de communes conformément aux dispositions de la loi.

Les dispositions prévues pour les élections à l'Assemblée constituante trouvent ici leur application, sous réserve des adaptations nécessaires.

Article 127.—Les communes et associations de communes sont placées sous le contrôle de l'Etat. Ce contrôle se borne à vérifier si l'administration est bien conforme aux lois.

Article 128.—Les contestations juridiques entre communes, associations de communes et organes de l'Etat, sont de la compétence des tribunaux administratifs.

IIIe PARTIE

DISPOSITIONS FINALES ET TRANSITOIRES

Article 129.—Les libertés et les droits constitutionnels ne peuvent être invoqués contre les décisions qui ont pour but l'extirpation du national-socialisme et du militarisme et la réparation des torts causés par eux.

Article 130.—L'Assemblée constituante sera considérée, à dater de la promulgation de la Constitution, comme la première Assemblée selon la Constitution et la Commission d'administration provisoire de la Sarre fera fonction de gouvernement intérimaire jusqu'à l'entrée en fonction d'un gouvernement conforme à la Constitution.

Article 131.—Toutes les lois et ordonnances antérieures nécessitant une adaptation aux principes de la Constitution restent provisoirement en vigueur.

Article 132.—La présente Constitution entre en vigueur à dater de la promulgation au Journal officiel du Gouvernement.

EXTRACT FROM THE PROCEEDINGS OF THE MOSCOW CONFERENCE OF FOREIGN MINISTERS

XXVIII—MEMORANDUM DE LA DELEGATION FRANÇAISE CONCERNANT LE REGIME DE LA SARRE (10 AVRIL 1947)*

*La Conférence de Moscow, Documents rélatifs à l'Allemagne emanant du Conseil des Ministres des Affaires Etrangères (2 mars–11 avril 1947), Ministère des Affaires Etrangères, Notes Documentaires et Etudes, No. 620 (Textes Diplomatiques.—XIX) (Section étrangère), Paris : Direction de la Documentation, 12 mai, 1947.

Le régime prévu pour le Territoire de la Sarre a essentiellement pour base des données économiques : priver l'Allemagne d'une partie de son potentiel de guerre, intégrer la Sarre dans l'unité économique et monétaire de la France.

I

Le rattachement économique et monétaire de la Sarre à la France implique :

1. Que le territoire de la Sarre sera englobé avec l'ensemble de ses ressources dans le système douanier français, c'est-à-dire que les frontières douanières de la France se trouveront portées aux frontières de la Sarre et que sur ces frontières les lois et règlements douaniers français seront automatiquement applicables ;

2. Que la Sarre et la France seront en union monétaire, que le franc français aura seul cours légal en Sarra et que la réglementation française du contrôle des changes s'appliquera automatiquement en Sarre ;

3. Que les niveaux des prix et des salaires en Sarre seront rajustés aux niveaux français ;

II

Le rattachement économique et monétaire, décrit ci-dessus, entraîne nécessairement un certain nombre de conséquences sur le plan politique et administratif ;

1. La Sarre échappera à la compétence du Conseil de Contrôle de Berlin et cessera de faire partie du territoire de l'Allemagne, et, en particulier, les services publics de la Sarre seront détachés de ceux de l'Allemagne ;

2. La Sarre constituera un territoire dont les habitants auront une citoyenneté propre, mais ses relations extérieures et la protection des ressortissants et des intérêts sarrois à l'étranger seront assurés par la France ;

3. Une constitution sarroise déterminera l'organisation des pouvoirs publics ; le pouvoir législatif et le pouvoir exécutif seront fondés sur le principe du suffrage universel, direct et secret ;

4. Ces pouvoirs ne seront limités que par les dispositions instituant un haut-commissaire de la République Française en Sarre, chargé d'assurer sur le plan législatif et administratif le respect par les autorités sarroises des principes du rattachement économique et monétaire. Sur le plan juridictionnel, des institutions judiciaires seront établies pour veiller

à l'observation de ces mêmes principes par les tribunaux sarrois. Le Haut-Commissaire sera, en outre, chargé de prendre les ordonnances nécessaires pour rendre applicables en Sarre les textes législatifs et réglementaires français indispensables au maintien de l'unité économique et monétaire;

5. En dehors de ces restrictions, les autorités sarroises seront compétentes pour administrer le pays.

III

La France aussurera la défense du territoire de la Sarre. A cet effet, une force militaire suffisante pour garantir la tranquillité intérieure et la surveillance des frontières y sera stationnée en permanence.

AGREEMENTS BETWEEN THE FRENCH REPUBLIC AND THE SAAR TERRITORY, SIGNED ON MARCH 3, 1950

I. GENERAL CONVENTION BETWEEN FRANCE AND THE SAAR TERRITORY

The Government of the French Republic of the one part, and

The Government of the Saar Territory of the other part,

Desiring to assure the application of the principles established in the Preamble to the Constitution of the Saar Territory,

Have agreed upon the following provisions:

ARTICLE 1

The Saar Territory is autonomous in all legislative, administrative and jurisdictional matters.

Such autonomy shall be exercised within the limits of the Constitution, including the Preamble, and of the agreements entered into by the Saar Territory and the French Republic.

ARTICLE 2

The Representative of the French Republic in the Saar Territory shall have full statutory powers to ensure the enforcement of French monetary and customs laws in the Saar Territory. Such powers shall be exercised by means of ordinances and decrees to be published in the Official Bulletin of the Saar Territory.

ARTICLE 3

The French Representative in the Saar Territory shall only have the power to oppose laws and regulations of the Saar Territory in case the contemplated measures

—constitute a menace to the monetary and custom union; or

—disregard an international obligation of the Saar Territory; or

—are of a nature to infringe the political independence or the external security of the Saar Territory.

The procedure for the opposition is outlined in a Protocol attached to the present Convention.

ARTICLE 4

The Saar authorities shall have the power to repeal ordinances and regulations promulgated by the French Representative prior to the enforcement of the present convention, by means of laws and ordinances clearly and explicitly stating such repeal.

Nevertheless, no law or regulation concerning obligations falling upon the Saar Territory in consequence of the war, and specifically no law or ordinance relating to the freezing and control of assets or to demilitarization may be repealed or modified but with the consent and agreement of the French Representative.

171

Before proceeding to the repeal of ordinances and decrees relating to the requisition of property, the Government of the Saar Territory, with the agreement of the French Representative, shall work out proper measures intended for placing the buildings required for housing personnel and services, at the disposal of said Representative and of the military authority.

ARTICLE 5

The granting of Saar nationality by naturalization shall be within the exclusive competence of the Saar Government.

Nevertheless, with a view to taking into account the conditions for the settlement of Saar nationals in France, Saar nationality shall be granted only after agreement with the French Representative in the Saar Territory in those exceptional cases when the naturalization is granted as a reward for extraordinary services in pursuance of paragraph 4 of Section 2 of Article 9 of the law of July 15, 1948, concerning Saar nationality, modified by the law of June 15, 1949.

ARTICLE 6

The members of the French Representation in the Saar Territory shall enjoy diplomatic privileges and immunities.

ARTICLE 7

The maintenance of peace and order in the Saar Territory shall be the responsibility of the Saar police.

The Saar police shall have jurisdiction over all persons domiciled or residing in the Saar Territory.

Nevertheless, no inquiries regarding personnel of the French Army or officials as described in Article 9 below shall be conducted but in co-operation with the French police in the Saar Territory. Furthermore, no search or arrest concerning army personnel or officials falling into the category outlined in Article 9 below shall be effected without previous consultation with the French Attorney General to the Court of Appeal of the Saar Territory.

The French Attorney General to the Court of Appeal of the Saar Territory shall have the power to refer all matters concerning French officials included in a list drawn up by the French Representative, to the French police in the Saar Territory. From then on, the inquiry shall be conducted in co-operation with the Saar police.

The above provisions shall not interfere with the right of the Saar police to take action against persons caught in the act.

The watch over the frontiers of the Saar Territory shall be kept in accordance with the conditions laid down in the agreement reached between the two governments on December 31, 1949.

The French Custom House and the competent French administrative services shall continue to be responsible for the enforcement in the Saar Territory of French customs laws and regulations, as well as of the laws and regulations enumerated in Articles 1 and 3 of the fiscal and budgetary Convention between France and the Saar Territory. The conditions for the enforcement of said laws and regulations in the Saar Territory shall be the same as those obtaining in France. The Saar authorities shall co-operate with the French administration in carrying out these provisions.

The Saar police may appeal to the French police for the repression of crimes and offenses whenever such repression makes it necessary that inquiries be conducted in France and abroad as well as in the Saar Territory.

ARTICLE 8

The armed forces shall be employed for the maintenance of law and order only upon request or with the consent of the Saar Government.

ARTICLE 9

Pursuant to Article 31 of the Agreement on mutual legal assistance, the Government of the French Republic shall have the right to maintain in the Saar Territory functionaries entrusted with the prosecution of crimes and offenses against the external security of France or of French troops stationed in the Saar Territory. Said functionaries shall notify without delay the competent Saar authorities of all the searches and arrests that they effected.

Nevertheless, arrests of Saar nationals and searches of the premises of Saar nationals may be effected only in the presence of functionaries of the Saar police, except in cases of impending danger to national interests and defense.

ARTICLE 10

A state of siege may be proclaimed in the Saar Territory only in case of events likely to constitute a menace to the external security of said Territory or of the French Republic, and in particular in case of war or of impending danger to the independence of the Saar Territory.

The state of siege shall be proclaimed by an ordinance issued by the Representative of the French Republic after consultation with the Saar Government.

ARTICLE 11

In accordance with the Constitution of the Saar Territory, the representation of the Saar abroad and the defense of its interests are ensured by the French Republic.

A representation of the Saar Government whose members will enjoy diplomatic privileges and immunities shall be established in Paris.

Saar officials shall be admitted to perform some duties in French consular offices established in countries where the Saar Territory has interests of a certain importance. These officials shall be appointed by the Saar Government, after approval by the government of the French Republic; they shall have the same status as French officials with similar rank. The number of said Saar officials, the consular posts in which they shall exert their functions, their ranks, their duties, and the ways by which they shall correspond with the Saar authorities shall be determined by mutual agreement between the two governments.

The duties to be performed by French consuls owing to the fact that France represents Saar interests abroad shall be defined in sets of instructions agreed upon by the two governments and dispatched to French consular posts by the French Government.

The French Government shall hereafter benevolently consider any request to the effect that Saar officials be admitted in a capacity as advisers to French officials carrying out special tasks in foreign countries where the Saar Territory has interests of a certain importance.

ARTICLE 12

In case some disagreement should arise between the two governments as to the interpretation or the application of the present Convention, said governments, upon request from either one, shall proceed to a joint examination of the dispute.

ARTICLE 13

The present Convention shall be drawn up in the French and German languages, the French text being authentic in case of dispute. It shall enter into force upon its publication in the two countries.

In faith whereof the respective Plenipotentiaries have signed the present Convention and have hereto affixed their seals.

Done in duplicate at PARIS, March 3, 1950

II. AGREEMENT ON THE ENFORCEMENT OF THE ECONOMIC UNION BETWEEN FRANCE AND THE SAAR TERRITORY

The Government of the French Republic of the one part, and

The Government of the Saar Territory of the other part,

Considering that the Constitution of the Saar Territory makes provisions for an economic, monetary, and customs union of the Saar Territory with the French Republic from which the free circulation of capital and goods between the two countries ensues;

Considering that the French law of November 15, 1947, concerning the introduction of the French franc in the Saar Territory, the fiscal and budgetary Convention between France and the Saar Territory, and the related regulations providing for the extension of the French regime of foreign exchanges and of French laws on credit to the Saar Territory have made it possible to carry out the monetary and customs union between France and the Saar Territory;

Desiring to specify the conditions for the operation of the economic link of the Saar Territory with France;

Considering the provisions of the fiscal and budgetary Convention between France and the Saar Territory,

Have agreed as follows:

ARTICLE 1

The French Government and the Saar Government shall avoid any discrimination between French and Saar economic products in their respective territories.

ARTICLE 2

The French Government shall grant to Saar economic interests the same consideration as to French economic interests when negotiating or enforcing treaties or tariffications regarding the foreign trade of the Franco-Saar Union.

In the case of commercial agreements especially affecting economic interests of the Saar Territory, a representative of the Saar Government shall be called to take part in an advisory capacity in the work preliminary to the negotiation of said treaty.

The French Government shall, as far as possible, keep the Saar Government informed of the progress of the negotiations and, in case the development of the conversations should make it necessary, the Saar Government shall be allowed to express their observations.

Said agreements, treaties, or tariffications shall come into force simultaneously in France and in the Saar Territory; those agreements, treaties, or tariffications shall become applicable after they have been signed and ratified by France in the name of both countries.

As far as the execution of said agreements, treaties, and tariffications is concerned, and in particular with respect to the apportioning of quotas for the various commodities, to the issuing of licenses, to the allotment of foreign exchange, the two signatories shall be submitted to the same regime.

ARTICLE 3

The Saar Government shall take all necessary measures to ensure that Saar business concerns may operate under conditions similar to those under which French business concerns operate in consequence of laws and regulations in force in France. Said Government shall abstain from adopting, or shall forbid the adoption of, measures which might disorganize the domestic and foreign trade of the Franco-Saar economic union, or might upset the normal play of economic forces in favor of or to the detriment of one of the two countries.

In particular,

a) The rates of taxes and duties laid upon cost prices shall be kept in the Saar Territory at such levels as to insure that the levies made from each category of establishments will not result in considerable disparity in favor or to the detriment of products and services of the Saar economy as compared to those of the French economy. The same criteria shall apply with respect to social security dues.

b) In order to avoid a substantial disparity between the salary rates prevailing in France and in the Saar Territory respectively, a set of rules similar to those in force in France shall be enacted in the Saar Territory.

Social security benefits, including annuities and pensions, shall be kept in the Saar Territory at such levels as to avoid upsetting the labor market of the Franco-Saar economic union.

c) With regard to economic controls and subsidies, all necessary legislative measures shall be adopted in order to place the Saar economy under conditions similar to those prevailing in the French economy, due allowance being made for special local conditions.

ARTICLE 4

All problems arising from the effort to bring the economies of the two countries into harmony with each other, in particular with respect to legislative and administrative measures, and all problems arising in the course of works for outlining and executing economic plans and programs may be submitted for study to the Commission set up by Article 5 below.

The two contracting governments undertake to do as soon as possible everything in their power to promote agreements between French labor, professional, and management organizations and their counterparts in the Saar Territory with a view to setting up all organs and to starting all procedures apt to ensure a close economic co-operation among said bodies.

ARTICLE 5

A Franco-Saar Economic Commission is hereby established. Said Commission shall be composed of the following members:
—The Minister of Foreign Affairs of the French Republic, or a representative of his, Chairman;
—three titular members and three substitutes appointed by the Government of the French Republic;
—four titular members and four substitutes appointed by the Government of the Saar Territory.
The Commission shall meet in Paris.

ARTICLE 6

Any dispute arising in the course of putting the present Convention into effect may be referred to the Franco-Saar Economic Commission by either of the contracting parties.

The Commission shall settle the dispute and decide as to the measures to be adopted by a majority vote of the members present. In case of draw the vote of the president shall decide.

The decisions of the Commission shall be binding for both France and the Saar Territory; the two Governments undertake to put them into effect.

ARTICLE 7

The present agreement shall be drawn up in the French and German languages, the French text being authentic in case of dispute. It shall enter into force upon its publication in the two countries.

In faith whereof the respective plenipotentiaries have signed the present agreement and have hereto affixed thir seals.

Done in duplicate at PARIS, March 3, 1950

III. AGREEMENT BETWEEN FRANCE AND THE SAAR TERRITORY CONCERNING THE OPERATION OF SAAR RAILWAYS

The Government of the French Republic of the one part; and
The Government of the Saar Territory of the other part,
Desiring to define the status of Saar state railways within the limits of the economic union between France and the Saar Territory and without prejudice to the provisions of the peace treaty,
Have agreed as follows:

ARTICLE 1

The provisional administrative regime of the Saar railways as laid down by:
—Ruling No. 116 of the General Administrator of the military government for the French Occupation Zone of Germany, of December 22, 1946;
—Ordinance No. 126 of the General Supreme French Commander in Germany, of November 16, 1947;
—Decree No. 47-183 of the Governor of the Saar Territory, of December 24, 1947;
—Decree No. 15 of the Governor of the Saar Territory, of March 30, 1947;
shall be ended as of the date when the present Agreement will come into force.

ARTICLE 2

1. An undertaking endowed with legal status and financial autonomy and charged with the administration and operation of the railway lines in the Saar Territory once the property of the former Reichsbahn is hereby established. The name of said undertaking shall be "Saar Railways."

2. Said undertaking shall have its headquarters at Saarbrücken. The Saarbrücken Courts shall be the competent tribunal for all litigations concerning the agency.

3. The Saar railways perform a public service. Nevertheless, their commitments shall normally be governed by the principles of common law.

ARTICLE 3

1. The Saar Government shall put all the equipment needed for the operation of the Saar railway system at the disposal of "Saar Railways."

2. The Saar Government undertakes to put the Saar railway system in good working condition, and to supply it with the financial means needed for this purpose.

3. The Saar Government undertakes to equip the Saar railway system with the land installations and the rolling stock necessary to cope with the exigencies of traffic.

4. The Saar Government undertakes to make up contingent operational deficiencies.

5. The rolling stock of the Saar railway system shall include:

a) engines and railway cars formerly the property of the Deutsche Reichsbahn and bearing the mark "Saar" on the date when the present agreement shall come into force;

b) engines and railway cars which might be allotted to the Saar railway system by international agreements in order to make up the rolling stock mentioned above; and

c) engines and railway cars purchased by the Saar railway system.

ARTICLE 4

1. "Saar Railways" shall take up all Saar personnel on the active list on the date when the present agreement shall come into effect.

2. They shall take up all obligations resulting from vested interests of said personnel and of all personnel retired under the provisional administration mentioned in Article 1, Section III.

3. They shall be bound to pay the pensions due to the personnel referred to in the paragraph above as well as the pensions provided for in Article 6 of Ordinance No. 116 of the General Administrator for the Military Government of the French Occupation Zone of Germany, dated December 22, 1946.

ARTICLE 5

The technical rules for the construction and operation of railways in the Saar Territory are established by law.

The member of the Saar Cabinet in charge of transportation shall wield a general supervision over the agency, and shall have the powers of approval described in Article 8, Section III.

ARTICLE 6

"Saar Railways" shall be administered by a Board of Directors consisting of twelve members, to wit:

Six Saar members appointed by the Saar Government, among whom a high rank official who shall act as chairman; and

Six French members appointed by the Government of the French Republic, among whom a high rank official who shall act as vice-chairman.

Included among the Saar members of the Board of Directors shall be two representatives of the agency's staff and one representative of the Saar Chamber of Commerce and Industry.

Included among the French members of the Board of Directors shall be one representative of the Saar mines.

The directors shall be appointed for terms of five years by their respective governments which, however, shall have the right to replace them even before the expiration of their mandate.

ARTICLE 7

Within the Board of Directors a Permanent Committee shall be set up, composed of the chairman, the vice-chairman, and a French and a Saar representative designated by their respective governments.

Said Permanent Committee shall have the task to investigate and prepare topics to be submitted to the Board of Directors.

ARTICLE 8

The Board of Directors shall represent "Saar Railways" in every field, including judicial matters.

It shall be endowed with the powers needed for administering the agency. Nevertheless, those decisions which entail commitments whose financial consequences exceed a limit to be fixed by the Saar Cabinet member in charge of transportation, shall be submitted to the latter for approval.

The Board of Directors may in turn delegate some of their powers to the General Manager of the railway system.

The Board of Directors shall submit to the Saar minister in charge of transportation for his approval:

—any plan for conventions or agreements that "Saar Railways" may be led to make with other French or Saar public agencies;

—the prospective budget, the income and expenditures account, as well as all applications for loans and all plans for maintenance and construction works; and

—their proposals for appointments of high rank officials.

The Board of Directors shall especially take into consideration in their decisions the necessity to secure in the best possible conditions those transports which are of direct interest to the mines, and the necessity to comply with requests made by French agencies responsible for the security of the Saar Territory.

The Board of Directors shall submit their decisions regarding rates to the Saar minister in charge of transportation for his ratification. Such ratification shall take into account the rules outlined in Article 13, Section III.

ARTICLE 9

The Board of Directors shall be convened by its chairman. It shall meet at least ten times a year. The chairman shall call an extraordinary session of the Board whenever one-third at least of the members so request.

The Board of Directors shall draw up their own rules of procedure.

ARTICLE 10

1. The General Manager of "Saar Railways" shall be appointed by the Saar Government in consultation with the French Government.

2. The General Manager of "Saar Railways" shall be in charge of carrying out the decisions of the Board of Directors.

3. The General Manager may not be a member of the Board of Directors; he shall attend the meetings of the Board of Directors and of the Permanent Committee. ·

4. The number of French technicians attached to the General Manager's office may not exceed five. One of said technicians shall act as liaison officer between "Saar Railways" and the National Company of French Railways (S.N.C.F.).

ARTICLE 11

The General Manager shall be the hierarchical superior of all members of the staff of "Saar Railways."

He will be in charge of personnel appointments and promotions within the limits of the powers delegated to him.

ARTICLE 12

The two contracting governments undertake to promote, within the limits of their respective competence, the enactment of rules regarding the co-ordination between the Saar railways and other means of transportation of any nationality, adopted by mutual agreement.

ARTICLE 13

The rates for domestic transportation on the Saar railway system shall at any time be the same as the rates in force in France for domestic transportation. Nevertheless, the Saar railways, in order to take account of local needs and with the consent of the French minister in charge of transportation, shall have the right to adopt special rates for certain goods and for certain connections.

Whenever the French railway rate system requires a maximum and a minimum charge to be quoted, the decision as to the rate to be charged by the Saar railways shall be made in agreement with the French minister in charge of transportation.

The direct Franco-Saar railway traffic shall be maintained, and shall automatically undergo whatever changes may occur in French rates.

The application of common rates between the Saar railways and other foreign railway systems shall take place after approval by the French minister in charge of transportation.

No diversion of traffic which would normally make use of either the French or the Saar railway system shall be encouraged by measures adopted by the management of either of the two systems.

ARTICLE 14

All technical and material aid which may be necessary to ensure the successful operation of Saar railways shall be provided by the National Company of French Railways under conditions to be agreed upon in a protocol between "Saar Railways" and the National Company of French Railways.

ARTICLE 15

In case the Board of Directors should be unable to reach a decision on a subject the dispute, upon request by the chairman or the vice-chairman, shall be submitted to the Commission contemplated in Article 5 of the Agreement on the enforcement of the Franco-Saar economic union.

ARTICLE 16

The present Agreement shall be drawn up in the French and German languages, the French text being authentic in case of dispute. It shall enter into force upon its publication in the two countries.

In faith whereof the respective plenipotentiaries have signed the present Agreement and have hereto affixed their seals.

Done in duplicate at PARIS, March 3, 1950

IV. AGREEMENT BETWEEN FRANCE AND THE SAAR TERRITORY CONCERNING THE WORKING OF SAAR MINES

The Government of the French Republic of the one part, and

The Government of the Saar Territory of the other part,

Considering that the Saar Territory has well-founded claims to the ownership of the coal mines situated in its territory, and that the Government of the French Republic undertakes to uphold the Territory's rightful claims to said ownership at the time when the German peace settlement will be discussed;

Considering that until said peace settlement is reached, and under reservation of the ratification of said rights of the Saar Territory by the same settlement, the Saar Government which, under the Constitution of December 15, 1947, exerts sovereign rights over the Saar Territory, is already empowered to determine the conditions for the working of said mines in agreement with the Government of the French Republic;

Considering that France, due to the experience that she has acquired in the working of the Saar coal basin, and also in view of the technical and commercial opportunities which she is in a position to extend to the Saar mines to their advantage, is well qualified to control the working of said mines;

Considering that the development of the Saar basin is a long-term project which can be successfully carried out only on condition that the development system be suited for the adoption of long-term plans chiefly with regard to capital investments;

On the basis of the above considerations, and conscious of their mutual obligations resulting from the Charter for the economic union of the Saar Territory with the French Republic,

Have agreed as follows:

ARTICLE 1

Without prejudice to the stipulations of the peace settlement, in particular as far as the ownership of Saar mines is concerned, it is hereby agreed that the responsibility for the operation of the Saar coal fields is entrusted to the French State. Said operation shall be guaranteed by the Saar Mines Administration [Régie des Mines de la Sarre].

The fields referred to in the preceding paragraph are the fields, conceded or not, located within the boundaries of the Saar Territory.

The operation shall be conducted by means of the mines installations, of the industries connected with the mines, and of associations already in existence or to be established.

The Saar Mines Administration shall have its headquarters at Saarbrücken. The new conditions under which it will operate are defined by the provisions of the present Agreement.

ARTICLE 2

The present Agreement shall come into force as soon as it is ratified by the two contracting parties,* and shall remain in force until the peace settlement becomes effective. If at that time the ownership of the coal mines is acknowledged to the Saar Territory, the present Agreement shall be automatically extended for such a period as will be necessary to bring its full duration, from the date of its entry into effect, to fifty years.

In the course of the Agreement far-reaching technical, economic, or social changes having profound effects upon the working of the mines and connected establishments may be pleaded by either of the contracting parties and may eventually be made the subject of additions to the present Agreement.

ARTICLE 3

The Saar Government shall leave at the disposal of the Saar Mines Administration during the whole course of the present Agreement all material and immaterial properties which are administered by said agency at the time when the present Agreement comes into force.

The Saar Government undertakes to put at the disposal of the Saar Mines Administration during the course of the present Agreement all material and immaterial properties owned by said government which shall be considered necessary to the successful operation and development of the mines and their connected establishments.

The Saar Mines Administration, on the other hand, shall have a right to appeal to all laws and regulations in force in the Saar Territory in support of its right to occupy or to acquire by way of dispossession grounds belonging to third parties and deemed useful for the operation or development of the mines and appendages thereof. The Saar Mines Administration shall continue to honor, in the owner's place and stead, all obligations that it had undertaken on the ground of similar actions prior to the date when the present Agreement shall come into force.

ARTICLE 4

During the course of the present Agreement the Saar Mines Administration shall have, as part of its normal administrative functions, the right to effect,

* In force, January 1, 1951.

on all grounds indicated in Article 3, all constructions, transformations, demo-
litions, and other works which it may consider useful.

Said Administration shall likewise have the right to lease said grounds and
installations, to establish all *de facto* claims on them, to transfer them by way
of sale or exchange, to dispose—gratuitously or for a consideration—of all
movable goods and immaterial rights put at its disposal pursuant to Article 3
above. All real estate properties purchased or built during the course of the
present Agreement shall become the property of the Saar Territory, and as
such shall be inscribed in the Register of Deeds. In case the direct working
of some sections of the coal fields on the part of the Saar Mines Administration
should prove difficult or too onerous, said agency, with the assent of the Saar
Government, shall have the power to wholly or partly transfer its working
rights as well as its rights over the installations it owns or holds in custody for
the duration of the present Agreement or part thereof.

The dues paid to the Saar Mines Administration as compensation for the
transfer of said working rights shall be passed on to the Saar Territory.

ARTICLE 5

The Saar Mines Administration shall pay all debts, honor all obligations,
and cash all credits of the Saargrüben Company originating from its activity
prior to January 1, 1948, in the name and interest of said company.

After the final settlement of the liquidation of the Saargrüben Company, the
Saar Mines Administration shall take over all debts and credits resulting from
the liquidation.

ARTICLE 6

The conditions for the hiring, employment, and promotion of the personnel
of the mines and connected establishments shall be determined at all levels by
professional skills.

ARTICLE 7

The Saar Mines Administration shall have all acknowledged rights of
private industrial and commercial companies, and shall be permitted to carry
out all actions that said enterprises are permitted to carry out pursuant to
French and Saar laws. Within these limits said agency shall plan and direct
the working of the mines in such a way as to ensure, up to the expiration of
the present Agreement, the proper utilization of the coal fields according to
the best mining rules and the preservation of the installations; it shall observe
safety rules in force at the time when the present Agreement comes into effect,
except for measures adopted exclusively in consequence of the state of war.
New safety measures may be adopted under the conditions outlined in Article
13, page 184.

ARTICLE 8

The Saar Mines Administration shall manage shipments, decide upon allot-
ments, and fix sale prices for the products of the mines and connected establishments in the mutual interest of the French and Saar economies, and with
due consideration for the supply needs of Saar industries.

ARTICLE 9

The Saar Mines Administration shall each year evaluate its profits for the
assessment of taxes. Said agency shall be exclusively subject to general fiscal

stipulations applicable to industrial establishments pursuant to Article 16 of the Fiscal and Budgetary Convention.

The above-mentioned profits are understood to be net operation profits, including profits carried forward from previous years and after deduction of general expenses and other outlays including the dues described in Article 10 below as well as industrial depreciation allowances and all reserves and justified provisions. Said depreciation allowances shall be calculated at 15 percent of total transactions before deductions during the first five years following the entry into force of the present Agreement, and at 11 percent of the same figure thereafter.

From profits as defined above, the amounts needed for the payment of possible arrears of the dues described in Article 10 below, of the above-mentioned taxes, and of charges resulting from the amortization of loans or advances made by the French Government shall be deducted in this order.

Twenty percent of the balance shall be utilized for social aims. The details of the way in which these amounts are to be disbursed shall be decided upon by the operator in agreement with the Saar Mines Council established by Article 12 of the present Agreement.

ARTICLE 10

The Saar Territory shall receive each year a total payment consisting of two parts. The first part shall be independent of the annual net output. The second part shall depend on the net output obtained by the Saar Mines Administration in excess of ten million tons per year.

The two parts of the payment as described above shall vary in the same proportion as the average sale prices of *"Noix III flambant 15/35"* and *"Criblés gras A 80"* on the first day of the year for which the payment is made.

The average basic price of the fuel, as defined above, being the price prevailing on the first day of January of the first year of application of the present Agreement, the basic values for the two parts of the payment are fixed as follows: the first part, 300 million francs; and the second part, 30 francs per each net ton of coal mined in excess of ten million tons.

From the sixth year on, the amount of the second part of the payment as defined above shall be augmented by an additional payment of 20 francs per ton to be applied to the total net tonnage of coal mined.

The first part of the payment shall be made in any case on the 30th day of June of the year following that to which the payment applies and shall be considered as actually paid on that date.

The second part of the payment, likewise due at the same date regardless of the financial results of the year under consideration, shall be paid without delay if the budget for said year shows sufficient profits.

If this is not the case, the payment of the second part of the amount due may be carried over. The payment of the principal plus interest for the period of delay, evaluated on the basis of the discount rate of the Banque de France increased by one point, shall have first priority among the payments to be made at the expense of profits from subsequent working years.

ARTICLE 11

At the expiration of the present Agreement, including possible extensions of the same, the Saar Mines Administration shall gratuitously deliver to the

Saar State all the material and immaterial properties that it holds, in the situation and conditions in which they are at that time.

Any contingent assets extant at the closure of the accounts of the Saar Mines Administration shall become the property of the Saar Territory. Should the closure of the agency's accounts reveal a deficit, the latter shall be taken over by the Saar State.

ARTICLE 12

The Higher Saar Mines Council [Conseil Supérieur des Mines de la Sarre] and the Saar Mines Committee [Comité des Mines de la Sarre] are hereby eliminated.

A Saar Mines Council [Conseil des Mines de la Sarre] is hereby established.

Said Council shall consist of 18 members, to wit: 9 members appointed by the Government of the French Republic and 9 members appointed by the Saar Government. All members shall be appointed for three years and may be reappointed.

The minister of the French Republic in charge of mines, or a representative of his, shall be the chairman of the Saar Mines Council.

The Council shall meet at least six times a year; the meetings shall be called by the chairman. In case of emergency, the Council shall meet upon request of nine of its members. The General Manager of the Saar Mines Administration and the State Controller shall attend the meetings.

The following documents shall, when requested, be submitted to the Council for its consideration: estimated revenue and expenditures account, plans for new works and for the establishment of new installations and new industrial branches, statements of losses, staff regulations, plans for financial participations, loans with more than five years duration.

The Council may deliberate on other matters regarding the operation of the mines proposed for discussion by at least five of its members.

The Saar Mines Council shall submit proposals and express its opinions regarding all above matters and regarding all matters on which it may be consulted by the minister of the French Government in charge of mines.

ARTICLE 13

A Franco-Saar Co-operation and Consultation Body with headquarters in Saarbrücken is hereby established. Said body shall be called Franco-Saar Mines Office [Office Franco-Sarrois des Mines].

The Franco-Saar Mines Office shall consist of 6 French members appointed by the Government of the French Republic and 6 Saar members appointed by the Saar Government. Their mandate will last three years, and they may be reappointed. The chairmanship of the Office shall fall alternatingly to a French member and a Saar member who shall be elected by their colleagues for one year. The Permanent Secretary-General of the Franco-Saar Office shall be designated by the French Government in consultation with the Saar Government.

The Office shall be consulted regarding all laws and regulations on economic, technical, financial, fiscal, and social matters which might influence operational conditions and operation costs of the mines.

On the other hand, the Office of its own initiative may examine and propose to the two contracting governments the signing of agreements as well as the adoption of laws and regulations meant to ensure the satisfactory operation of the mines from the technical, economic, financial, administrative, fiscal, and social viewpoint.

In case of disagreement between the operator and the Saar Mines Service regarding a decision or a ruling of the latter, the operator's recourse to the minister in charge of mines of the Saar Government shall cause the suspension of the measure except in case of immediate danger according to Article 199 of the mines law. Before deliberating on the recourse, the Saar minister in charge of mines shall consult the Franco-Saar Office. In case the Franco-Saar Office should prove unable to formulate a proposal of settlement by majority vote, the Saar minister in charge of mines shall decide the controversy after reaching an agreement on the matter with the French minister in charge of mines. The Saar minister in charge of mines shall follow a similar procedure in case he should decide not to accept the advice of the Franco-Saar Office.

On the basis of powers delegated to it by the two contracting governments, the Office shall control the bookkeeping and the administrative management of the mines to make sure that books and accounts are kept properly and conform to the bookkeeping plan adopted by the Saar Mines Administration and that the budget is truthful and correct.

Expenses of the Office shall be covered by a contribution paid by the Saar Mines Administration.

ARTICLE 14

Any dispute that might arise regarding the application or the interpretation of the present Agreement shall be submitted, upon request of either of the contracting parties, to the Commission provided for in Article 5 of the Convention concerning the application of the Franco-Saar economic union.

ARTICLE 15

The present Agreement shall be drawn up in the French and German languages, the French text being authentic in case of dispute.

V. AGREEMENT BETWEEN FRANCE AND THE SAAR TERRITORY CONCERNING THE SETTLEMENT OF NATIONALS OF THE TWO COUNTRIES AND THE CONDUCT OF PROFESSIONAL ACTIVITIES

The Government of the French Republic, of the one part; and

The Government of the Saar Territory of the other part,

Considering that the economic union of the Saar Territory to France and the principle of free circulation of people and goods from one of the two countries to the other, which is a corollary of said union, have caused relations of a peculiar nature and basically different in character from the relations existing between France and foreign countries to be established in the economic field between France and the Saar Territory;

Being desirous of regulating within the framework of said union the problems arising from the settlement of and the conduct of professional activities on the part of their respective nationals in the territory of the other country,

Have agreed as follows:

SECTION I

General Stipulations

ARTICLE 1

Nationals of one of the contracting Parties shall be permitted to freely enter the territory of the other Party, to travel or establish their domicile in said territory, and to leave it at any time, with reservation of the provisions of police and security regulations.

ARTICLE 2

Nationals of one of the contracting countries shall enjoy in the territory of the other the same treatment as nationals as regards the right to acquire, to own, and to rent real and personal property, and to dispose thereof.

ARTICLE 3

Nationals of one of the contracting Parties in the territory of the other shall have free access to Courts pursuant to the provisions of the Convention on mutual aid in legal matters.

ARTICLE 4

Each of the two contracting Parties undertakes not to adopt with respect to property, rights, and interests legally owned in its territory by nationals of the other Party any measure or provision of public interest which would not be applicable to its own citizens under the same circumstances. The same criteria shall apply with regard to indemnifications to which said measures would give rise.

ARTICLE 5

Nationals of one of the contracting Parties in the territory of the other Party, in peacetime as well as in wartime, shall be subject only to such requisitions as are imposed upon nationals, and shall be entitled to the same indemnifications accorded the latter by local laws.

SECTION II

Concerning the Practice of Industrial or Commercial Professions and the Performance of Craftsmanlike Work Without Fixed Wages

ARTICLE 7

Taken into consideration in the present Section are commercial, industrial, or craftsmanlike activities not rewarded with a fixed wage, conducted by nationals of one of the contracting Parties in the other Party's territory. Nevertheless, the present provisions are not applicable to such professions and activities as:

—stock exchange agents and real estate brokers,
—maritime brokers,
—wine and liquor retail dealers,
—fishermen on board foreign boats in territorial waters,
—employment in maritime shipment of merchandise in the interest of the State, of groups, or of companies being grantees of public utility services,
—employment in air transports.

Article 7

French nationals domiciled in the Saar Territory, and Saar nationals domiciled in France, as well as French and Saar nationals wishing to take domicile in the country of which they are not citizens, shall enjoy the same treatment as the nationals of the country in which they wish to settle with respect to the establishment of a commercial or a manufacturing business or of a craft, except when a special regulation is provided for by stipulations of the present Agreement.

Article 8

No restrictions provided for by the laws of one of the contracting Parties with regard to the conduct by aliens of professional activities envisaged in the present Section shall apply to the nationals of the other contracting Party who are already domiciled or wish to settle in the territory of said Party for the purpose of conducting such professional activities.

Specifically, persons having the title of Saar citizens pursuant to the law of July 15, 1948, regarding Saar nationality, modified by the law of June 25, 1949, shall not be subject in France to the following provisions of the Ordinance of November 2, 1945, regarding the conduct of various professional activities on the part of aliens:

—Chapter I, Article 7, paragraph 2;
—Chapter II, Article 15, paragraph 3, and Article 17, paragraphs 3 and 4;
—Chapter V, wholly.

Article 9

Saar citizens may benefit by the stipulations of the law of June 30, 1926, on commercial ownership notwithstanding the stipulations of Article 19 of said law, under reservation, however, of the provisions of Article 53, Section IX, of the present Agreement.

Article 10

Nationals of one of the contracting countries, in order to be allowed to conduct a professional activity in the other country will have to be of age if said activity is a commercial or industrial one, and will have to be at least 24 years of age if said activity is a craft. They will have to comply with the standards of professional respectability required by the laws of the country in which they wish to become established.

Article 11

Unless other provisions are applicable pursuant to the following paragraph, and under reservation of the provisions of Article 46 of the present Agreement, the parties concerned will have to prove their professional proficiency on the basis of no less than five years of previous activity in a similar line in the case of industrial or commercial professions, and of no less than seven years of previous activity in a similar line in the case of crafts. Said activity may not necessarily have been conducted in a capacity as independent employer or self-employer. Said proof shall consist of a certificate of the competent Chamber of Commerce and Industry, or Chamber of Crafts (Chambre des Métiers). Such expressions as industrial or commercial profession and craft as employed in the present article shall be taken in the same meaning as they have in the country in which the prospective activity will be set up.

The Joint Commission provided for by Article 58 below shall have the power to prescribe special standards regarding professional skills in certain professions.

ARTICLE 12

Trading licenses as commercial travelers issued to Frenchmen by French authorities shall be valid in the Saar Territory.

Likewise, trading licenses issued to Saar commercial travelers by Saar authorities shall be valid in France.

Trading licenses as commercial travelers issued to French and Saar nationals abroad by French diplomatic and consular officials shall be valid in both countries.

ARTICLE 13

Hawking and peddling shall be governed in the territory of either of the contracting Parties by the provisions of general or local laws regulating said activities.

Nevertheless, in the enforcement of said provisions no distinction shall be made between nationals of the two countries on the ground of nationality.

ARTICLE 14

Commercial activity at markets and fairs shall be permitted to French nationals in the Saar Territory and to Saar nationals in France on the same conditions as to nationals. No discrimination on the ground of nationality may be raised against them by general police or municipal regulations.

ARTICLE 15

Civil and commercial companies constituted in accordance with the laws of one of the contracting Parties shall be recognized as legally existent by the other Party with the proviso that nothing in their constitution or their objectives be contrary to public order as defined by the laws of the latter Party.

ARTICLE 16

For the purpose of implementing the present Agreement, the nationality of companies shall be defined in connection with their headquarters as stated in their statutes, provided said companies fall under French or Saar control.

The Joint Commission provided for in Article 58 below shall have the power to extend the provisions of the present Agreement to companies for which conditions outlined in the foregoing paragraph are not fulfilled.

ARTICLE 17

Regulations on business establishments concerning partners and administrators as well as principals shall apply to Saar nationals and to Saar financial participations in France under the same terms and conditions as to French nationals and participations, and vice versa.

ARTICLE 18

The stipulations of Article 17 shall not apply to the companies listed below:
—companies manufacturing and trading war materials; and
—companies being grantees of or charged with public utility services.

ARTICLE 19

Company branches shall have to comply with the laws in force in the country in which they are established as regards legal formalities for taking up residence and the conduct of their operations.

The laws in force in the country of residence shall apply with respect to the establishment of large department or five-and-ten [*prix uniques*] stores, as well as with respect to the right of companies whose purpose is manufacturing and selling common goods to establish retail sale branches.

ARTICLE 20

French nationals domiciled in the Saar Territory as well as Saar nationals domiciled in France shall have the right to vote in and to be candidates for Chambers of Commerce on the same conditions as nationals.

French nationals established in the Saar Territory as craftsmen or as wage earners in craft shops, and Saar nationals established in France as craftsmen or as wage earners in craft shops, shall have the right to vote in and to be candidates for Chambers of Crafts (Chambres des Métiers) on the same conditions as nationals.

ARTICLE 21

Individuals and legal persons [*personnes morales*] of either of the two contracting Parties shall have the right to tender for all awards of public auctions in the other Party's territory in the same conditions as national establishments, and shall enjoy the same treatment without any discrimination for reason of nationality.

SECTION III

Bankruptcy and Dissolution by Courts

ARTICLE 22

The provisions of the present Section refer to bankruptcy and dissolution by Courts of individual traders and commercial companies whose assets or creditors are in either of the two contracting countries.

Said provisions do not apply to bankruptcy of noncommercial establishments.

The Courts to which the application is submitted shall decide in accordance with the law whether the definition as trader or commercial company applies to the entity under consideration.

ARTICLE 23

Competent Courts in matters of bankruptcy or dissolution shall be:

1. The Court of the place where the main establishment is located in the case of individuals; and

2. The Court of the place where social headquarters are located in the case of legal persons. In case social headquarters are not located within the territory of the Franco-Saar economic union, the competent Court shall be the Court of the place where the main establishment within the territory of the Franco-Saar economic union is located.

If bankruptcy or dissolution by judicial process is declared in both countries, the earlier decision alone shall be taken into consideration.

ARTICLE 24

The consequences of bankruptcy or dissolution by Court action declared in either of the two countries by the Court competent in accordance with the provisions of the foregoing article shall extend to the territory of the other country as well.

The receiver or receivers, in consequence of the judgment or of the decision by which they were appointed, shall have the power to take in either country any action they deem necessary, as representatives of the bankrupt individual or estate, and especially to request the authorities of either country to take any provisory or conservatory measure. Nevertheless, seizure or distraint may be carried out only after exequatur of the decision or the judgment declaring bankruptcy or dissolution. Said exequatur shall be issued in accordance with the simplified procedure provided for in Article 21 of the Convention on judicial organization of January 3, 1948.

ARTICLE 25

The entirety of an estate in bankruptcy or dissolution by Court action shall be one and indivisible.

ARTICLE 26

Claims against the bankrupt shall be submitted and proved in accordance with the rules of the Court which declared the bankruptcy.

Likewise, the receiver or receivers shall proceed to the liquidation of the bankrupt's estate in conformity with the rules of the Court which declared the bankruptcy.

ARTICLE 27

Bankrupts, in good faith or fraudulent, shall be subject in each of the two countries to forfeitures, interdictions, or incapacitations provided for by the laws of said country.

ARTICLE 28

All public announcements regarding bankruptcy, including entries in official registers in each of the two countries, shall conform to the laws in force in said country.

ARTICLE 29

All judgments and decisions in matters of bankruptcy or dissolution by judicial process rendered in one of the two countries, and especially decisions relating to ordinary composition [*concordat*] and to rehabilitation, shall have the authority of a final decision [*chose jugée*] in the other country. Nevertheless, said decisions shall become mandatory in the other country only after exequatur in accordance with the simplified procedure provided for in Article 21 of the Convention on judicial organization of January 3, 1948.

SECTION IV

Professional Organizations

ARTICLE 30

The present stipulations are applicable exclusively to French nationals and Saar nationals enjoying their civil rights and political franchise in the territory of one of the two contracting Parties.

ARTICLE 31

Nationals of each of the two countries shall reciprocally have the right to be admitted to labor and management organizations of the other country on the same conditions as the latter's nationals, with reservation of the rules of statutes and bylaws of said organizations.

ARTICLE 32

With a view to promote the development of the Franco-Saar economic union, management organizations rightfully established in one of the two countries may join corresponding management organizations of the other country, due account being taken of statutory provisions governing said organizations.

SECTION V

Professional Wage-earning Occupations

ARTICLE 33

French nationals wishing to hold professional wage-earning jobs in the Saar Territory shall be exempt from the need of administrative work permits. Nevertheless, they shall have to comply with the provisions of the law on the sojourn of aliens of July 25, 1948.

ARTICLE 34

Individuals having the status of Saar citizens in accordance with the law on Saar nationality of July 15, 1948, modified by the law of June 25, 1949, and wishing to settle in France for the purpose of obtaining there professional wage-earning jobs in accordance with the provisions of the present Section of the Agreement, shall be exempt from the necessity of complying with certain provisions of the law on professional wage-earning work for aliens of November 2, 1945, to wit:

—Chapter I, Article 5, paragraphs 2 and 3; and Article 7;
—Chapter II, Article 15, paragraph 3; and Article 17, paragraphs 3 and 4;
—Chapter V, wholly.

ARTICLE 35

Conditions for the application of the law on protection of domestic labor of August 8, 1932, to employers hiring foreign labor in France shall be specified, as far as Saar workers are concerned, in an exchange of letters between the two governments.

SECTION VI

Creation of a Common Labor Market Between France and Saar

ARTICLE 36

The Ministry of Labor and Social Security of the Government of the French Republic, and the Ministry of Labor and Social Insurance of the Saar Government shall periodically exchange general information on the conditions of labor markets in the two countries.

ARTICLE 37

Statistical data and information on the quality of labor demand and supply on hand shall be the subject of communications periodically exchanged between the competent departments of the two governments.

ARTICLE 38

Information regarding identity and skills of workers able to fill jobs offered in the conditions outlined in Article 37 shall be directly forwarded, as far as employment offers in France are concerned, by the Ministry of Labor and Social Insurance of the Saar Government to interregional clearing services especially designated for the purpose. As far as employment offers in the Saar Territory are concerned, said information shall be forwarded by the Departmental Office of Labor and French Manpower of the place in which the applicant is domiciled to the Ministry of Labor and Social Insurance of the Saar Government.

ARTICLE 39

Applications for employment that French and Saar employment offices might not have been able to fulfill locally or by way of exchanges and that are of a certain importance on account of their being due to mass dismissals, or because they originate from workers in trades suffering from a shortage of manpower in the other country or from groups or technicians willing to work in said trades, shall be the subject of periodical exchanges of information between France and the Saar Territory.

ARTICLE 40

Employment offers likely to be made to employment seekers as described in the foregoing article shall be channeled in the same way as those described in Article 38 above so that the competent services may be in a position to give the workers reliable and detailed information regarding the kind of work and the working conditions in the job under consideration.

ARTICLE 41

A Joint Commission composed of representatives of both contracting Parties being experts in questions of manpower shall have the task of facilitating the enforcement of the provisions of the present Section. Said Commission shall keep fluctuations of the labor markets in the two countries under close observation. It shall have the authority to make suggestions regarding all modifications of social legislation and administrative policies in the two countries which may be deemed necessary in order to make possible the proper enforcement of the provisions of this Section, and also to eventually submit said proposals to the Joint Commission provided for in Article 58.

SECTION VII

I. Professional Training and Technical Education

ARTICLE 42

The Government of the French Republic and the Government of the Saar Territory, in order to strengthen the economic and cultural co-operation between their two countries, agree to promote to the highest possible degree the professional training of their respective nationals in business establishments and professional training institutions of the other country.

ARTICLE 43

Nationals of the two countries shall have to comply with the laws on education of the country where they reside, and may be admitted under the same conditions as nationals to public and private institutions of professional training, with the exception of those establishments which are under the supervision of national defense authorities.

ARTICLE 44

Whenever regulations for the admission to the professional training institutions described in the foregoing article or regulations for taking public examinations of one of the contracting countries require that certificates be submitted, the competent minister of that country shall decide, in consultation with the competent minister of the other country, which foreign certificates will be required in each individual case.

ARTICLE 45

Diplomas or certificates of professional aptitude issued in one of the two countries shall ensure the recognition of the concerned professional qualifications for their holders in the other country. The competent ministers of the two countries shall determine by means of mutual agreement the certificates required in the two countries for admission to the various professions.

ARTICLE 46

French craftsmen [*professionels*] whose claim to professional skill is based on holding skill certificates [*diplômes de capacité*] provided for in the law of March 10, 1937, or mastership diplomas [*brevets de maîtrise*] issued by the "Chambres des Métiers" of the districts [*départements*] of Bas-Rhin, Haut-Rhin and Moselle, or other certificates endowing them with a title to said qualification to be defined in accordance with the provisions of the foregoing article, shall rightfully be considered as master craftsmen [*artisans maîtres*] in the Saar Territory.

Saar craftsmen holding mastership diplomas [*brevets de maîtrise*] issued by the "Chambre des Métiers" of the Saar Territory shall be recognized as master craftsmen in France.

Wage earners working in craft shops and holding certificates as journeymen [*compagnons*] issued by "Chambres des Métiers" or certificates of professional aptitude provided for by French laws, or having been skilled workers in their trade for three years shall be recognized as journeymen [*compagnons*].

II. Admission of Stagiaires into France and the Saar Territory

ARTICLE 47

For the purpose of putting into effect the provisions below, the word *stagiaire* shall be meant to indicate nationals of one of the two countries going to the other country for a limited time in order to improve their knowledge of the language or of the commercial or professional usages in said country, while holding a job there.

Stagiaires shall be permitted to hold jobs regardless of the situation of the labor market.

ARTICLE 48

Both governments shall make efforts to facilitate the employment of *stagiaires* in the other country.

ARTICLE 49

Within one month from the date when the present provisions come into effect each of the two governments shall make known to the other government the authority or authorities charged with gathering applications of their nationals and to expedite applications from nationals of the other country.

ARTICLE 50

The conditions for the enforcement of Articles 47, 48, and 49 shall be defined in an Annex to the present Agreement.

SECTION VIII
Conduct of Farming Activities

ARTICLE 51

Saar nationals established in France as farmers shall wholly benefit from the provisions of the law on farm leases, except only for special provisions on the acquisition of fixed property on the part of lessees.

ARTICLE 52

The French and Saar Governments shall grant French and Saar nationals wishing to settle as farmers in France or in the Saar Territory complete freedom of search for suitable farming operations and every help for obtaining administrative licenses needed to conduct their operations.

SECTION IX
Transitional and Final Provisions

ARTICLE 53

The title to commercial ownership in France, instituted by the law of June 30, 1926, shall be granted to Saar nationals domiciled in France before the publication of the present Agreement only in so far as they did not avail themselves of the statute on Saar refugees. Saar nationals domiciled in France shall be allowed to avail themselves of the provisions of the present Agreement regarding business only in case a new lease or an extension of an old lease is subscribed to after the present Agreement comes into force.

ARTICLE 54

With respect to the application of Articles 33 and 34, the governments of the two contracting Parties, as an exception and in case the risk of serious disturbances in the labor market should arise, may prohibit the exercise of certain wage-earning professions in certain regions.

ARTICLE 55

The present Agreement shall be applicable, so far as France is concerned, in the metrópolitan territory, in Algeria, and in French overseas districts. Its application may be extended by France to territories over which she exerts international responsibility.

ARTICLE 56

If, in consequence of changes made in the laws and regulations of the two contracting countries and of the enforcement of such laws and regulations subsequent to the application of the present Agreement, individuals or companies of one of the two countries should find themselves at a disadvantage compared to the nationals of the other country, negotiations shall be started with a view to ensure that both sides are afforded the same treatment on the basis of the more liberal regime.

Once said measures are agreed upon, they shall be enforced by the governments concerned in the territory of each of the two countries.

In case the negotiations provided for in the first paragraph above should not lead to results within six months from the day one party informed the other of its intention to start them, the government which initiated them may, at its own option, either apply like measures to the nationals of the other country or denounce the present Agreement. The denunciation shall become effective three months after notification thereof was sent.

ARTICLE 57

Matters connected with the present Agreement and concerning the régime of road transports between France and the Saar and the régime of weights and measures, inland navigation, and the trade of pharmaceuticals shall be made the subject of special agreements.

In addition, the two governments shall have the right to settle, by means of arrangements between services, various technical problems concerning in particular the restoration of normal conditions in certain professions and arising from the enforcement of the principles of the economic union and from the provisions of the present Agreement.

ARTICLE 58

All difficulties arising from the application of the present Agreement shall be submitted to a Joint Commission composed as follows:

for France, five members appointed by the French Government; and

for the Saar Territory, five members appointed by the Saar Government.

The chairmanship shall fall alternately at one session to a member of the French and at the next session to a member of the Saar delegation.

ARTICLE 59

The Joint Commission shall decide by majority vote. Its decisions shall have executory power as soon as they are published in France and in the Saar Territory. The publication shall be made in the customary form of official publications.

ARTICLE 60

The present Agreement shall be drawn up in the French and German languages, the French text being authentic in case of dispute. It shall come into force upon its publication in both countries.

The Agreement shall remain in force for one year from the day when one of the contracting Parties notifies the other of its desire to suspend its effects, subject to the provisions of Article 56, paragraph 3, above.

ANNEX

Admission of Stagiaires into France and the Saar Territory

ARTICLE 1

In accordance with the provisions of Articles 47, 48, and 49, Section VII, Chapter II, concerning the admission of *stagiaires* into the Saar Territory and France, the conditions under which French and Saar *stagiaires* shall be authorized to take jobs in the Saar Territory or in France are defined in the articles below:

ARTICLE 2

The number of *stagiaires* who may be admitted into each of the two countries shall not be over 500 per year.

Said limit shall not include *stagiaires* of one of the two countries already domiciled in the territory of the other country. Said limit may be attained whatever the duration of authorizations issued during each year and whatever the length of time for which same authorizations are made use of.

If the whole contingent of 500 authorizations is not utilized during a certain year by *stagiaires* of one of the two countries, said country may not curtail the number of authorizations to be issued to *stagiaires* of the other country, nor carry over to next year the nonutilized share of its own contingent.

For the evaluation of the contingent of 500 *stagiaires*, the year shall start on January 1 and end on December 31. The contingent may be modified by agreement to be reached between the two contracting Parties, upon proposal from one of them, submitted at the latest on December 1 of the year under consideration.

ARTICLE 3

Stagiaires may be male or female. As a general rule, they shall not be above thirty years of age.

ARTICLE 4

In principle, the authorization shall be granted for one year. In exceptional cases it may be extended for another six months.

ARTICLE 5

Stagiaires may be admitted by competent authorities only if the employers who hire them engage themselves to the said authorities to reward *stagiaires*, as soon as they render normal services, on the basis of wages prescribed by regulations on the matter or agreed upon by collective agreement, whenever such regulations or agreements exist, and on the basis of normal wages prevailing for the particular profession and in the particular region when said regulations or agreements do not exist.

In all other cases employers shall undertake to reward the services of *stagiaires* by providing for their needs of food and board either in kind or by way of a cash allowance.

ARTICLE 6

Stagiaires wishing to avail themselves of the present provisions shall file an application with the authority, in their place of residence, in charge of gathering said applications for each profession. They shall, in their application, supply all necessary information, and especially mention the establishment in which they expect to be employed. They shall at the same time submit the following documents:

(1) the pledge provided for in the second paragraph of Article 5 above;

(2) an official certificate of good health and good character;

(3) in some special cases, a declaration by which they engage themselves to leave the country wherein they wish to complete their period of training [*stage*] as soon as the latter has expired. Said declaration shall not be required of agricultural *stagiaires*.

The above-mentioned authorities shall decide whether it be necessary or advisable to forward individual applications to the corresponding authorities of the other country in view of the annual quota to which they are entitled, and if so, they shall actually forward said applications.

The competent authorities of the two countries shall ensure that applications are processed with the greatest possible dispatch.

BIBLIOGRAPHY

BIBLIOGRAPHICAL NOTE CONCERNING PRIMARY SOURCES

The indispensable source for the study of the Saar as an international problem during the rule of the Governing Commission is the *League of Nations Official Journal* for the years 1920–1936, which contains the regular quarterly as well as the special reports of the Saar Basin Governing Commission to the Council of the League. It also includes numerous documents appended to these reports, such as the texts of memorials and petitions from political and other organizations in the Saar Territory. Likewise, all the minutes of the Council and the League, the reports of subcommittees, and the correspondence between the Secretariat and various governments were published in the *Official Journal*. It should also be noted that international agreements were registered at the Secretariat of the League of Nations and were published in the Treaty Series.

The Governing Commission of the Saar itself published a monthly *Amtsblatt*, or official journal, in German, containing the texts of its ordinances, decrees, and proclamations. Finally, the proceedings of the Advisory Council were published regularly from the time of the Council's creation in 1922.

Publications of the British, French, German, and American governments likewise constitute important sources. In addition to *Parliamentary Debates*, certain of the British command papers have touched on the Saar question. The British Foreign Office also published in 1920 *Peace Handbook No. 31* on Lorraine and Saar mine fields. Also, the *Débats Parlementaires* published by the *Journal Officiel* of the French Republic can be consulted to advantage. The German government published in 1921 a paper entitled *Das Saargebiet unter der Herrschaft des Waffenstillstandsabkommens und des Vertrags von Versailles*. This White Book includes a variety of documents to show French activities in the Saar in an unfavorable light. The correspondence between the German government and the Allied and Associated Governments on the Saar section of the draft treaty of Versailles may be found in Volume I of Walther M. A. Schücking, *Kommentar zum Friedensvertrage*, 5 vols. (Berlin, 1920–1922). The replies of the Allies to the observations of the German government are given in French and English. The commentaries may also be found in English in *International Conciliation*, Nos. 143 and 144. Annotations of the text of the Treaty of Versailles and a summary treatment of subsequent events related to its provisions were published by the U.S. Department of State in 1947 in Conference Series 92, No. 2724.

For the more recent period, official American data may be obtained from the *Biennial Report of the Chief of Staff of the United States Army, July 1, 1943, to June 30, 1945, to the Secretary of War* (Washington, D.C., 1945); from "The Present Status of the Saar," *Documents and State Papers of the Department of State*, I, 7 (October 1948); and from *The European Recovery Program; Country Studies*, Chapter XVII, "Western Germany," issued by the Department of State (Washington, D.C., 1948).

Primary French sources for this period include *La Sarre et la sécurité française*, Ministère des Affaires Etrangères, Notes Documentaires et Etudes, No. 326 (Paris: Direction de la Documentation, June 1946); and

Trois ans de présence française en Sarre, Ministère des Affaires Etrangères, Notes Documentaires et Etudes, No. 991 (Paris: Haut-Commissariat de la République Française en Sarre, September 1948).

SELECTED SECONDARY SOURCES

Babelon, Ernest. *Au pays de la Sarre: Sarrelouis et Saarbruck*. Paris, 1918.

Baker, Ray Stannard. *Woodrow Wilson and World Settlement*. 3 vols. New York, 1922.
   A discussion of the Saar negotiations in Paris, which sets forth Wilson's position clearly and authoritatively and interprets the stand of the British and French from the American point of view.

Barthou, Louis. *Le Traité de Paix*. Paris, 1919.

Bauer, Hubert A. "The Geographic Background of the Saar Problem," *Geographical Review*, XXIV (October 1934), 5555–65.

Binkley, Robert C. "New Light on the Paris Peace Conference," *Political Science Quarterly*, XLVI (September–December, 1931), 343–44.

Bisschop, W. Roosegarde. *The Saar Controversy*. The Grotius Society Publications, No. 2. London, 1924.

Brooks, Alfred H., and Morris F. La Croix. *The Iron and Associated Industries of Lorraine, the Saar District, Luxemburg, and Belgium*. U.S. Geological Survey, Bulletin No. 703. Washington, D.C., 1920.

Bruns, Viktor. *Die Volksabstimmung im Saargebiet*. Berlin, 1934.

Capot-Rey, Robert. *Quand la Sarre était française*. Paris, 1928.
———. *La région industrielle sarroise: Territoire de la Sarre et bassin houiller de la Moselle; étude géographique*. Paris, 1934.

Chiny, Henri. *Le retour éventuel de la Sarre à l'Allemagne vu par les Allemands*. Paris, 1932.

Comité d'Etudes. *L'Alsace-Lorraine et la frontière du nord-est*. Travaux du Comité d'Etudes, I. Paris, 1918.

Cowan, L. G. *France and the Saar, 1680–1948*. New York, 1950.

Donald, Sir Robert. *A Danger Spot in Europe and Its Government by the League of Nations*. London, 1925.
   An indictment of the government of the Saar.

Engerand, Fernand. *Les frontières lorraines et la force allemande*. Paris, 1916.

Florinsky, Michael T. *The Saar Struggle*. New York, 1934.
   Good semipopular account covering most of the period of League of Nations' control.

Gallois, Lucien. "Alsace-Lorraine and Europe," *Geographical Review*, VI (August 1918), 89–115.

Grabowsky, Adolf, and Georg Wilhelm Sante (eds.). *Die Grundlagen des Saarkampfes*. Special number of the *Zeitschrift für Geopolitik*. Berlin, 1934.

Grimm, Friedrich. *Frankreich an der Saar: Der Kampf um die Saar im Lichte der historischen französischen Rheinpolitik*. Hamburg, 1934.

Haskins, Charles H. "The Saar Territory as It Is Today," *Foreign Affairs*, I (December 1922), 46–58.

Haskins, Charles H., and Robert H. Lord. *Some Problems of the Peace Conference*. Cambridge, Mass., 1920.
    One of the authors is the American expert who helped draft the Saar section of the Treaty of Versailles.

Held, C. C. *The Political Geography of the Saarland*. Ph.D. dissertation, Clark University. Worcester, Mass., 1949.
    This doctoral dissertation deals with the Saar region as a problem in political geography. It was found most useful for data on the postplebiscite period. The bibliography on the physical, human, and economic geography of the Saar is excellent.

House, Edward M., and Charles Seymour (eds.). *What Really Happened at Paris: The Story of the Peace Conference, 1918–1919*. New York, 1921.

Kloevekorn, Fritz (ed.). *Das Saargebiet: seine Struktur, seine Probleme*. Saarbrücken, 1929.

Lambert, Margaret. *The Saar*. London, 1934.

Lloyd George, David. *The Truth About the Peace Treaties*. 2 vols. London, 1938.

Maupas, Jacques. *La Sarre et son rattachement à l'Allemagne*. Paris, 1936.

Miller, David Hunter. *My Diary at the Peace Conference*, 21 vols. New York, 1924. (Privately printed.)

Oncken, Hermann. *The Historical Rhine Policy of the French*. New York, 1923.

Peyret, Henri. *L'Oeuvre Française en Sarre: Bilan économique de trois années, 1945–1948*. Special number of *L'Economie*, supplement to No. 162 (July 1948).

Priou, Jean. *Le Territoire de la Sarre: Etudes politiques et économiques*. Paris, 1923.
    A scholarly study of the constitutional and administrative organization of the Saar and of the social, industrial, commercial, and financial problems during the first years of the international regime.

Reischer, O. R. "Saar Coal After Two World Wars," *Political Science Quarterly*, LXIV (March 1949), 50–64.

Renaissance de la Sarre. Gouvernement militaire de la Zone Française de l'Occupation. Saarbrücken, 1947.

Reynolds, Bernard T. *The Saar and the Franco-German Problem*. London, 1934.

Rice, George S. "Destruction of French Coal Mines and Plants and Their Rehabilitation," *Journal of the Franklin Institute Devoted to Science and the Mechanic Arts*, CLXXXIX (June 1920), 737–78.

Röchling, Hermann. *Wir halten die Saar!* Berlin, 1934.
    The opinions of a prominent Saar industrial magnate and ardent German nationalist.

Russell, Frank M. *The International Government of the Saar*. Berkeley, Calif., 1926.

Russell, Frank M. "The Saar Basin Governing Commission," *Political Science Quarterly*, XXXVI (June 1921), 169–83.

Tardieu, André. *The Truth About the Treaty.* Indianapolis, 1921.
   The French case, as stated at the Peace Conference by a close adviser of Clemenceau. The official French position on the Saar is expounded by the author, who was the French member of the Committee of Three which drew up the Saar provisions of the Treaty of Versailles.

Vidal de la Blache, Paul. "La frontière de la Sarre d'après les traités de 1814 et de 1815," *Annales de Géographie*, XXVIII (July 1919), 249–67.

Vidal de la Blache, Paul, and Lucien Gallois. *Le basin de la Sarre; clauses du Traité de Versailles; étude historique et économique.* Paris, 1919.

Wambaugh, Sarah. *The Saar Plebiscite; with a Collection of Official Documents.* Cambridge, Mass., 1940.
   A scholarly and painstaking work by the foremost authority on international plebiscites, who was technical adviser and deputy member of the Saar Plebiscite Commission. This book is very helpful in achieving an understanding of the background of the Saar plebiscite and is indispensable for its detailed treatment of techniques employed in preparing and carrying out the plebiscite. The work includes 147 pages of relevant documents and a useful bibliographical note.

INDEX

Adenauer, Konrad, 124, 125
Advisory Council, 48, 49, 50, 62, 73
Allied and Associated Powers, 7
Aloisi, Baron Pompeo, 93, 101, 104
Alsace-Lorraine, 7, 9, 10, 11, 12, 13, 15, 18, 19
Anti-Semitism, 88, 90
Asquith, Herbert, 66
Aulard, François, 7–8

Balfour, Arthur James, 9–10, 64
Barthou, Jean Louis, 101
Baruch, Bernard, 15, 17
Beneš, Eduard, 103
Bevin, Ernest, 111
Bidault, Georges, 110, 111
Bismarck, 6
Boch, Alfred von, 32
Boncour, Joseph Paul, 91
Bouillon, Franklin, 10
Bourgeois, Léon, 66–67
Branting, Hjalmar, 65, 67, 69, 77, 80
Braun, Max, 88, 99
Briand, Aristide, 79, 80, 83
Brissaud-Desmaillet, General Georges-Henri, 40
Bürckel, Joseph, 96, 100–101, 106
Byrnes, James F., 111

Cecil, Lord Robert, 66, 67, 70, 71, 72, 73–76, 77
Chambres de Réunion, 3
Christian Peoples party, 116–17
Clay, General Lucius, 114
Clemenceau, Georges, 7, 11, 13, 14, 26, 27
Committee of Three, 16, 17, 93, 95, 100, 101, 102
Communist party, 117–18, 129
Constitution of the Saar, 118–22; *see also* Appendix C for text in French
Conventions of March 3, 1950, 124–27; *see also* Appendix E for texts in English
Council of Europe, 122–25

Département de la Saare, 5
Deutsche Front, 88, 98, 103, 104

Eden, Anthony, 96–97
Ehrenrooth, M. von, 81
Engerand, Ferdinand, 8

Franc, 55–58, 114
Freiheitsfront, 98–99, 100
French garrison troops, 42; attitude of League of Nations Council, 62–63, 73–74, 84; demand for removal, and recruitment of local gendarmerie, 43–45
French government: aide-memoire, 99–102; attitude toward political parties in the Saar, 116; draws new Saar boundaries, 110–12; encourages and guides drawing up of a Saar Constitution, 117–22; influence on League of Nations Council, 32; initiates conversations leading to Conventions and Accords of March 3, 1950, 124–25; measures toward economic recovery, 112–13; position at Peace Conference, 10–17; Schuman Plan, 127–28; secret conversations with Russian government relating to Saar, 8–9; supports candidacy of Saar for admission to Consultative Assembly of Council of Europe, 123–24; treaty rights in the Saar, 27–34
French Left, 79–80
French mines, 12, 15, 21
French Mines Administration, 35; payment of employees in francs, 55–56, 74, 85, 86; recent output, 113; reopening of Saar mines by French in 1945, 108; schools, 51–54, 55
French Revolution, 4–5
Foch, Marshal Ferdinand, 12

Gaulle, Charles de, 109, 110
German government: comments on the Saar section of the Treaty of Versailles, 26–28; criticisms of the Governing Commission, 41, 43, 44, 52–53, 62, 63, 79, 80; and propaganda in the Saar, 84, 85, 87; and Saar officials, 40–41; *see also* National Socialism
Gouin, Felix, 110
Governing Commission, 21, 23–24, 25 26; initial problems and policies, 34–41; instructions from the Council of the League of Nations, 30–31; League pressure on Commission, 62–64; measures of the Commission in connection with the depression of 1929–30, 84–85; personnel, 31–33; problems with the advent of National Socialism in Ger-

203

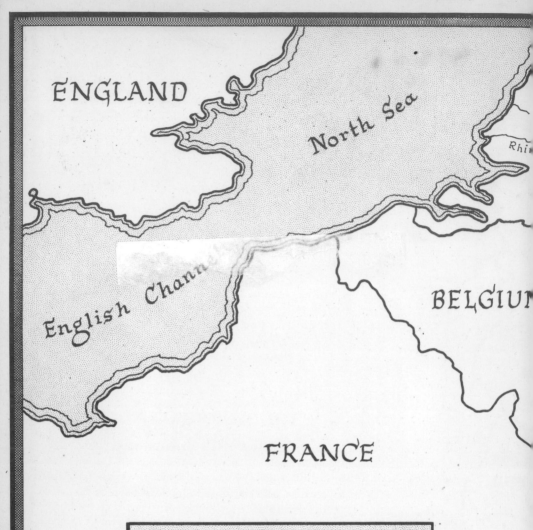

ENGLAND

North Sea

Rhi

English Channel

BELGIUM

FRANCE

The
STRATEGIC POSITION
of the
SAAR